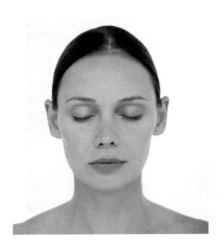

SECRETS OF
STAYING
YOUNG

CHARMAINE YABSLEY

SECRETS OF STAYING YOUNG

NATURAL WAYS TO COMBAT THE EFFECTS OF AGING AND ENHANCE YOUR BEAUTY

dbp

DUNCAN BAIRD PUBLISHERS

LONDON

Secrets of Staying Young
Charmaine Yabsley

Distributed in the USA and Canada by
Sterling Publishing Co., Inc., 387 Park Avenue South, New York, NY 10016-8810

This edition first published in the UK and USA in 2010 by
Duncan Baird Publishers Ltd, Sixth Floor, Castle House, 75–76 Wells Street, London W1T 3QH

Library of Congress Cataloging-in-Publication Data

Yabsley, Charmaine.
  Secrets of staying young : natural ways to combat the effects of aging and enhance your beauty / Charmaine Yabsley.
      p. cm.
  Includes index.
  ISBN 978-1-84483-911-7
  1. Longevity. 2. Beauty, Personal. 3. Nutrition. 4. Health. I. Title.
  RA776.75.Y33 2010
  613.2--dc22
                            2009029515

ISBN: 978-1-84483-911-7

10 9 8 7 6 5 4 3 2 1

Typeset in Helvetica Neue
Color reproduction by Scanhouse, Malaysia
Printed in Malaysia for Imago

For information about custom editions, special sales, premium and corporate purchases, please contact Sterling
Special Sales Department at 800-805-5489 or specialsales@sterlingpub.com.

Publisher's note: The information in this book is not intended as a substitute for professional medical advice and
treatment. If you are pregnant or breastfeeding or have any special dietary requirements or medical conditions, it is
recommended that you consult a medical professional before following any of the information or recipes contained in
this book. Duncan Baird Publishers, or any other persons who have been involved in working on this publication,
cannot accept responsibility for any errors or omissions, inadvertent or not, that may be found in the recipes or text,
nor for any problems that may arise as a result of preparing one of these recipes or following the advice contained in
this work. Essential oils must be diluted in a base oil before use. They should not be taken internally and are for adult
use only. The detox plan on pages 134–137 should be avoided by children, elderly people and women who are
pregnant or breast feeding.

All the recipes in the book use imperial measurements. However, metric measurements have occasionally been used
where this system is more appropriate to the small quantities described, i.e. when supplying nutritional information.

For my parents

contents

KEY TO SYMBOLS

✔ Foods to eat

✘ Foods to avoid

♥ Treatments

● Problems

❗ Information/Warning

★ Nutrients

✚ Supplements

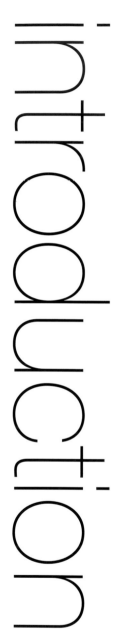

About five years ago, if you had taken a look inside my beauty cabinet you would have been brained by falling bottles, so full was it crammed. I truly thought that it was impossible to be beautiful without the numerous lotions and potions I painstakingly and vigorously applied morning and night. I believed everything that beauty companies told me and followed the make-up and exercise programs published in the women's magazines that I faithfully bought each month.

However, through my work—initially at a holistic health farm in Australia and later as editor for a health magazine and as a freelance health writer—I have discovered the importance of nutrition and the role it plays, not only in the way we feel, but also in the way we look.

the path to health

I first became interested in food and its health benefits as a teenager. I had suffered from children's rheumatoid arthritis since the age of three and had spent years under the supervision of doctors and physiotherapists. While these experts were quick to recommend medicines to help alleviate the pain I was suffering, none recommended changing my diet or even taking supplements as part of my daily routine. Then, one morning, after laying out several medicines for me to take, my father decided that these medicines weren't helping me in any way. Of course, they were helping to dull the pain of my swollen joints, but they certainly weren't helping to prevent it.

My parents then embarked on a journey to discover how I could live medicine-free. This project involved my taking copious amounts of aloe vera juice and celery seeds, cutting out tomatoes for months on end, and even practising meditation. It may have seemed an exercise in futility at the start but, as the months went by, the number of "attacks" (as we referred to them) occurred less and less often. And when they did occur, they seemed less severe. As the years went by, I became more and more interested in holistic medicine (treating the body and mind as one) and how foods can create not only a healthy body, but also a healthy mind.

Whether or not it was owing to my healthy diet, at the age of 21 we discovered that I no longer had arthritis. It may have been that I had outgrown the illness, as can sometimes happen, but I do believe that if it weren't for my parents and their determination to trust in nature and the healing benefits of food, I would never have recovered in the way I did.

Ever since learning this important life lesson, I have always found that food is the answer to most of our problems. Tired? Then it's most likely that you haven't eaten for hours. Irritable? You probably need a natural sugar burst. Feeling run-down? When was the last time you ate a well-balanced meal of protein and vegetables bursting with goodness?

make a friend of food

Food is not our enemy. Despite being bombarded with messages that deprivation is good, it's important to realize that without food we cannot function.

From childhood, food is used primarily as either a bribe or a punishment—rather than for its nutritional uses. How many times did you hear, "If you're good, you can have a sweet?" or "You're not leaving the table until you've eaten all your vegetables." Without even being aware of it, as we have moved into our adult years, we have become conditioned to think of food as something to reward ourselves with or to deprive ourselves of. Instead, let's look at what food is. Food is a living organism, and we should consider the benefits that food, good food, makes to our everyday lives. For instance, when you eat a carrot, you are not only receiving all of its nutritional benefits, but also its energy and life. And if you regard every foodstuff that you eat in the same way, it's easier to get into the habit of eating fresh, wholesome food, bursting with goodness and health, instead of fatty snacks and junk food takeaways. Not only does a crunchy vegetable salad taste much better than a bar of chocolate (yes, really!), it will make you feel much happier and healthier as well.

Eating well and, more importantly, enjoying the foods we prepare and eat, is certainly the most naturally beautiful way to live.

how to use this book

Now that you've decided to embark on a natural, more holistic way of life, it's important to understand how this book works.

The book is divided into four sections: *Chapter One, The Path to Natural Beauty*, explores the concepts of natural beauty and looks at the intrinsic connection between external beauty and internal health. *Chapter Two, Beauty Food Pharmacy*, is a chapter on the foods we should eat and how to eat them. Within each section is a *Star Food* (in some cases there are more than one). These foods are highlighted because of their optimum levels of health-giving nutrients and also the ease with which we can use them in everyday cooking. If a food can be applied topically—that is, to the skin—then I have also explained how to do so.

If you are looking for a particular remedy or recipe plan for a specific health problem such as acne, then turn to *Chapter Three, Natural Beauty Clinic*. Here, I have explained each skin problem and how and why it occurs and what steps can be taken to treat it or prevent it recurring. This chapter not only contains recipe references to *Chapter Four*, but also includes beauty treatments to apply. Not all beauty problems will have a diagnosed beauty treatment, but all ailments have recommended recipes to follow, and where applicable, first aid hints or tips.

Chapter Four, Recipes, Treatments, and Therapies, comprises more than a hundred beauty-enhancing ways of using these various foods. The recipes have detailed preparation and cooking instructions and, where possible, serving suggestions as well. There is a balance of vegetarian and non-vegetarian recipes, with options available for all dietary requirements. I have pinpointed the main beauty benefits of a dish, although all the dishes are extremely nutritious and recommended for overall good health and well-being. More than 40 beauty treatments show you how to use natural ingredients to help keep your skin, hair, and nails in tip-top condition. And the chapter concludes with a variety of therapies, including a home spa and a seven-day detox plan, aimed to help you put your newly-learned knowledge into practice. As with all new health plans, it's important to check with your doctor before dramatically changing your diet. Experiment with my suggestions—I hope you enjoy discovering your own natural beauty, as much as I have enjoyed writing this book.

Eat wisely, eat well—and enjoy!

Charmaine Yabsley

the path to natural beauty

Have you ever met someone who is naturally beautiful? Someone whose beauty is obvious to all, but seems to defy conventional notions of esthetic perfection? They may not have perfectly proportioned features, but there is a radiance about them, a sense of vitality and well-being that is hard to define. Look a little closer and you see that their hair is glossy and thick, skin soft and smooth, eyes clear and bright. Not only do they look good but they exude qualities of calm and contentment, and a sense of harmony both within and without. This is natural beauty—a state of physical, mental, and emotional health—that we can all aspire to, regardless of our genetic heritage. The first step is learning to take care of our bodies with a nutritious diet, natural beauty products, and a program of exercise, relaxation, and sleep.

The following chapter will set you on the path to natural beauty. We begin with a discussion of the concept of natural beauty, before tracing the connections between the substances that we eat and apply to our bodies, and our state of health, both inside and out. We examine the importance of relaxation and the impact of the mind and emotions on physical health, as well as highlighting some of the pitfalls of the modern-day pursuit of beauty. The chapter concludes with the case for the natural route, and offers detailed advice for getting the most out of this book.

A HEALTHY BODY IS A BEAUTIFUL BODY

Every year many of us (women in particular) spend large amounts of disposable income on cosmetics and other beauty products in a bid to achieve clear, glowing skin; thick, lustrous hair; and sparkling eyes. While these treatments may enhance beauty, they often fail to tackle the root causes of many beauty problems that are, in fact, intimately connected with our internal health.

The word "health" comes from the same root as "wholeness." Therefore, you can conceive of health as a state of wholeness or integration at all levels of your being. To understand how this integration operates, it helps to think of your body as a complex network of interdependent and dynamic systems, rather than simply as a set of individual component parts or organs. Changes in one system inevitably impact on all the other systems of your body.

The integration of the various bodily systems is clearly evident in the integumental system, which encompasses the skin and its components—hair, nails, sweat, and sebaceous glands (see pages 70–83). The skin covers the entire surface of the body, and forms a self-repairing and self-renewing interface between your internal and external environment. Functioning as a selectively permeable barrier, skin helps to protect your body from the effects of injury, sunlight, smoking, environmental pollution, and infection, while allowing for the absorption of certain chemical substances and the elimination of waste products.

As a potential entry point for invading microbes, the skin provides an important site for immunosurveillance and the activation of the body's immune response. It is also the target of a number of hormones that affect the appearance and function of its components, such as the sebaceous glands, pigment-producing cells, and hairs. The skin plays an important role in the regulation of body temperature. This is achieved by sweating and by the constriction and dilation of the blood vessels that pass close to the surface of the skin. In addition, the skin serves as a major sensory organ, for it is richly supplied with nerve receptors for detecting light touch, pressure, vibration, temperature, and injury.

From this we can begin to develop a sense of how the integumental system is intimately connected with other bodily systems—such as the immune system, the endocrine system, the circulatory system, and the nervous system. This means that problems involving the body's internal systems can have a negative impact on the quality of your skin. For example, a failure to break down and eliminate toxins effectively can lead to a blemished complexion. Poor absorption of nutrients through the wall of the digestive system can result in thinning hair.

From this it is clear that to enhance your outward appearance, you must tend to the health of all your internal body systems. Just as plants require the right amounts of sunshine, water, and fertilizer in order to thrive, so your body needs optimum levels of water, nutrients, exercise, and fresh air if it is to function effectively. The amounts may vary from person to person, but the nature of the essential requirements remains the same. As well as catering for these needs, it is important to protect your body from the damaging effects of environmental pollution, including smoking, alcohol, and pesticides, and guard against processed foods and excessive exposure to sunshine.

At the same time, it is important to address psychological and emotional stressors, which have a negative impact on the body at a physiological level, depleting the immune system and inhibiting the digestion and absorption of nutrients.

Therefore, achieving a beautiful body depends on adopting a balanced and healthy lifestyle: eating regular, well-balanced meals consisting of unprocessed organic produce; drinking plenty of filtered water; exercising at least four times a week; limiting your exposure to sunshine, cigarette smoke, and alcohol; and engaging in some form of stress-relieving activity, such as meditation or yoga.

In reward for all your efforts, you will not only develop smooth, glowing skin, shining hair, clear eyes, and strong, well-shaped nails, you will also feel a greatly increased sense of vitality and a zest for life. Your self-image will improve, and as a result your confidence and self-esteem will grow. Feeling and acting at your best, you are likely to attract people to you—for there is nothing more beautiful than vibrant health.

EAT FOR BEAUTY INSIDE AND OUT

Eating three well-balanced, nutritious meals a day, containing fruit, vegetables, and protein, and snacking between times on fruit, nuts, or seeds, will help you achieve the daily intake of nutrients and vitamins your body needs. Choosing organic products, where possible, and eating at regular meal times can help support your digestive system. Drinking at least 3 pints of water a day keeps the body well hydrated, which not only keeps the skin looking great but also gives you more energy. And as water helps fill you up, it means you're less likely to snack on sugary treats.

the role of supplements

Walk into any health food store and you'll be confronted by a vast array of vitamins, minerals, and tinctures, all promising better health. Of course, in theory, if you follow a well-balanced, nutritious diet, exercise regularly, and drink plenty of water, you're unlikely to need supplements. However, owing to external factors such as stress, pollution, central heating, and air-conditioning, all of which place a strain on your body by robbing it of precious stores of vitamins and minerals, supplements can be of benefit.

The important thing to remember, as my friend and nutritionist Natalie Savona says, is that "supplements" are just that: they *supplement* a healthy diet, not replace it.

Vitamins such as A, C, and E—all antioxidants—that are required by the skin for repair and renewal and to help protect it against premature aging, are found in many fruits and vegetables. However, people who don't eat adequate amounts of these vitamins may have to include supplements in their daily health routine. These vitamins also help protect the skin against pollution and other environmental enemies. Such factors cannot be controlled very easily, so it may be necessary to supplement your diet with protective vitamins in order to maintain maximum defence. Other vitamins and minerals may be needed because of individual requirements.

For example, they can help to restore flexibility to the joints, relieve menopausal symptoms, or regulate blood sugar levels, and it may not be possible to meet these demands through diet alone. If you do think that your diet needs supplementation, I recommend that you seek the advice of a registered nutritionist or your doctor.

natural treatments

You visit a skin specialist, attend regular yoga classes, eat healthily and never, ever go to bed without removing your make-up. So you'd consider yourself to be taking a fairly holistic approach to your beauty routine, wouldn't you? But have you considered adopting a more natural approach to skin care? Embracing a natural beauty routine may be one of the best decisions you can make for your body. Nature is filled with wonderful healing ingredients that can be utilized to soothe, heal, and enhance your natural beauty.

We spend billions of dollars a year on cosmetics, including make-up, moisturizers, cleansers, and face masks. When we buy a beauty product, the last thing we're paying for is the contents of the jar. We are actually shelling out for tax, duty, packaging, advertising, marketing—and even for the service we are receiving when buying it. Considering that the majority of products we purchase tend to gather dust on the bathroom shelf, or are discarded the moment another "miracle" product is released, perhaps it's time to look at a more natural—and yes, cheaper—alternative.

Making your own beauty products is not only a more sensible choice from the point of view of spending your hard-earned money, when you discover the healing power that comes from nature's cosmetic store, it can also seem like the only option. Plus, think of all the money you'll have to spend on more important items—like shoes!

what to use

Fruits, in particular, make excellent beauty treatments. Take a look at the many beauty products available today: most have a fruit extract included somewhere in their ingredients list. It seems that the commercial world has finally woken up to the healing powers of fruits. Owing to their various ingredients, fruits can be used to moisturize, nourish, and heal specific skin conditions, as well as being incorporated into a daily beauty routine. Some fruits have astringent qualities, helping to exfoliate and renew dead skin cells. Others have a nurturing and calming influence on skin conditions such as acne, pimples, injuries, and scars. When using fruits as part of your beauty treatment, find the freshest available and, if possible, choose organic products.

Vegetables, too, are an ideal ingredient to include in natural treatments, as they have an anti-inflammatory effect on damaged, inflamed, and sensitive skin. Most vegetables contain vitamin A, which is required by the skin, and in particular the surface layer (epidermis), for healing purposes. Vegetable masks and treatments tend to work quite quickly and are therefore an excellent tonic for sunburned skin, allergic reactions, eczema, or outbreaks of pimples.

The basic items you'll need for a natural beauty routine are:

- *Mixing bowl* made of plastic or glass (metal bowls oxidize when they come into contact with fruit or vegetable juices).
- *Storage jars* made of plastic or glass. Store natural beauty products in the refrigerator, unless otherwise specified. Recipes containing eggs or milk should be kept no longer than six hours.
- *Cotton balls* for cleansing before and after a treatment.
- *Hair band*—use the fabric kind (available from the pharmacy) to keep your hair away from your face.

The following are ideal ingredients for natural beauty products:

- *Bathing salts*, which contain magnesium to help heal stresses and strains. Always keep a supply in your bathroom.
- *Camomile tea bags* for cooling tired eyes and calming inflamed or sensitive skin.
- *Cucumber* is an excellent base for use as a toner or lotion.
- *Eggs* are nourishing and add thickness to a recipe, making it easier to apply.
- *Honey* is used in masks as a healing aid and to bind ingredients.
- *Lemon* is an astringent and therefore an ideal toner or exfoliant.
- *Milk* makes an excellent cleanser and skin-softener.
- *Oatmeal*, cooked or raw, can be combined with lemon juice or honey to make a deep-cleansing and exfoliating treatment.
- *Olive oil* is extremely nourishing, and ideal for treating dry skin.
- *Strawberries* are good for toning the skin and for removing caffeine and nicotine stains from the teeth.
- *Sugar* makes a good emergency exfoliator.
- *Water*—use tepid water on the skin, unless otherwise stated.
- *Yogurt* helps to balance and nourish the skin.

THE ROLE OF RELAXATION

Beauty is a state of mind. There's nothing more attractive than a confident, well-groomed person who exudes good health. I'm sure you know someone just like that. There's something about such people that draws you to them: some call it charisma, I call it natural beauty. If you're serious about following a naturally beautiful lifestyle, it's vital to maintain a healthy and balanced state of mind.

Advances in technology, instead of saving us time, are actually forcing us to do, and achieve, more than ever before. Think about your day. How many e-mails did you write, read, and answer? How many times were you interrupted by your cellphone? These communication tools may help make your job and life easier, but they are constant, and in many cases unnecessary, interruptions in your everyday life. A recent survey found that two out of three people claimed to be stressed, citing work, home life, finances, or family as factors. Stress is becoming the greatest cause of ill-health in modern society.

Short-term stress can be good for you, sharpening your mental abilities and observational skills. But in the long term, stress can lead to high blood pressure, an impaired immune system, and lack of libido, and can cause many people to skip meals or binge eat. Certain foods that you may consume can put your body under chemical stress. Similarly, if your diet is unbalanced you may be stressing your body by depriving it of essential nutrients. Eating too much over long periods leads to weight gain, which reduces stamina and puts the heart, lungs, and other organs under stress.

The following substances can increase stress in your body:
● *Caffeine*—this is a stimulant. One reason you probably drink it is to raise your level of arousal (i.e. stress). If you are drinking too many cups of coffee a day, reduce your stress by switching to decaffeinated kinds (or alternative drinks, such as fruit juices).
● *Alcohol*—in small amounts this may help you relax. In larger amounts it can disrupt sleep (and cause hangovers!) and increase stress. Over the long term, excess alcohol damages your body.
● *Nicotine*—in the very short term, this may relax you, too, but its toxic effects raise the heart rate and stress the body (as well as causing numerous other ill effects). If you smoke, take your pulse before and after a cigarette, and notice the difference. Most ex-smokers report feeling generally more relaxed once they quit.

● *Sugar-rich foods*—they can raise short-term energy levels. But the body copes with excess sugar by secreting more insulin, which reduces the amount of sugar in the blood. This extra insulin can persist and continue acting even after it has normalized blood sugar levels, causing an energy dip.

By eating a well-balanced diet, you can minimize the effects of stress on your health. In particular, vitamin C helps control the release of the stress hormones adrenalin and cortisol in the body. Good sources of this vitamin include oranges, bell peppers, papaya, cabbage, kiwi fruit, broccoli, and cauliflower. B-complex vitamins—found in bananas, wholewheat bread, beans, eggs, and dairy products—also help balance stress levels.

how to relax

An ideal way to relax is to take time to pamper yourself. When you're stressed, you tend to focus on the endless list of tasks that you have to complete. The last thing you'll think of is relaxing, or even breathing correctly! People tend to frown constantly when under stress, which can cause small lines to form around the forehead and eyes, leading to premature aging. A massage, which many may consider an indulgence, actually helps to decrease levels of stress hormones in the body. Massage relaxes muscle fibers and stimulates the lymphatic system, which is your body's first line of defense against disease. Massage also calms the nervous system by inducing the brain to release chemicals called endorphins—natural painkillers and mood-enhancers.

If you suffer from stress on a day-to-day basis, there are ways to avoid feeling overstretched and overwhelmed.

● Take short, regular breaks, even if this is just a matter of stopping what you are doing or getting up from your desk. Fetch yourself a glass of water at the same time to ensure that you're replenishing your body's fluid levels.

● Remember to breathe! A few deep breaths will do wonders for reducing adrenalin levels and releasing the tension in your face, neck, and shoulders.

● Eat regular meals. When you skip meals, your blood sugar levels drop, which can make you irritable, tired, and, ultimately, even more stressed.

● Schedule time for yourself. When you are writing your endless list of tasks for the day, make sure you include something pleasurable for yourself. This is not to say that relaxation is another duty you must complete! Rather, it is a necessary exercise to ensure that you stay healthy and clear-headed in order to get through your day. You might choose to walk to the park at lunchtime, read your favorite magazine over a cup of herbal tea, or have a long, hot bath filled with relaxing oils—these are all treats that help make the stressful periods of life more bearable.

● Make time to exercise. After a long day at work, heading to the gym, or to an exercise class, may be the last thing you feel like. Yet exercise helps reduce stress and, more importantly, this is one time when nobody can interrupt you! Go for a swim, join that yoga class, or put on your running shoes. You'll not only feel better for it, you'll also be better equipped to handle whatever the next day brings.

where to relax

Once you've found time for relaxation, it's important to create the right environment. Set aside an area of the home specifically for relaxation. Whether it's in the garden, your bedroom, or any other area you feel comfortable in, ensure that it is used only for this purpose and that other members of the household are aware of this. Disconnect the telephone, sit on a comfortable chair or cushion, and light a candle or oil burner containing a relaxing scent, such as lavender, camomile, *may chang,* or lemon grass. If it helps, play a meditation or relaxation CD to set a calming mood.

Close your eyes and begin to breathe slowly and evenly. Don't worry if hundreds of random thoughts rush through your mind—this is a natural part of the relaxation process. Spend a few minutes doing and thinking of nothing but your breath. If a thought comes into your mind, just acknowledge it and then leave it be. I've found that focusing on the number of breaths I take is a good way to prevent unwanted "noise" interfering with my relaxation. You can stay like this, concentrating on your breath, for as long as you like, or you can follow one of the relaxation programs outlined in Simple Stress-Busters (page 128).

Stress needn't run your life. Utilize it wisely and you'll feel all the better for it.

BEAUTY FADS, BEAUTY DANGERS

In today's image-obsessed society, it seems that in order to be considered beautiful, we must be thin. We need only look at our "role models" in the media—actresses and fashion models—to see how this quest for beauty has been taken to extremes. During the past ten years, what is considered an "acceptable" weight for women has plummeted to dangerous levels. One piece of research has shown that even our retail store mannequins have lost weight. Thirty years ago the average window dummy was a size six. Today, clothes are exhibited on figures that border on sizes two to four. These figures are unachievable and misleading in every way—particularly when you consider that over this period humans have actually grown larger! In the 1940s women were, on average, a size six and weighed around 121 lb. Today, the average American woman is a size 12 and weighs between 144 and 154 lb. While our sedentary lifestyle has something to do with the weight gain, it is also true that humans have naturally grown upward and outward. With girls as young as eight reportedly going on diets and with the number of women suffering from anorexia and bulimia growing every day, it's time we reassessed our understanding of what beauty is all about.

dieting pitfalls

When we diet, we place unnecessary strain on our body. Of course, if you are overweight, cutting down on sugary foods and snacks is a good idea, but this shouldn't be called a diet, as it really necessitates a permanent change of eating habits. However, any nutritional deprivation will express itself through various avenues, such as dry, sallow-looking skin, lifeless hair, and cracked, white-spotted nails.

I'll let you in on a little secret. Dieting actually makes you fat! Unbelievable I know, but nevertheless it's true. Anyone who has dieted for years, only to become heavier than ever, will agree with me. But why is this? It's important to realize the fundamentals of dieting. If we go "on" a diet, it follows that eventually we must come "off" this same diet. This

usually means a return to bad eating habits and lack of exercise. (Not always, but usually!)

When you diet, your body panics and worries about where its next meal is coming from. So, when you do eat, instead of utilizing the food as energy and distributing it to the various organs, the body places this food in fat stores. The body thinks that it may be some time before it receives more food, and is protecting itself against starvation and deprivation. (In women, our fat stores tend to be around our hips, thighs, buttocks, and abdomen: in men, it's mainly the abdomen that stores fat.) However, when you eat regularly, therefore providing yourself with enough food to use as fuel and energy, your body is less likely to store fat as it is confident that there will be another food delivery shortly!

fad diets

You've heard of them all. In fact, it's difficult to avoid the coverlines hailing another "celebrity" diet, along with pictures of once normal-looking women, who are now little more than skin and bones, being applauded by the media as though they have achieved something worthwhile. No wonder we're confused! Whether it's eating by colors, according to your blood group, no meat, all meat, no bread, all bread, dinner for breakfast, or nothing but grapefruit or cabbage soup for days on end, the diet industry is big business—and no wonder. Diets don't work, so we eagerly welcome a new way of losing the pounds, without actually considering what we may be doing to our bodies.

Any diet that cuts out a food type risks leading to a deficiency of a particular nutrient. For example, vegans or vegetarians may lack vitamin B12, mainly derived from meat products, and are thus susceptible to anemia. It's important that they include grains and legumes, which contain B12, in their diet. (B12 also strengthens hair and nails.)

Cutting out carbohydrates means you risk burning up too much fat, and this may produce potentially toxic substances called ketones. Complex carbohydrate foods, such as brown rice and oats, are rich in essential nutrients that help to balance energy, moods, and weight. As there is evidence linking obesity and non-insulin-dependant diabetes with diets high in fat and low in carbohydrates and fiber, it is important to ensure that you are receiving at least 30 percent of your daily intake from carbohydrates. And if you are avoiding dairy foods and eating a strict detox diet of fruit and vegetables, you may be lacking calcium, which is imperative for good bone health, and placing your body at risk of osteoporosis. If you are avoiding dairy foods, replace these with nuts, seeds, and soy products.

cosmetic surgery— yes or no?

Cosmetic surgery was once available only to the very rich, or the very famous. Now main street pharmacies offer Botox treatments during lunch hours, and a trip to the plastic surgeon is becoming as common as a visit to the dentist. With around 800,000 people in the US alone having Botox each year, it seems that this quick-fix route is becoming the norm. But is it harmful? Well, yes and no. Botox is derived from a naturally occurring toxin, produced by the *Clostridium botulinum* bacterium, and can be lethal if ingested. However, only a tiny amount is injected, so adverse effects are unlikely. In more than 30 years of therapeutic use, botulinum toxin has proved remarkably safe. Side effects may include excessive muscle weakness at the injection site or adjacent muscles. These effects typically resolve quickly. Occasionally, patients report flu-like symptoms but these are usually short-lived.

Botox is relatively non-intrusive and lasts only three months. Surgery, such as face-lifts, rhinoplasty (nose jobs), and breast enlargement, should be taken more seriously. Bearing in mind that cosmetic surgery can go horribly wrong, if you're considering such treatments it's important to find the best and most experienced surgeon. This is not the time to shop around for the cheapest deal.

I neither condone nor recommend cosmetic surgery—I think it is a matter of individual choice—however, I think it's important to look at all the options. I would suggest that anyone considering surgery should ask themselves *why* they think they want it and *how* they think it would improve their life. Many women say they believe that it would give them more confidence. But confidence comes from within and surgery cannot give you this. If you've always hated the size of your breasts or your crooked nose, then surgery may help you feel happier about your appearance. But, like confidence, true beauty comes from inside you—and no amount of time spent "under the knife" can help you achieve that!

WHY FOLLOW THE NATURAL ROUTE?

Considering how easy it is to reach for a jar of moisturizer, or a pre-prepared meal, it's no wonder that, as consumers, we are tending to opt for the quick-fix, ready-made option when it comes to our health and beauty. However, as recent research has shown, we may be doing more harm than good to our skin.

Most of us are aware of the damage caused to our skin and our health by external environmental dangers, such as secondhand cigarette smoke and pesticides on fresh produce.

But we should also think about the beauty products we use. A study by Mount Sinai School of Medicine in New York found an average of 91 industrial compounds, pollutants, and other chemicals in the blood and urine of volunteers. Some chemicals were known carcinogens (cancer-causing chemicals), while others were banned or untested for potential health hazards. Even more disturbingly, some of these chemicals were traced back to beauty products. And, according to another source, it's estimated that more than 5,000 chemicals are used in personal care products.

The skin, the body's largest organ, is the main absorption point of everyday toxins. Up to 60 percent of ingredients in body products, such as lotion, cream, and bubble bath, will be absorbed through the skin and into the bloodstream. The chemicals then accumulate in target organs, or are metabolized through the system, in some instances over a period of years.

how do I know if it's a "natural" or "organic" product?

It's difficult to know whether a product is truly natural or organic. For example, if a product such as shampoo contains "lemon extract for shiny hair," this does not necessarily mean that pure lemon juice has been used. The best way to confirm whether a product is truly natural is to check the label. Ingredients are listed in descending order with the largest quantities first. In truly organic products, synthetic fertilizers, pesticides, and other chemicals are strictly prohibited. In most cases, a small amount of preservative

may have been added to prohibit the growth of bacteria. But the amount is so small that it's barely noticeable. Some companies actually list the percentage of pure organic ingredients. But watch out for those that are labelled "pesticide free." This does not mean that the product is 100 percent natural, as the company may still have used ingredients that have been grown with fertilizers, which may still cause harm to you and your skin.

which ingredients to watch out for

Some of the most problematic ingredients in your beauty products may appear listed as propylene glycol, mineral oil, alcohol, petrolatum, isopropyl myristate, triethanolamine (TEA), and glycerine. These ingredients do not benefit the skin in any way and may even be harmful. They can smother the skin, clogging the pores and hindering its ability to remove toxic waste products and really "breathe."

● *Propylene glycol* is relatively inexpensive and widely available and so is the most common "moisture-carrying" substance found in cosmetics. But it actually absorbs moisture from your skin. It has been reported to cause sensitive reactions, such as a red rash or small bumps very much like pimples, in some people. Propylene glycol is used extensively in industry as a component of brake fluids and anti-freeze preparations, and also plays a part in the production of varnish.

● *Some manufactured exfoliants* can disrupt the skin's natural life cycle by removing mature skin cells, leaving the immature cells below vulnerable to premature exposure to the environment. Once exposed, these immature cells can dry out and age more rapidly than they naturally would.

● *Bentonite mineral and kaolin clay* are widely used in facial masks, where they dry out the skin and form an impenetrable barrier. This barrier traps toxins, including carbon dioxide, in your skin, while keeping the vital oxygen out. If your skin can't breathe, it can't stay healthy.

● *Alcohol* is the main active ingredient in astringents and other facial cleansers. It makes your face feel cool and refreshed, but it is actually causing quite a lot of damage to your skin. As it cleanses, it strips away the natural oils that are there to protect your face. After the skin surface has been stripped, it can take almost 24 hours for your skin to repair itself. Your face needs moisture to stay healthy and young-looking—not harsh chemicals.

● *Liquid foundations* often contain mineral oil, a substance that suffocates and dries out the face, plus petrolatum and isopropyl myristate. Petrolatum can't be absorbed by the skin and so it clogs the pores. Isopropyl myristate is a fatty compound that has been shown not only to clog pores but also to cause blackheads and pimples. When isopropyl myristate comes into contact with a di- or trie-thanolamine compound, it produces a nitrate substance such as n-nitrosodiethanolamine, a suspected carcinogen. Moisturizers for the face and body are applied over a large portion of the skin and remain there for several hours. This exposure is significant. Many powder foundations contain talc and zinc stearate, both of which can be carcinogenic. Most blushers contain talc zinc stearate and also mineral oil.

● *Glycerine* is commonly used in moisturizers to help the cream glide easily and smoothly onto your skin, but it can also have detrimental side effects in that it draws moisture from the skin and holds it on the surface, effectively drying the skin from the inside out.

natural is best

As you can see, using natural products, particularly those that you have concocted yourself, is really the safest beauty program for your skin. After all, if you're following a holistic lifestyle, exercising regularly (not just aerobic exercise but also practising yoga or tai chi), and eating as healthily as you can, then it makes sense that you complete this circle with natural beauty products. Making your own cosmetic products may feel like just one more chore you have to set aside time for. But most of the recipes and treatments in this book are relatively quick and easy to make, and the majority of ingredients used are already present in your kitchen.

Try to regard the time and effort you spend mixing together a particular treatment as an important part of your pampering program—it will help to focus your thoughts and ready body and mind for a wonderful, relaxing escape.

beauty food pharmacy

Eating well is not just an indulgence, or something that you do purely for the sake of your physical well-being, it's also an essential part of maintaining smooth, glowing skin, shiny hair, and strong nails. Unlike your internal organs and inner health, the skin is something that you see every day. It is therefore easy to determine how well you are merely by looking in the mirror. By eating the freshest foods and using natural ingredients as part of your daily skin-care routine, you'll help to maintain a strong immune system, and ensure that you look, and feel, your best.

The most wonderful thing about eating well is that it is so easy. It really is just as simple to reach for an apple as it is to open a bag of potato chips. Plus, you'll feel healthier and happier, which is one of the first steps to achieving natural beauty.

The following chapter explains the various benefits of foods—all of which are available from your supermarket, local grocery store, and—in the case of herbs—your own garden. Each section includes information on the vitamins and other nutrients that these various foods contain, as well as how and why they are good for you. And there are in-depth profiles of star foods that provide extra special health benefits. To help you make the most of each foodstuff, there is a list of easy-to-follow recipes to try, plus various beauty treatments with which to pamper yourself. Eating well has never been easier, or as much fun!

fruits and vegetables

SOFT FRUIT AND BERRIES

APRICOTS *(Prunus armeniaca)*

★ VITAMINS B2, B3, B5, C; BETA CAROTENE; CALCIUM, BORON, IRON, MAGNESIUM, POTASSIUM, ZINC; SOLUBLE FIBER, SUGARS

● PROTECT EYES AND BLOOD VESSELS; HELP PREVENT RED, IRRITATED EYES AND DRY, SPLITTING HAIR AND NAILS

Fresh or dried, apricots are an excellent health and beauty food. Three small fresh apricots contain more than 50 percent of the recommended daily intake (RDA) of beta carotene, a potent antioxidant. Beta carotene prevents the build-up of plaque deposits in the arteries, protects the eyes from sun damage, and deactivates free radicals that, if left unchecked, accelerate the aging process and increase the risk of cancer. The body converts beta carotene into vitamin A, which is vital for good vision and for keeping the eyes lubricated. Those at risk of dry eyes, such as contact-lens wearers, should include plenty of apricots in their diet. Apricots contain significant levels of iron, essential for hemoglobin, the oxygen-carrying pigment in red blood cells. Iron deficiency leads to anemia, pale skin, and thinning, undernourished hair.

RECIPES oatmeal with prunes and apricots (page 92), Italian salad (page 104), lentil and red onion quiche (page 109)

BLUEBERRIES *(Vaccinium corymbosum)*

★ VITAMIN C; ANTHOCYANINS, BETA CAROTENE; CALCIUM, POTASSIUM, FIBER

● ANTI-AGING PROPERTIES; HELP PREVENT DRY SKIN, GUM DISEASE, THREAD VEINS, WRINKLES, MOUTH ULCERS, BLOODSHOT EYES

The many health benefits that blueberries offer can be achieved by eating just a handful a day. They are richest in antioxidants of all the fruits and vegetables. The antioxidants in blueberries are called flavonoids (polyphenols) and they neutralize free radicals and so help slow down the aging process. The flavonoids in blueberries strengthen the collagen in the walls of the tiny blood vessels in the eyes, so helping to reduce the risk of cataracts and glaucoma.

Blueberries are also rich in vitamin C, which helps maintain strong capillary walls. Capillaries are the tiny blood vessels that keep the skin well supplied with oxygen and nutrients, thus helping it to regenerate, and also keep its elasticity and plumpness for longer. Blueberries contain anthocyanins, which combat bacteria and strengthen blood vessels in the gums, so helping to protect against gum disease and plaque build-up. Blueberries supply fiber to bulk up food waste and hasten its passage through the colon. Therefore, adding blueberries to your morning smoothie or oatmeal keeps you regular and reduces the risk of colon cancer. Like cranberries, blueberries help prevent urinary tract infection.

RECIPES fresh fruit salad (page 92), smooth and sweet honey and berries (page 93), strawberry spread (page 93)

PRUNES *(Prunus domestica)*

★ BETA CAROTENE; IRON, POTASSIUM, CALCIUM, SELENIUM; FIBER

● PROMOTE STRONG FINGERNAILS, SHINY HAIR, SKIN HEALING

A glass of prune juice or a handful of dried prunes helps relieve constipation by speeding up the passage of stools through the digestive tract. Prunes also contain sorbitol—a type of sugar that has a laxative effect. A 3½ oz serving of prunes provides 20 percent of a woman's daily iron intake, which is especially important for vegetarians who, as they do not eat meat, miss out on a rich source of iron. Therefore, prunes provide an easy and healthy way to avoid anemia symptoms, such as fatigue, sallow skin, poor concentration, dry and flaking nails, and dull, lifeless hair.

RECIPES oatmeal with prunes and apricots (page 92), marinated chicken with prune salsa (page 106)

RASPBERRIES *(Rubus idaeus)*

★ VITAMIN C; ANTHOCYANINS; POTASSIUM; FIBER

● PROTECT EYES AND GUMS; PREVENT SPLITTING NAILS, DRY SKIN

Raspberries should be part of every woman's diet. They can help with irregular menstrual cycles, and are believed to aid in childbirth by encouraging labor. These sweet, red fruits contain ellagic acid, a phytonutrient that helps neutralize carcinogens (cancer-causing substances), and so helps to protect the body against cigarette smoke, processed foods, and barbecued meats. Raspberries help increase fluid intake. This is vital for healthy nails, which are composed of 16 percent water and so need to be kept well-hydrated or they become brittle, and prone to splitting. Raspberries also help fight fungal infections of the nails. Like blueberries, raspberries are rich in anthocyanins, which help to strengthen the blood vessels in the eyes. A handful of raspberries contain almost 80 percent of the recommended daily intake (RDA) of vitamin C, which is vital for healthy skin. Raspberries are an excellent mood-booster, and should be eaten in abundance during the winter months to avoid the symptoms of seasonal affective disorder (SAD), also called "winter blues," such as lethargy and depression.

RECIPES fresh fruit salad (page 92), mixed fall fruits with pancakes (page 112), strawberry starter smoothie (page 114), skin healer (page 114), an apple a day (page 115)

EXOTIC FRUIT

BANANA *(Musa acuminata)*

★ BETA CAROTENE; TRYPTOPHAN; CARBOHYDRATE; POTASSIUM

● ANTI-AGING, MOISTURIZING; HELPS PREVENT HAIR LOSS, ACNE

A banana contains around ¾ oz of fruit sugar, which is quickly absorbed into the bloodstream, giving an almost immediate energy boost. However, diabetics should avoid ripe bananas—under-ripe ones contain less sugar and so raise blood sugar levels more slowly. High blood pressure sufferers benefit from eating bananas, as the potassium in these fruits regulates blood pressure. Potassium also promotes cellular growth, and, as it is important in the balance of fluids in the body, keeps the skin hydrated. Bananas contain tryptophan, nature's very own sleeping pill, which has a sedative effect on the body, calming the nervous system and so helping to combat stress. This means bananas are an excellent beauty food, as stress can cause premature aging, hair loss, and skin disorders such as eczema or dermatitis.

RECIPES: fresh fruit salad (page 92), apple, vegetable, and quorn curry (page 108), mixed fall fruits with pancakes (page 112), get up and glow (page 114), strawberry starter smoothie (page 114), an apple a day (page 115). TREATMENTS banana and cream anti-aging mask (page 122), banana hair mask (page 123)

KIWI FRUIT *(Actinidia chinensis)*

★ VITAMINS A AND C, FOLATE; FIBER

● ANTI-AGING, BOOSTS IMMUNE SYSTEM, PREVENTS WRINKLES

Originally from New Zealand, kiwi fruit (also known as "Chinese gooseberries") are now extremely popular worldwide. This is not only owing to their sweet and tangy taste, but also because they contain high levels of vitamin C. Eating one kiwi fruit a day means you have achieved your recommended daily intake (RDA) of this vitamin. Kiwi fruit loses little of its nutritional value even after lengthy storage. A deficiency of vitamin C makes you more susceptible to colds, flu, and other infections, and wounds take longer to heal. Vitamin C helps to strengthen capillary walls, which, when ruptured, can cause skin bruising and tiny thread veins. Maintaining strong capillaries also ensures that a good supply of oxygen and nutrients can reach the skin, which is important for cell regeneration and for helping to maintain optimum levels of elastin and collagen—the structural components of the skin that confer strength, plumpness, flexibility, and elasticity.

RECIPES fresh fruit salad (page 92), strawberry spread (page 93), perfect start (page 114), happy and healthy (page 115), an apple a day (page 115)

strawberry

STRAWBERRIES OFFER MANY BEAUTY BENEFITS. THE MASHED PULP CAN BE APPLIED DIRECTLY TO SUNBURN TO ALLEVIATE REDNESS AND CAN ALSO BE USED TO HELP FADE FRECKLES. WHEN MADE INTO A JUICE, STRAWBERRIES CAN BE APPLIED DIRECTLY TO THE TEETH TO HELP REMOVE THE STAINS CAUSED BY RED WINE OR TOBACCO.

History of the strawberry

In the Victorian language of flowers, the strawberry (*Fragaria* x *ananassa*) represents absolute perfection. Strawberries have many sexual connotations: in provincial France, strawberries were regarded as an aphrodisiac of the highest quality. Traditionally, newlyweds were served soup of thinned sour cream, strawberries, borage (a herb with a taste similar to that of cucumber) and powdered sugar. Medieval stonemasons carved strawberry designs on altars and around the tops of pillars in churches and cathedrals, symbolizing perfection and righteousness. At about the same period, strawberries were served at important state occasions and festivals to ensure peace and prosperity.

If you're looking to meet Mr or Mrs Right, legend holds that if you break a strawberry in half and share it with a member of the opposite sex, you will both soon fall in love!

Health profile

Strawberries contain the antioxidant vitamins A, C, and E—making them excellent immune-boosters, thereby helping the body fight against cold, flu, and other infections. Antioxidants also repair cell damage caused by free radicals, so may help to prevent some cancers. Strawberries are high in fiber, which helps to bulk stools, moving them faster through the colon. It is believed that this helps reduce the risk of colon cancer—and it is good news, too, if you suffer from constipation. They also contain the plant chemicals p-coumaric acid and chlorogenic acid, which prevent carcinogens forming in the stomach and thus guard against stomach cancer.

Beauty-boosting properties

These luscious berries are a star source of vitamin C, one of the most important nutrients for maintaining healthy skin. This vitamin is critical to the formation of collagen—a key structural element of the connective tissue that keeps skin firm, plump, and flexible. Vitamin C also helps prevent the tiny capillaries beneath the skin's surface from breaking and promotes wound healing. Strawberries are especially recommended for acne sufferers, as they are mild digestive cleansers, helping the body rid itself of any toxins that may trigger an acne outbreak. They are rich in potassium, which helps regulate the body's water balance. They help the body retain a healthy level of fluids, keeping the skin well hydrated, as well as nourishing the nails and hair follicles.

BEAUTIFUL FOOD PROFILE	
HEALTH COUNTER 100 G	CALORIES 37; CARBOHYDRATE 9 g; FRUCTOSE 2 g; FAT 2 g; FIBER 2 g
VITAMINS AND MINERALS	VITAMINS A, C, AND E, FOLATE; CAROTENES; CALCIUM, POTASSIUM
GOOD FOR	HEALTHY DIGESTION; SKIN; STRONG NAILS AND HAIR GROWTH; PREVENTING ACNE, FRECKLES, SUNBURN

inside out: recipe

STRAWBERRY AND BALSAMIC VINEGAR PUDDING

1 punnet strawberries (organic if possible)
superfine sugar to taste
4 fl oz good quality balsamic vinegar
7 oz mascarpone cheese

Arrange the strawberries in a deep dish. Sprinkle with the sugar and add the vinegar. Stir, cover, and leave to stand for 6 hours. Serve with the mascarpone cheese. Serves 4–6.

outside in: treatment

STRAWBERRY ROSE BODY POLISH

Designed to exfoliate, nourish, and lighten dark or discolored areas of skin. The natural acids and plant oils will leave you with a healthy glow.

12 oz/½ pt strawberries, rinsed,
   tops removed, and thinly sliced
2 fl oz/¼ cup plain yogurt
1 tsp vegetable glycerine
2 tbsp raw honey
1 tbsp castor oil

8 oz fine sea salt
3 oz almond oil
5 drops rose essential oil
5 drops rose geranium essential oil
5 drops rosewood essential oil

Prepare the strawberries and combine with the yogurt, glycerine, honey, and castor oil in a blender and blend until smooth. Set aside. Pour the sea salt into a bowl. Add the almond oil and stir. Add the strawberry mixture and mix well. Add the essential oils last and stir well. Leave the mixture to set for about 30 minutes. Run a warm bath and drench your entire body. Rub the mixture all over, making sure you exfoliate areas such as the tops of the arms, the elbows, and the shins. Leave the scrub on for 5 minutes. Shower, and when dry apply a rich moisturizer all over.

pomegranate

POMEGRANATES ARE NOT ONLY GOOD FOR YOU—THEY ARE THOUGHT TO BE APHRODISIACS, SO INCLUDE THEM IN A ROMANTIC MEAL!

History of the pomegranate

The pomegranate (*Punica granatum*) has been revered as a symbol of health, fertility, and rebirth throughout history. Some cultures believed it held profound and mystical healing powers; others chose to use it in more practical ways, such as decoration or in a dye. Many scholars suggest that it was a pomegranate, and not an apple, that Eve used to tempt Adam in the biblical Garden of Eden. The religious connections continued into the Middle Ages. For example, in medieval tales of the unicorn, pomegranate seeds were said to "bleed" from the animal's horn, symbolizing Christ's suffering. The pomegranate tree represented eternal life.

Health profile

The juice from pomegranates is one of nature's most powerful antioxidants. In fact, studies show that pomegranate juice contains more potent antioxidants than any other drink. In addition to vitamin C, pomegranates contain a group of antioxidants called flavonoids (also known as polyphenols). This large group of plant chemicals is known to have a wide range of beneficial actions, including as anti-inflammatories, antibacterials, and antivirals. Their most important effect

is as antioxidants. These guard the body against free radicals, the harmful molecules formed by natural metabolic processes in the body, and by pollution and cigarette smoke. Free radicals increase the risk of heart disease, stroke, cancer, and Alzheimer's disease, and can cause premature aging. So pomegranates truly are nature's very own medicine chest!

Beauty-boosting properties

When the body is attacked by free radicals, among the many detrimental effects this can cause, the system is robbed of the nutrients that are required for skin repair and renewal. If you continue to lack these nutrients, the skin becomes dull, dry, and loses its elasticity, all effects that lead to premature aging. In India, the leaf of the pomegranate is used to treat cuts, as it contains a natural healing and soothing agent. The

skin-saving benefits of pomegranates have recently been discovered by cosmetic houses, which have included the fruit in moisturizers, sunscreens, and cleansers, among other products.

BEAUTIFUL FOOD PROFILE

HEALTH COUNTER/100 g	CALORIES 120; FAT 5 g; FIBER 1 g
VITAMINS AND MINERALS	VITAMIN C; FOLATE; CAROTENES; CALCIUM; IRON; SODIUM; POTASSIUM
GOOD FOR	ANTI-AGING, HEART DISEASE, WRINKLES

inside out: recipe

POMEGRANATE SOUP

5 oz/⅝ cup lentils
3 tbsp butter or margarine
1 medium onion, chopped
8 cups water
1 cup long-grain rice
1 tsp turmeric
salt and freshly ground pepper
    to taste

1 oz/½ cup fresh parsley,
    chopped
3 oz/½ cup scallions, chopped
1 cup pomegranate juice
2 tbsp fresh mint, chopped
1 tbsp raisins

Rinse the lentils several times and set aside to drain. Melt 2 tablespoons of butter or margarine in a large saucepan. Add the onion. Sauté until the onion is tender. Add the water, drained lentils, rice, turmeric, salt and pepper. Bring to the boil. Reduce the heat and cover. Simmer over a low heat for 40 minutes or until the lentils and rice are tender. Add the parsley, scallions, and pomegranate juice. Simmer for another 15 minutes. Melt 1 tablespoon of butter or margarine in a small skillet. Add the mint. Sauté until the butter or margarine is golden brown. Pour over the soup. Sprinkle with the raisins. Serves 6–8.

outside in: treatment

POMEGRANATE AND CRANBERRY SHAMPOO

2 fl oz/¼ cup liquid castile soap (available from health stores)
2 tsp pomegranate juice
4 tsp cranberry juice
1 tsp liquid glycerine

Mix all the ingredients together and pour into clean bottles. Shake well before each use. Apply lotion to wet hair and lather well. Rinse, and follow with your chosen conditioner. This mixture should be kept refrigerated. Store for 10 days maximum, and then discard.

MANGO *(Mangifera indica)*

★ VITAMINS B3, C, AND E; BETA CAROTENE; POTASSIUM, IRON; INSOLUBLE FIBER

● ANTI-AGING; AIDS NIGHT VISION; GUARDS AGAINST ACNE, STYES, DERMATITIS, DRY SKIN, LIFELESS COMPLEXION, SUN DAMAGE

A juicy, ripe mango is a summer delight, rich in three powerful antioxidants, vitamins B3, C, and E, and beta carotene. These vitamins are vital for healthy skin and B3 also protects against conditions such as dermatitis. Beta carotene diffuses the sun's rays and strengthens the skin against ultraviolet (UV) damage. It is converted into vitamin A in the body and is essential for healthy skin, good vision—especially night vision—and strong, healthy teeth. Mango is an excellent detoxifying tool as it helps to cleanse the blood and the kidneys. Detoxifying clears the complexion, enhances skin radiance, and wards off wrinkles.

RECIPES fresh fruit salad (page 92), mango, apple, and passion-fruit sorbet (page 112)

PINEAPPLE *(Ananas comosus)*

★ VITAMIN C, FOLATE; BETA CAROTENE, BROMELAIN, P-COUMARIC ACID; POTASSIUM; FIBER

● EXFOLIANT; HELPS PREVENT WRINKLES, BLEMISHES, SUN SPOTS, AGE SPOTS, CLEARS BLOCKED PORES

Pineapple contains chemicals called alpha-hydroxy acids (AHAs), which are widely used in the beauty industry as an "exfoliant." When applied to the skin, AHAs help to speed up skin cell renewal, as they slough off dead skin, making way for younger, smoother cells, and aiding skin healing and repair. AHAs are particularly recommended for age or sun spots, softening the appearance of wrinkles, unblocking pores, and treating blemishes. Pineapple has many healing qualities internally, too, owing to the fact that it contains an enzyme called bromelain. This extract, when used medicinally, has been shown to be effective in treating blood clots that might otherwise lead to thrombosis. When blood clots do not dissolve naturally, they can block blood vessels, leading to a heart attack or stroke. Bromelain also helps to treat bruising, speeds up the healing process, and may even aid digestion, as it helps break down proteins in the stomach.

RECIPES passion-fruit pineapple sorbet with mint sauce (page 113), skin healer (page 114). TREATMENTS face the day mask (page 122)

WATERMELON *(Citrullus lanatus)*

★ VITAMINS C AND A; BETA CAROTENE, LYCOPENE; CALCIUM, IRON, MAGNESIUM, POTASSIUM

● SUN PROTECTION, REHYDRATING, HELPS PREVENT WRINKLES

Watermelon—and watermelon juice—is the tastiest, most thirst-quenching treat you can have on a summer's day. And watermelons don't just taste good. The red color of watermelon is caused by the phytochemical lycopene—a substance also present in tomatoes—that may help protect the body against cancer. Along with lycopene, watermelons contain beta carotene, which, together with its high levels of vitamin C, helps to protect the skin against the damaging rays of the sun. As there is such a high water content in this fruit, watermelon is an ideal way to keep the skin well hydrated and so ensure it stays smooth and supple. We lose around 17 fl oz of water each day, and just one slice of watermelon provides 12 fl oz of fluid.

RECIPE make yourself some watermelon juice and drink at least one glass a day

CITRUS FRUIT

LIME *(Citrus aurantifolia)*

★ VITAMIN C, FOLIC ACID; LYCOPENE, POTASSIUM; FIBER

● GOOD FOR GUMS, WOUND HEALING AND DIGESTION; HELPS
  PREVENT PIMPLES AND BLEMISHES

Traditionally limes—and other citrus fruits—were taken to sea by ancient mariners to help prevent scurvy on long voyages because they contain such high levels of vitamin C. Today, limes are still highly recommended for keeping gums healthy, healing wounds, preventing bruising to the skin, and helping to protect the eyes against cataracts. The vitamin C in limes helps to cleanse the digestive system, which promotes clear skin and even weight loss. Vitamin C also aids the absorption of iron from plant sources of this mineral, particularly important for non-meat eaters. Limes are well known for their capacity to block the effect of carcinogens (cancer-forming substances) in the stomach. The fiber in citrus fruits helps to increase the size and weight of stools, aiding their passage through the colon. In the long term, this may help prevent colonic cancer. Like pineapple, limes contain alpha-hydroxy acids (AHAs). Applied topically, limes (and lemons) may help to prevent wrinkles and are an effective anti-pimple treatment.

RECIPES Thai sweet and sour soup (page 95), lime, tomato, and scallop salad (page 102)

OTHER FRUIT

APPLE *(Malus domestica)*

★ VITAMINS C AND E; QUERCETIN; POTASSIUM; CARBOHYDRATES,
  FIBER, CELLULOSE

♡ IF YOU'VE FORGOTTEN TO BRUSH YOUR TEETH, BITE INTO AN
  APPLE. THIS IS AN EXCELLENT WAY TO KEEP YOUR TEETH CLEAN
  AND YOUR BREATH FRESH

● EXFOLIATING, ANTI-AGING, MOOD-ENHANCING; HELPS PREVENT
  PIMPLES AND CELLULITE

Apples are a good source of vitamins C and E, antioxidants that help the body to mop up the free radicals caused by factors such as smoking, pollution, and poor nutrition, and so help fight heart disease and cancers. Continued exposure to free radicals can lead to premature aging, wrinkles, and dull-looking skin. Antioxidants help the skin's cells to renew and repair themselves, so that the skin does not look tired and lifeless. Vitamin C is needed to help heal wounds. It also aids in the absorption of calcium into the body, and so is vital for building strong, healthy bones and teeth. Apples are high in dietary fiber and so contribute to regularity. The effects of a sluggish digestive system tend to reveal themselves in the skin, often in the form of pimples around the mouth. For maximum health benefits, eat apples unpeeled (but carefully washed) since the most important nutrients are in the skin. The scent of a freshly cut apple is also believed to help lift the spirits.

Apples contain silicon and malic acid, which help keep hair and nails strong and healthy, and restore vitality to the skin, leaving it softer and smoother, reducing wrinkles and blemishes, and lightening age spots. Malic acid is believed to help flush out the toxins that might otherwise lead to cellulite. Applied to the skin, apple is a good exfoliant, helping to remove dead skin cells and leaving your skin feeling wonderfully soft and refreshed. Peel an apple and—holding the peel skin side out—rub over your face to reveal smooth glowing skin.

RECIPES apple, vegetable, and quorn curry (page 108), mango, apple, and passion-fruit sorbet (page 112), apple and almond fruit fool (page 113), boysenberry and apple muesli-style crumble (page 113), Bramley apple and blackberry layer (page 113), perfect start (page 114), perfect skin (page 115), happy and healthy (page 115), an apple a day (page 115)

PEAR *(Pyrus communis)*

★ VITAMIN C; BETA CAROTENE; POTASSIUM; PECTIN; CARBOHYDRATES

● AIDS WOUND HEALING, HELPS PREVENT MOUTH ULCERS, ACNE,
  HAY FEVER

Pears are a useful fruit for people of all ages. As they are the least likely to cause an allergic reaction, they are an ideal fruit to give to babies or young children. Pears are high in fiber. In particular, they contain pectin, a soluble fiber that acts as a gentle laxative to keep the digestive system regular and healthy. Fiber is an excellent detoxifier. By detoxifying your digestive system, you will keep your skin clear and smooth, your eyes will sparkle, and you'll have more energy. Try eating only pears for one day to feel the difference. Pears also contain quercetin, which reduces inflammation. Applied to inflamed skin, pears help speed up the healing process.

RECIPES fresh fruit salad (page 92), mixed fall fruits with pancakes (page 112), perfect start (page 114)

lemon

**LEMON HAS EXCELLENT CLEANSING AND ASTRINGENT PROPERTIES
—FOR BOTH INSIDE AND OUT. LEMON JUICE IS A NATURAL EXFOLIANT,
LEAVING THE SKIN TINGLING FRESH. IT ALSO HELPS REDUCE THE
APPEARANCE OF FINE LINES AND WRINKLES.**

History of the lemon

The lemon (*Citrus limon*) and other citrus fruits are native to
southern China and Southeast Asia where they have been
cultivated for around 4,000 years. Arab traders brought citrus fruits
to eastern Africa and the Middle East between AD 100 and 700.
Superior varieties from Southeast Asia arrived in Europe with
Portuguese traders in the 16th century. By the 1800s citrus fruits
were found worldwide. In Europe, demand for them increased after
the 1890s when physicians found that scurvy (a disease common
among sailors, now known to be caused by vitamin C deficiency)
could be prevented by drinking the juice of citrus fruits.

Health profile

Lemon is an internal cleanser. Practitioners of Ayurveda (an ancient
Indian health system) recommend drinking hot water with lemon
juice first thing in the morning to aid internal cleansing and
to kick-start the digestive system. This is also believed to
help clear blemished skin. Citrus fruits contain high levels of vitamin
C, an important antioxidant that has been shown to help protect
the eyes against cataracts. Studies have also shown that people
who regularly include citrus fruits in their diet reduce their risk of
stomach cancer by about 60 percent. The fiber in lemons is
believed to help bulk up stools, helping to avoid constipation and
reducing the risk of colon cancer.

Beauty-boosting properties

If you suffer from pimples, lemon juice is more effective than any
anti-blemish medication. It is a natural astringent, helping to
remove bacteria from an infected area and promote wound
healing. Lemon juice applied directly to cold sores can speed up
the healing process—although it does sting! Lemons are also
nature's very own hair highlighter, adding rays of sunshine to blond
hair. You can also use lemon juice on your nails to remove garlic
or onion odors, and to cleanse the nail bed.

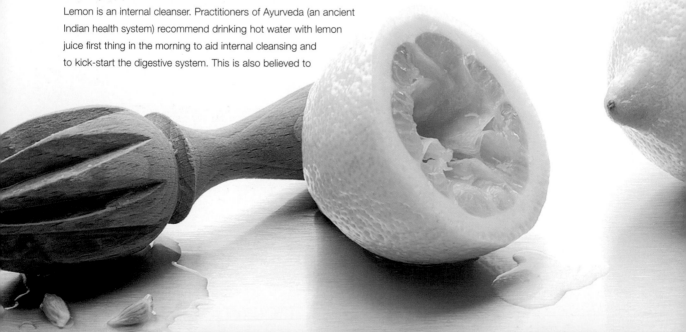

BEAUTIFUL FOOD PROFILE	
HEALTH COUNTER/100 g	CALORIES 14; CARBOHYDRATE 2 g; FRUCTOSE 1 g; FAT 2 g; FIBER 2 g
VITAMINS AND MINERALS	VITAMIN C; CAROTENES; CALCIUM, POTASSIUM
GOOD FOR	EXFOLIATING, LIGHTENING HAIR, HAIR GROWTH, COLD SORES, SORE THROATS

inside out: recipe

CHICKEN AND LEMON SALAD

4 chicken breasts
1½ oz baby tomatoes
½ avocado
1½ oz organic cheese
8 oz baby spinach
1 lemon

Cook the chicken breasts in a small pan (you can either slice them or keep them whole). While they're cooking, slice the tomatoes, avocado, and cheese and arrange over the spinach leaves. Drizzle lemon juice on the avocado to prevent it going brown. When the chicken is almost cooked, add the lemon juice to the chicken in the pan, turning the chicken over until the juice is soaked up. Allow to cool slightly and then serve atop the salad leaves. Add more lemon juice if desired. Serves 4.

outside in: treatment

LEMON JUICE ASTRINGENT

This mixture helps to cleanse, freshen, and tone the skin. The strong natural astringent in the lemon juice also inhibits harmful bacterial action on the skin.

½ lemon
4 fl oz camomile hydrolat (available from health food stores)

Juice the lemon and add to the camomile. Store in the refrigerator in a covered container or bottle. Apply to the face, using cotton balls.

GREEN LEAFY VEGETABLES

ASPARAGUS *(Asparagus officinalis)*

★ VITAMINS B1, C, AND E, FOLIC ACID, ASPARAGINE; GLUTATHIONE; IRON, PHOSPHORUS, POTASSIUM, ZINC; FIBER

● ANTI-BLOATING; GUARDS AGAINST DRY, SCALY SKIN, WHITEHEADS, BLACKHEADS, DRY HAIR, FLAKING NAILS, HIGH BLOOD PRESSURE, CATARACTS

The active ingredients in asparagus include asparagine, which stimulates the kidneys and produces a diuretic effect (increasing urine output), making this an excellent anti-bloating vegetable. If you tend to suffer from bloating as part of your menstrual cycle, try including asparagus in your meals around ten days before your period is due. The beta carotene present in asparagus helps prevent dry, rough, and scaly skin. It is also beneficial if you are prone to whiteheads and blackheads. Beta carotene is a great nail strengthener and helps add moisture to dry hair. Eating asparagus regularly may help regulate blood pressure levels, which is particularly important if you suffer from high blood pressure, or if this condition runs in your family. Asparagus also contains glutathione, which may guard against cataracts (a deficiency of glutathione has been noted in people suffering from this disease).

RECIPES lime, tomato, and scallop salad (page 102), Italian salad (page 104)

BROCCOLI *(Brassica oleracea)*

★ VITAMINS C AND E, FOLIC ACID; BETA CAROTENE; CALCIUM POTASSIUM, SODIUM

● GOOD FOR SKIN, HAIR, NAILS

With its high content of antioxidants and fiber, broccoli is a wonderful cleansing vegetable, acting on the digestive system to keep it regular and free of bacterial build-up. Broccoli also purifies and stimulates the liver, which strengthens the body's immune system. The liver is the most important organ for healthy bodily functions. Preventing a build-up of toxins internally produces results that can be seen externally, in the form of smooth, glowing skin. Broccoli contains vitamin B2, which is required for strong, healthy growth of the hair, skin, and nails. Women who suffer from low iron levels as a consequence of heavy menstruation, or anemia, should increase their intake of broccoli, as this vegetable contains high levels of iron and beta carotene, a substance that, along with vitamin C, helps the body absorb iron into the bloodstream. Smokers, too, should include broccoli in their diet as its high vitamin C content may help protect against the carcinogenic effects of cigarette smoke. Vitamin C helps protect the skin against premature aging, particularly caused by smoking.

RECIPES steamed lemon grass chicken and rice rolls (page 98), beef and noodle salad with chili lemon grass dressing (page 102), green machine (page 114)

CELERY *(Apium graveolens)*

★ VITAMINS B1, C, AND E; BETA CAROTENE, PHENOLIC ACIDS; CALCIUM, POTASSIUM; FIBER

● DETOXIFYING, HYDRATING, AIDS SKIN AND NAILS

Celery is probably most often eaten as part of a calorie-controlled diet. Nonetheless, it has many other beneficial properties. It detoxifies the kidneys, which helps to keep the eyes clear and the skin glowing. Celery also has a high water content, so helping to keep the skin hydrated by replacing some of the fluids lost each day. Well-hydrated skin is smooth and supple and less likely to age prematurely. Keeping the body well-hydrated also helps ensure strong nails—dehydration can lead to brittle, splitting nails. Celery contains phenolic acids, which have been shown to block the actions of prostaglandins, chemicals linked to inflammatory conditions such as arthritis. Celery is also believed by many to be effective in the treatment of rheumatoid arthritis. It is thought that celery's neutralizing effects in the body help to renew joints and connective tissue. However, there are no scientific studies to support these claims.

RECIPES mushroom and bean soup (page 95), chicken salad with soy dressing (page 102), green machine (page 114), perfect start (page 114), perfect skin (page 115)

ZUCCHINI *(Cucurbita pepo)*

★ VITAMIN C; BETA CAROTENE; SODIUM, POTASSIUM; FIBER

● PREVENTS SENSITIVE SKIN, BROKEN CAPILLARIES, CATARACTS

Adding zucchini to your daily vegetable intake is a tasty way to increase your consumption of vitamin C. Reduced levels of vitamin C can lead to colds, flu, and other infections, so it's important to keep your immune system strong and healthy. It is good to include extra vitamin C in your diet if you have sensitive skin. This vitamin

strengthens the capillaries and bolsters the immune system against irritants. Zucchini contain beta carotene, which is converted into vitamin A in the body. Low levels of beta carotene are linked to eye disorders such as cataracts and macular degeneration. So adding zucchini to your dishes is one way to maintain healthy eyes.

RECIPES *mediterranean oven-roasted vegetable soup (page 94), vegetable and bean soup (page 96), vegetarian flan (page 99), tofu vegetable salad (page 102), oven-baked vegetable salad (page 105), shredded beet and feta salad (page 105), multicolored rice salad (page 105), rice jumble (page 109)*

LETTUCE *(Lactuca sativa)*

★ VITAMIN C, FOLIC ACID; BETA CAROTENE; CALCIUM, IRON, POTASSIUM; FIBER

● SKIN HYDRATING, ANTI-AGING; HELPS PREVENT OSTEOPOROSIS AND INSOMNIA

There are several varieties of lettuce, including butterhead, lollo rosso and iceberg, all of which are high in nutrients and low in calories. Opt for the darker varieties, as they contain more antioxidant vitamins than lighter types. Lettuces contain iron, vitamin C, and beta carotene, all of which are necessary for cell renewal and for ensuring well-nourished skin. Owing to their high water content, lettuces offer an ideal way to keep you hydrated, thus helping to ensure your skin stays soft and supple. Lettuce is also high in fiber which, together with the many antioxidants present in the leaves, helps to reduce the risk of colon cancer.

Women in particular should enjoy lettuce as part of a healthy eating plan, not just because of the low-calorie content, but also because it provides large amounts of calcium—important for strong bones. Lettuce is a good source of folate (the plant form of folic acid), which makes for strong nails. All women who are—or may become—pregnant are recommended to increase their intake of folic acid to help reduce the risk of spina bifida, a malformation of the spinal column that can occur in unborn babies.

Regular sleep plays a vital part in natural beauty by aiding relaxation, reducing stress, and encouraging cell renewal. Lettuce contains a natural sedative called lactucarium. If eaten just before bedtime, lettuce helps ward off insomnia and so aids restful sleep.

RECIPES *tasty tuna snack (page 99), Italian salad (page 104), shredded beet and feta salad (page 105), warm chickpea and tuna salad (page 105), warm winter salad (page 106), barbecue pork san choy bau (page 108)*

SPINACH *(Spinacia oleracea)*

★ VITAMINS C AND E, FOLIC ACID; BETA CAROTENE, CALCIUM, IRON, POTASSIUM; FIBER

● HELPS PREVENT MOUTH ULCERS, WHITE SPOTS, DISCOLORED NAILS, AND DRY, IRRITATED EYES

The vitamin C in spinach helps the immune system fight infections in the body, including those that cause eye disorders such as inflammation of the eyelid linings, blocked tear ducts, and eye dryness. Vitamin C also helps ensure the skin cells receive a constant supply of oxygen, helping to build collagen and promote regeneration of new cells. The beta carotene in spinach is thought to help neutralize free radicals caused by environmental factors such as excess exposure to the sun. Spinach is an excellent nail food, especially important if you suffer from discolored, irregularly shaped nails. Folate (or folic acid, a B vitamin, so-called because it is found in foliage) is needed for the formation of the red, oxygen-carrying blood pigment hemoglobin, which provides a healthy, pink color to the nail bed, as well as strengthening the nail itself. Folate also helps to prevent white spots on the nails.

Spinach is one of the richest plant sources of iron, which makes it an ideal addition to a meal for women suffering from a drop in iron during their menstrual cycle, anemia, and low blood sugar. Spinach is also high in calcium. Calcium is needed for strong bones and therefore helps protect against osteoporosis. Women of all ages, but particularly those aged 30 and upward, should try to include spinach regularly in their diet.

RECIPES *sesame beef rice and paper rolls (page 99), tofu vegetable salad (page 102), baby spinach, potato, and egg salad (page 103), spinach salad with warm garlic dressing (page 107)*

WATERCRESS *(Nasturtium officinale)*

★ VITAMINS C AND E, BETA CAROTENE, NICOTINIC ACID; ISOTHYOCYANATE; CALCIUM, IRON, POTASSIUM

● CLEANSING; HELPS PREVENT WATER RETENTION, EYE SENSITIVITY, NIGHT BLINDNESS, AND CANCERS OF THE LUNG, THYROID, COLON, AND RECTUM

Watercress makes a tasty addition to salads and sandwiches and is a useful garnish. It has a cleansing and restorative effect on the body, acting mainly as a diuretic. This helps reduce fluid retention, which might otherwise lead to bloating and facial puffiness. Watercress contains vitamin C and high levels of beta carotene, which may help protect against sensitivity to sunlight. Beta carotene can also help prevent night blindness. The calcium present in watercress is necessary for strong bones, teeth, and nails, and for helping to prevent muscle cramp. It is thought that the isothyocyanates in watercress detoxify nicotine and so may help protect the lungs against cancer. Other antioxidants present may guard against cancers of the thyroid, colon, and rectum.

RECIPE hard as nails (page 114)

VEGETABLE FRUITS

BELL PEPPERS *(Capsicum anuum)*

★ VITAMINS C AND E, FOLATE; CAROTENES, CAPSAICIN; POTASSIUM

● HYDRATING; PROMOTE HEALTHY SKIN, STRONG NAILS, GOOD NIGHT
    VISION; STRENGTHEN IMMUNE SYSTEM

Bell peppers are rich in carotenoids and vitamin C. The hot flavor of bell peppers is caused by the chemical capsaicin, which is present in all three varieties, yellow, red, and green. Capsaicin is sometimes given medicinally, applied to the skin to desensitize the nerves and so help control the pain of arthritis. A medium-sized bell pepper provides more than three times the recommended adult daily intake (RDA) of vitamin C. Bell peppers are therefore an ideal food for winter, when most people are more likely to suffer from colds and blocked sinuses.

Bell peppers are an excellent skin and nail food. They have a high water content and so are particularly useful for keeping the skin and nails hydrated. Dry nails are prone to flaking and are more likely to split. Yellow bell peppers contain lutein, which helps maintain healthy vision, especially at night. Poor night vision means you are more likely to squint in low light, for example when driving at night on poorly lit roads, and this can encourage the formation of fine lines and wrinkles around the eyes.

RECIPES stuffed bell peppers (page 99), tofu vegetable salad (page 102), multicolored rice salad (page 105), rice jumble (page 109)

PUMPKIN *(Cucurbita maxima)*

★ VITAMINS B1, C, AND E; ALPHA AND BETA CAROTENES; POTASSIUM;
    FIBER

● ANTI-AGING; GOOD FOR NAILS, HAIR, FERTILITY, HELPS PREVENT
    COLDS

The deep-orange color of pumpkins indicates that this vegetable is packed full of alpha and beta carotenes, along with other antioxidants, such as vitamins C and E. Carotenes play an important part in the battle against free radicals, which can damage cells, including those in blood vessel walls, thereby accelerating the aging process and causing wrinkles and sagging skin. Alpha and beta carotenes are also useful weapons in the body's fight against cancer. In particular, they may help reduce the risk of prostate cancer. The combination of vitamin C and beta carotene means regular servings of this vegetable can boost the immune system, helping to guard against colds and flu.

A strong immune system promotes skin healing and expresses itself through shiny hair and strong nails. Pumpkins are an excellent source of essential fatty acids (EFAs), required by the skin to maintain moisture, combat dryness, and improve muscle tone. As the word "essential" suggests, EFAs can't be made by the body and must come from food, so it's important to include as many sources as possible in your diet. For those trying to start a family, nutritionists recommend including pumpkin and pumpkin seeds in the man's diet, as the seeds especially are rich in iron and zinc, which are believed to help improve sperm mobility. Pumpkins can also help cleanse the digestive tract and purge the intestinal walls of harmful bacteria. If you have been suffering from a chesty cough, a bowl of pumpkin soup aids breathing by helping to clear mucus from the bronchi (tiny tubes) in the lungs.

RECIPES pumpkin soup (page 94), couscous medley (page 106).
TREATMENT pumpkin face mask (page 45)

TOMATO *(Lycopersicon sp.)*

★ VITAMINS C AND E; BETA CAROTENE, LYCOPENE

● ANTI-AGING; HELPS PREVENT CANCERS, IMPROVES SKIN AND
    DIGESTION

A ripe, juicy tomato helps to hydrate the skin and lubricate the digestive system. Tomatoes can provide around 40 percent of an adult's recommended daily intake (RDA) of vitamin C. This vitamin, along with its fellow antioxidant vitamin E, also present in tomatoes, helps protect the skin and other tissues against free radicals, and reduces the risk of cataracts. The bright red pigment in tomatoes is called lycopene, and it also acts as an antioxidant. In a study conducted by Harvard University, it was found that men who consumed ten servings of tomatoes a week could cut their risk of prostate cancer by up to 45 percent. Tomatoes are also thought to lower the risk of stomach, colon, and rectal cancers by around 60 percent. New research suggests that tomatoes may even help prevent lung cancer. Two powerful compounds found in tomatoes—coumaric acid and chlorogenic acid—are thought to block the effects of nitrosamines, some of the most powerful carcinogens found in tobacco smoke. By inhibiting these compounds, the chances of lung cancer are reduced significantly. Lycopene also helps protect against heart disease. Another advantage of tomatoes: if your hair has turned slightly green from the effects of chlorine in the water after swimming, apply a mask of tomato sauce to tone down the unsightly shade!

RECIPES healthy fry-up (page 92), smoked haddock kedgeree with grilled tomatoes (page 93), weekend omelet (page 93), mediterranean oven-roasted vegetable soup (page 94), sundried tomato soup (page 96), classic tomato sauce (page 101), tofu vegetable salad (page 102), lime, tomato, and scallop salad (page 102), baked feta and roasted tomato pasta salad (page 103), lima bean, tomato, and rocket salad (page 104), Italian salad (page 104), oven-baked vegetable salad (page 105).
TREATMENT milk and tomato juice cleanser (page 116)

ROOT VEGETABLES

BEET *(Beta vulgaris)*

★ VITAMINS A AND C, FOLATE; CALCIUM, IRON; ANTHOCYANINS, FIBER

● BOOSTS IMMUNITY; PROTECTS AGAINST SKIN BRUISING, VARICOSE
  VEINS, SUN DAMAGE, PREMATURE AGING

Beet is a favorite of naturopaths, owing to its excellent healing qualities. The many nutrients and vitamins in beet stimulate the liver, kidneys, gallbladder, spleen, and bowel, as well as strengthening the immune system. It is believed that a strong and healthy liver and kidneys encourage healthy skin, assisting the cells in renewal and self-repair. Beet also contains anthocyanins, which are members of the flavonoid family. Flavonoids have anti-inflammatory and antioxidant properties, making them an important nutrient for skin health. They help protect the skin against bruising, as well as guarding against free-radical damage. All women hoping to become pregnant are encouraged to include beet in their diet, as it contains folate (folic acid), which is believed to reduce the risk of spinal abnormalities, such as spina bifida, in children.

RECIPES shredded beet and feta salad (page 105)

CARROTS *(Daucus carota)*

★ VITAMIN C, FOLIC ACID; CAROTENES; POTASSIUM; FIBER

● ANTI-AGING; ENHANCES EYESIGHT; HELPS PREVENT MOUTH
  ULCERS AND CANCERS

Remember when your mother told you that eating carrots would help you see in the dark? Well, she wasn't just saying that to get you to clean your plate! Night blindness can be caused by lack of beta carotene, and carrots have an abundance of this nutrient. High levels of beta carotene are also useful in helping the body guard against cancers—particularly of the stomach and lungs. Recent research has shown that carrots may help to protect against cancers of the mouth and rectum, too. External factors in everyday life such as cigarette smoke, pollution, and stress can deplete your levels of vitamin C, leaving your skin dry and susceptible to pimples and premature aging. The vitamin C in carrots helps to replace these daily losses, boosting the collagen levels in your skin. Collagen is essential for the formation of bones, ligaments, and teeth and is also the "glue" that holds the skin together. Without collagen your skin will begin to age and sag. Need more incentive? In ancient Greek times, it was believed that carrot juice increased sexual appetite, especially in men!

RECIPES *carrot soup (page 94), tofu vegetable salad (page 102), shredded beet and feta salad (page 105), apple, vegetable, and quorn curry (page 108), happy and healthy (page 115).*

TREATMENTS *cooling toner (page 117), all-over body pamper (page 118)*

ONION *(Allium cepa)*

★ VITAMINS B6, C, AND E, FOLIC ACID; QUERCETIN, ALLICIN; CALCIUM, POTASSIUM

● ANTI-AGING, DETOXIFYING, IMMUNE-BOOSTING; PROTECTS AGAINST NETTLE RASH, NAIL INFECTIONS, MOUTH ULCERS, HAY FEVER, LIFELESS HAIR

Onions are best known as a cold remedy (the French swear by onion soup as a cure-all for the sniffles), yet they boast many other health-boosting properties. One of the main properties of onion is quercetin, a powerful antioxidant that is believed to slow the aging process, fight cataracts, and possibly lower the risk of cancer of the colon and stomach. Onions are a natural detoxifier and can strengthen the immune system, promoting shiny hair, strong, pink nails, and smooth, glowing skin. The natural antiseptic and antibiotic properties of onions help to repair tissue and cell damage in the skin, protecting against premature aging. A study at the University of Bern, Switzerland, found that onions increase skeletal mass and inhibit the natural breakdown of bone, making them an excellent protection against osteoporosis. Onions may also protect against inflammatory joint conditions, such as gout and rheumatoid arthritis. Researchers have found that onions have a mild blood-thinning effect. This may help guard against thrombosis (abnormal blood clots), which can lead to heart attacks and strokes.

RECIPES *pumpkin soup (page 94), vegetable and bean soup (page 96), stuffed bell peppers (page 99), vegetarian flan (page 99), classic tomato sauce (page 101), lima bean, tomato, and rocket salad (page 104), couscous medley (page 106), exotic kedgeree (page 107), baked fillet of sole (page 107), barbecue pork san choy bau (page 108), lentil and red onion quiche (page 109)*

SWEET POTATOES *(Ipomea batatas)*

★ VITAMINS C AND E, FOLIC ACID; CAROTENES; POTASSIUM, CALCIUM; FIBER

● ANTI-AGING; GUARDS AGAINST ACNE, CONGESTED SKIN, BROKEN CAPILLARIES, CONSTIPATION, COLON AND RECTAL CANCER

An excellent alternative to the traditional white potato, sweet potatoes are only now receiving the attention they deserve. They are an excellent source of antioxidants—and the best low-fat source of vitamin E—thus helping the skin to repair itself and neutralizing free radicals. Sweet potatoes have excellent skin- and circulation-boosting properties and are particularly recommended for those suffering from eczema or psoriasis. They are a good source of fiber, reducing the risk of constipation, and of colon and rectal cancer. A diet rich in fiber can also help prevent narrowing of blood vessels and the formation of blood clots, which can lead to heart disease. Lack of fiber may even contribute to acne and other skin congestion problems.

RECIPES *sweet potato soup (page 95)*

FUNGI

MUSHROOM *(Polyporaceae)*

★ VITAMIN B3, B5, BIOTIN, FOLATE; LENTINAN; COPPER, IRON, POTASSIUM

● ENHANCES ENERGY LEVELS AND IMMUNE SYSTEM; STRENGTHENS BONES; PREVENTS DRY, SCALY SKIN

There are around 38,000 types of mushroom, not all of them edible! Those that can be eaten are packed full of goodness and have health-giving properties. Mushrooms contain the B vitamin biotin, which helps to increase energy levels, alleviate muscle pain, and repair dry, scaly skin. It may also help prevent hair loss. Maiitake mushrooms, in particular, have been shown to boost the immune system by stimulating white blood cell activity. Mushrooms contain copper, which also helps strengthen the immune system, and plays a major part in blood and bone development. The phytonutrient lentinan found in mushrooms may help suppress tumor growth. Wild mushrooms thin the blood and so help prevent abnormal blood clots. (Never eat wild mushrooms you have picked yourself unless you are quite sure they are safe.)

RECIPES *mushroom and bean soup (page 95), warm winter salad (page 106)*

avocado

A TASTY AND VERSATILE FOOD, THE AVOCADO IS ONE OF THE MOST IMPORTANT FRUITS TO INCLUDE IN A NATURAL BEAUTY DIET. IT IS PACKED WITH NUTRIENTS SUCH AS VITAMINS A AND E THAT OFFER NUMEROUS HEALTH-GIVING PROPERTIES. AND IT'S NOT JUST GOOD FOR YOUR INSIDES! RICH IN SKIN-SAVING OILS, AVOCADO IS AN IDEAL INGREDIENT TO INCLUDE IN FACE MASKS AND HAIR TREATMENTS.

History of the avocado

It is believed that the ancient Aztec and Inca civilizations enjoyed avocado, not just for its taste but also because of its many health benefits, including as an aphrodisiac and a cure for toothache! The Spanish conquistadors discovered the avocado tree growing in swampland and so nicknamed it the "alligator pear." The fruit was introduced into Mauritius in 1780 and by the mid-19th century had spread throughout Asia. Avocado (*Persea americana*) is now grown in most tropical and subtropical countries including South Africa and Australia. It is used in many cosmetic preparations.

Health profile

An avocado contains a whopping 1 oz of fat and 731 calories. Despite these drawbacks, nutritionists say adding a little avocado to your diet each day packs a beneficial punch that outweighs the fat and calories. Its health-giving qualities include properties of particular benefit to the skin. For example, it is especially rich in monounsaturated oils and vitamins A and E. The oils in avocado help maintain the integrity of the membrane that surrounds skin cells, and so may reduce the inflammation associated with skin conditions such as acne, eczema, and psoriasis. Avocados contain folate and potassium, and are very high in fiber. The monounsaturated fats in avocados include oleic acid, which has been found to improve levels of healthy fats in the body and help lower cholesterol. Look for Florida-grown avocados, which contain half the fat and two-thirds the calories of California-grown avocados. Those harvested between November and March contain one-third of the fat of those picked earlier in the season.

Beauty-boosting properties

Avocado truly is the skin-saver of the food world. Using avocados either internally or externally offers numerous benefits to the complexion. Fat provides the skin cells with the nourishment they need to prevent wrinkles and dryness. Without fat, vitamins A and E can't be delivered to the cells where they are needed most. Vitamin A in particular is required by the body to produce new cells—critical for keeping skin looking youthful.

BEAUTIFUL FOOD PROFILE

HEALTH COUNTER/100 g	CALORIES 190; MONOUNSATURATED FAT 12 g; POLYUNSATURATED FAT 2 g; FIBER 3 g
VITAMINS AND MINERALS	VITAMINS B5, B6, AND E; COPPER, POTASSIUM
GOOD FOR	ANTI-AGING, DRY AND SCALY SKIN, DRY AND DAMAGED HAIR, CONJUNCTIVITIS

inside out: recipe

GUACAMOLE

An ideal summertime dip, this recipe is highly nutritious, and tasty, too!

4 avocados, pitted and peeled
2 tbsp lemon juice
1 clove garlic, crushed
1 tomato, finely chopped
1½ oz/¼ cup onion, finely chopped
¼ tsp ground cumin
3–4 drops hot pepper sauce

Using a fork, coarsely mash the avocados with the lemon juice and garlic. Stir in the remaining ingredients to blend. Garnish as desired and serve with tortilla chips. Serves 2–4.

outside in: treatment

AVOCADO CLEANSER

Moisturizing and non-irritant, this cleanser is ideal for removing make-up at the end of the day. Suitable for all skin types, especially dry or dehydrated skin.

1 avocado
1 tsp fresh whipping cream

Remove the stone and then scoop out the avocado flesh. In a bowl, mash the avocado until smooth, then add the cream. Blend together with a fork until all the lumps have gone. Apply the mixture to your damp face. If you prefer, use circular motions to apply. This will help loosen dead skin cells. Using a soft cloth, gently remove the cleanser from your face with lukewarm water. Pat dry. Throw the remaining mixture away, as it will not keep.

oils, nuts, and seeds

All nuts and seeds are high in fats and oils, but they are the "good" fats, unsaturated ones that the body puts to very good use in many ways—to strengthen both the cardiovascular and central nervous systems, to regulate hormonal balance, and much more. They are also important for healthy, soft skin. Dry skin can indicate a lack of these important fats. Nuts and seeds are a good source of protein, too, especially important for vegetarians and vegans. Because of their high fat content, nuts and seeds should be eaten only in small amounts—ideally fresh, not roasted or salted. All forms of cooking transform good fats chemically so the body cannot use them as efficiently. Nuts and seeds can be eaten as snacks, sprinkled on salads or cereals, or to add an extra flavor and texture to casseroles, soups, and smoothies.

OLIVE OIL (Olea europea)

★ VITAMIN E; MONOUNSATURATED FAT

● GOOD FOR MASSAGE, IMPROVING SKIN TEXTURE, MOISTURIZING; TREATS SUNBURN AND MINOR SKIN ERUPTIONS

Olive oil forms a significant proportion of the fat eaten in a traditional Mediterranean diet, which has been linked to lower rates of heart disease and other chronic illnesses. It is good for the gallbladder and liver, as well as aiding healthy digestion and regular bowel movement. Keeping these systems working efficiently has a positive effect on the skin, as skin disorders such as acne can be linked to sluggish bowels and poor detoxification. Externally, olive oil is helpful for dry skin, minor burns, and minor inflammation. This is partly because it contains vitamin E, which is needed for skin elasticity and healing. Olive oil is the best oil to use in cooking, as it is the most stable; other vegetable and seed oils can be damaged by heat and so become less beneficial to health.

RECIPES *pea and fava bean soup (page 94), mediterranean oven-roasted vegetable soup (page 94), large shrimp and noodle soup (page 96), bruschetta with olives and tomatoes (page 97), baby spinach and radicchio salad (page 97), marinated chicken with prune salsa (page 106).* TREATMENTS *natural olive oil shampoo base (page 120), banana hair mask (page 123), hot hair mask (page 123)*

WHEAT GERM AND WHEAT GERM OIL (Triticum vulgare)

★ VITAMINS B1, B2, B6, AND E, FOLIC ACID; IRON, MAGNESIUM, SELENIUM, ZINC; FIBER, OMEGA-3 FAT, OMEGA-6 FAT, MONOUNSATURATED FAT

● PREVENTS DRY, SCALY SKIN, ANTI-AGING, HEALING

Wheat germ is a powerhouse of nutrients for all-round health, not least of the skin. It is a rich source of B-complex vitamins, which are vital for energy production. It also contains zinc, which, together with B6, is essential for daily skin repair and renewal. The vitamin E content in wheat germ and wheat germ oil nourishes the skin, enhancing healing and helping to maintain elasticity. Vitamin E is needed for healthy blood capillaries. These tiny blood vessels are responsible for ensuring a good supply of blood—plus the oxygen and nutrients it contains—to the skin, and clearing away waste products. Wheat germ oil is a rich source of unsaturated fats.

RECIPES *thirsty skin moisturizer (page 118)*

ALMONDS (Prunus dulcis)

★ VITAMIN E; CALCIUM, MAGNESIUM, MANGANESE, ZINC; FIBER, OMEGA-6 FAT, MONOUNSATURATED FAT

● ANTI-AGING, WOUND HEALING, DETOXIFYING, TREAT SCARS, CRACKED LIPS, PREVENT GRAYING HAIR

Almonds have a very long history of use in beauty care, and quite rightly, too, given their concentrated nutrient content. They have the highest level of fiber of any nut. This contributes to a healthy gut and hence aids efficient elimination of waste products from the body. The vitamin E content of almonds plays an important role in healthy skin, inside and out, helping to maintain its elasticity and promoting tissue repair. Almonds are a particularly rich source of the bone-building mineral calcium, along with its "partner" mineral, magnesium. However, people susceptible to cold sores or other herpes infections should avoid almonds, as they are rich in the amino acid arginine, which promotes activation of the virus.

RECIPES *carrot soup (page 94), apple and almond fruit fool (page 113).* TREATMENTS *family cleanser (page 117), rosewater and grapeseed toner (page 117), everyday moisturizer (page 118), all-over body pamper (page 118), cocoa butter cream (page 118)*

HAZELNUTS *(Corylus avellana)*

★ VITAMINS B6 AND E, FOLATE, COPPER; MANGANESE, MAGNESIUM, POTASSIUM, SELENIUM, ZINC; FIBER, OMEGA-6 FAT, MONOUNSATURATED FAT

● ANTI-AGING, SUN PROTECTION, HYDRATING, AID ELASTICITY

Hazelnuts are a particularly rich source of the skin-friendly antioxidant vitamin E. This nutrient confers elastic properties on the skin, helping to minimize the signs of aging, and also helps protect against the damaging effects of the sun, cigarette smoke, pollution, and other environmental factors. Potassium—a mineral abundant in hazelnuts—counteracts the level of sodium (salt) in the diet, and so helps to maintain a healthy fluid balance in the body. The high levels of monounsaturated fat in hazelnuts, when eaten in moderation, can help reduce the risk of cardiovascular disease. Hazelnuts also provide an excellent source of plant sterols, which are believed to play a role in the prevention of certain diseases, including cancer and heart disease.

RECIPES pork fillets with date and hazelnut stuffing (page 106)

PECANS *(Carya illinoensis) (right, back)*

★ VITAMINS B6 AND E; MAGNESIUM, MANGANESE, ZINC; OMEGA-6 FAT, MONOUNSATURATED FAT

● HYDRATING, ANTI-AGING; REGULATE HORMONES

Pecans contain one of the highest levels of fat of any nut (as much as 75 percent). Even though the fat is of the "good" variety, they should still be consumed in moderation. The vast majority of the fat in pecans is monounsaturated (as in olive oil), which has been found to be protective against heart disease, as well as nourishing the skin, keeping it soft and supple. Pecans are one of nature's richest sources of vitamin B6, which is required for countless uses in the body, including energy production and cell replication (the layers of skin constantly renew themselves). It also plays a part in regulating hormone levels. This is crucial for healthy skin, as skin problems are often caused by a hormonal imbalance.

RECIPES lentil and red onion quiche (page 109)

CASHEW NUTS *(Anacardium occidentale) (right, front)*

★ VITAMINS B3, B6, AND E; MAGNESIUM, MANGANESE, POTASSIUM; OMEGA-6 FAT, MONOUNSATURATED FAT

● GOOD FOR HYDRATION, CELL RENEWAL, SMOOTH, GLOWING SKIN, HAIR GROWTH; PREVENT ACNE, WHITE SPOTS, GRAYING HAIR

The health properties of cashews are often overlooked, perhaps because these nuts are most often eaten roasted and salted, which detracts from their goodness. Raw, they are a fine source of fats and other nutrients including the important B vitamins, B3 (niacin) and B6 (pyridoxine). Both of these are widely used throughout the body, not least for energy production. This energy is used not only to power us through the day and help keep us feeling lively, but also for the chemical actions and reactions that occur in every cell. This fact is particularly important for the skin, which has a very rapid turnover and so needs a good supply of oxygen, nutrients, and fluid. The main fat in cashews is monounsaturated, so, like olive oil, cashews are good for soft skin.

RECIPES cashew stuffed potato boats (page 96), apple, vegetable, and quorn curry (page 108), fruit and nut risotto (page 111)

pumpkin seeds

LOOKING FOR A WONDER FOOD FOR THE SKIN? ENTER PUMPKIN SEEDS, PACKED WITH MINERALS SUCH AS ZINC, FOR SKIN REPAIR AND RENEWAL; VITAMIN B6, FOR CELL REPLICATION; FATS, FOR SMOOTH, ELASTIC SKIN THAT RETAINS WATER; AND FIBER, WHICH AIDS DETOXIFICATION AND SO INDIRECTLY HELPS THE SKIN.

History of pumpkin seeds

In China, the pumpkin seed is known as "the emperor of the garden" and as a symbol of fruitfulness, rebirth, and health. All varieties of pumpkins are now cultivated in many parts of the world. Both flesh and seeds can be eaten. The seeds have a long history of use as an important food source and for their health-promoting properties. Pumpkin seeds are great as a snack, just as they are, and they are also wonderfully versatile with sweet and savory foods. They can be blended in smoothies, sprinkled over soups, cereal, salads, or cooked vegetables; included in baked foods such as breads, muffins, and crumble toppings; or added to casseroles, rice salads, and—in fact—anything you fancy.

Health profile

Pumpkin seeds stand out as having particularly high levels of vitamins, minerals, healthy fats, and fiber. They are unusual seeds because they contain a sizable amount of both omega-3 and omega-6 fats. Pumpkin seeds (as with other nuts and seeds) are a good source of protein for vegetarians. They offer a rich supply of important minerals including zinc, needed for healthy growth and development; calcium and magnesium, needed for healthy bones, nerves, and muscles; and iron. Zinc is a powerful immune-booster

and, along with the fat in these seeds, helps prevent prostate enlargement. Pumpkin seeds are also used as a folk remedy for intestinal parasites.

Beauty-boosting properties

The range of vitamins, minerals, and fats in pumpkin seeds provides a unique beauty boost. The rich blend of omega-3 (one of the richest plant sources after flax and hemp) and omega-6 fats keeps skin soft, elastic, and more water-retentive, thus preventing dehydration. These fats also help keep hair glossy. The zinc in pumpkin seeds is needed for a healthy immune system, crucial for combating disease, including skin infections. Zinc is required for healthy skin renewal and so is particularly important for teenagers, who experience sudden growth spurts and can be lacking in this mineral. Zinc deficiency can contribute to skin problems such as acne. Pumpkin seeds are a rich source of iron, and therefore help combat anemia, which (as well as causing fatigue) leaves the skin looking dull and gray. They contain vitamins B3 and B6, important for skin cell renewal (working alongside zinc), and for hormonal balance, needed to maintain clear skin.

BEAUTIFUL FOOD PROFILE

HEALTH COUNTER/100 g	CALORIES 569; PROTEIN 24 g; CARBOHYDRATE 12 g; FAT 38.6 g; FIBER 5.3 g
VITAMINS AND MINERALS	VITAMINS B3 AND B6, FOLIC ACID; CALCIUM, IRON, MAGNESIUM, MANGANESE, SELENIUM, ZINC
GOOD FOR	STRONG NAILS, ECZEMA, PSORIASIS SUNBURN, THINNING SKIN, WHITE SPOTS, CRACKED LIPS, ACNE, FLAKY SCALP, THINNING HAIR, CONJUNCTIVITIS

inside out: recipe

ROASTED PUMPKIN SEEDS

1 medium pumpkin
½ oz butter or 1 tbsp olive oil
seasonings of choice

Preheat the oven to 300°F. Remove the seeds from the pumpkin (you can leave some strings and pulp on the seeds but not too much). Toss them in a bowl with the melted butter or oil, and season. Spread the seeds in a single layer on a sheet of baking paper. Bake for about 45 minutes, stirring occasionally, until golden brown.

outside in: treatment

PUMPKIN FACE MASK

1 medium pumpkin, cut into chunks, and cored to remove the stem
4 pineapple chunks (each about ½-in wide)
1 tbsp finely ground oats
1 tbsp finely ground almonds
1 tsp milk
1 tsp honey
2 drops rose geranium essential oil
1 drop rose essential oil

Slice the pumpkin chunks into 6–8 pieces and remove the skin. Place the pieces (including seeds and strings) in a microwave-safe dish with about ¼ cup of water. Microwave for 2 minutes, or until the flesh is soft. Allow to cool for a few minutes. Cut the pumpkin peel from around the flesh and discard it. Place the pumpkin flesh, seeds, and strings into a small food processor with the pineapple chunks and blend for 1 minute, or until smooth. Add the oats, almonds, milk, and honey, blending for a short time after each one. Add the essential oils and blend again. The texture should be rich and smooth, but slightly grainy from the almonds. Apply a layer to clean and toned face and neck skin. Leave for 15 minutes. Rinse well with warm water and follow with moisturizer.

WALNUTS (Juglans regia)

★ VITAMIN E; MAGNESIUM, MANGANESE, ZINC; FIBER, OMEGA-3 FAT, OMEGA-6 FAT, MONOUNSATURATED FAT

● GOOD FOR STRONG NAILS, HAIR GROWTH; TREAT ECZEMA, PSORIASIS, CONSTIPATION, PIMPLES, AND PALE, LIFELESS SKIN

Walnuts are the richest nut source of omega-3 fat, which is sadly lacking in most diets today. This family of fats has been linked to a healthy heart, smoother skin, improved brain power, and reduced inflammation (redness and itchiness) in conditions such as eczema and psoriasis. Walnuts are a good source of fiber—in China they are used as a gentle laxative—which is important for regular bowel movements and for cleansing the gut, both necessary to keep the skin glowing. Walnuts also contain plant sterols, which have been linked to lower levels of cholesterol in the body.

RECIPES alpine muesli with red and green grapes (page 93), black-eyed peas and walnut spread (page 98)

BRAZIL NUTS (Bertholletia excelsa)

★ VITAMIN E; MAGNESIUM, MANGANESE, SELENIUM, ZINC; OMEGA-6 FAT, MONOUNSATURATED FAT

● GOOD FOR SOFT, SMOOTH SKIN, STRONG NAILS, HAIR GROWTH; TREAT PSORIASIS

Brazil nuts are particularly rich in fats and oils (more than 60 percent). Even though these are of the "good" varieties, Brazils should be eaten only in small quantities, as a high-fat diet overloads the digestive system and liver. Brazils contain the all-important omega-6 fat, which is needed for soft skin as well as for maintaining hormonal balance. Brazils are the richest known source of selenium, an important antioxidant mineral that is often lacking in the modern diet. Brazil nuts contain the sulfur amino acids (protein constituents) methionine and cysteine—sulfur is needed for skin regeneration and also for liver detoxification.

RECIPES nutty oven-baked monkfish (page 111)

MACADAMIA NUTS (Macadamia integrifolia)

★ VITAMIN E; MAGNESIUM, MANGANESE; OMEGA-6 FAT, MONOUNSATURATED FAT

● GOOD FOR HAIR GROWTH AND STRENGTH; PREVENT WATER RETENTION, BLOATING, PUFFY EYES

Along with pecans, macadamias are the fattiest of nuts (nearly 75 percent). But, as in all nuts, these are the "good" fats that, in moderation, can contribute to good health. Macadamias are usually eaten roasted and salted (as are many nuts), but they are best avoided in this form. A high intake of salt can lead to water retention and puffiness around the eyes and ankles. Roasting the nuts converts the "good" fats they contain into ones the body cannot use properly. As with all nuts and seeds, macadamias can be a useful part of a diet aimed at balancing energy and blood sugar levels. Including such quality fats and proteins helps to provide a sustained release of energy from a meal or snack.

RECIPES alpine muesli with red and green grapes (page 93)

SESAME SEEDS *(Sesamum indicum)*

★ VITAMINS B1, B3, AND B6, FOLIC ACID; OMEGA-6 FAT; CALCIUM, MAGNESIUM, SELENIUM, ZINC

● SUN PROTECTION; HELP PREVENT FLAKY SCALP, CONJUNCTIVITIS, UNEVENLY RIDGED NAILS, WHITE SPOTS, ACNE, ECZEMA

Sesame seeds lend a delicious flavor to foods. Unfortunately, because they are so small, they often pass through the body undigested, which means their nutrient content is missed. However, when chewed thoroughly, or used as a paste (such as tahini) or oil, they are a rich source of fats that are important for glowing skin and healthy cardiovascular and nervous systems. The seeds contain powerful antioxidants such as selenium, zinc, and sesamin. Zinc is essential for regular skin renewal. Sesame seeds are rich in B vitamins, which are important for countless uses in the body including energy release and hormone production. Unlike most foods high in unsaturated fat, sesame contains a natural preservative called sesamol, which helps stop fat going rancid.

RECIPES steamed lemon grass chicken and rice rolls (page 98), sesame beef rice and paper rolls (page 99), ginger marinade sauce (page 101), chicken salad with soy dressing (page 102), salmon steaks with sesame seed crusts (page 109). TREATMENTS all-over body pamper (page 118), cocoa butter cream (page 118)

HEMP SEEDS *(Cannabis sativa) (far left, top)*

★ CALCIUM, MAGNESIUM, ZINC, OMEGA-3 FAT, OMEGA-6 FAT

● ANTI-AGING; TREAT PMS, ECZEMA, CONSTIPATION

Hemp seeds are the seeds of the marijuana plant (but legal!). They are a very rich source of omega-3 fat (20 percent of the total fat content). They have a tough outer shell so are best eaten ground (use a coffee grinder) or as an oil. Hemp seeds contain a unique blend of fats, not only omega-6 (linoleic acid) but also—unusually for an edible seed oil—its derivative, gamma-linolenic acid (GLA),

which is also found in evening primrose oil. GLA is valued for its ability to stave off PMS symptoms, as well as for helping eczema sufferers. Hemp seeds are also a rich source of fiber.

RECIPES fresh fruit salad (page 92)

SUNFLOWER SEEDS *(Helianthus annus) (far left, center)*

★ VITAMINS B1, B3, B6, AND E; CALCIUM, MAGNESIUM, SELENIUM, ZINC; OMEGA-6 FAT

● ANTI-AGING, DETOXIFYING; TREAT ECZEMA, FLAKY SCALP, THINNING HAIR, CONJUNCTIVITIS

Sunflower seeds (and pumpkin seeds) are a powerhouse of nutrients, only lacking in the omega-3 family of fats. Along with the omega-6 and monounsaturated fats they contain, the vitamin E in sunflower seeds helps reduce the risk of heart disease and is good for the elasticity and softness of the skin. Sunflower seeds contain the minerals calcium and magnesium, both important for relaxation and contraction of muscles (including the heart), as well as for bone health. The zinc and selenium in the seeds are important antioxidants, which help protect against the aging process—both externally (wrinkles!) and internally. Sunflower seeds contain the soluble fiber pectin, which helps to keep the intestines well cleansed, and so can contribute to clear skin.

RECIPES fresh fruit salad (page 92), alpine muesli with red and green grapes (page 93), strawberry spread (page 93), salmon steaks with sesame seed crusts (page 109), strawberry starter smoothie (page 114), an apple a day (page 115). TREATMENTS family cleanser (page 117)

FLAXSEEDS *(Linum usitatissimum) (far left, bottom)*

★ CALCIUM, MAGNESIUM, ZINC; FIBER, OMEGA-3 FAT, OMEGA-6 FAT

● TREAT PSORIASIS, THINNING SKIN, FLAKY SCALP, SINUSITIS

Flaxseeds (or linseeds) are one of the richest plant sources of omega-3 fat (nearly 60 percent of total fat content). Omega-3 is a member of the unsaturated fat family that is most often lacking in the diet (members of this family are also found in fish oils). Omega-3 fat has powerful anti-inflammatory properties, helpful for conditions such as eczema and psoriasis, and has been linked to reduced risk of heart disease and joint problems. Omega-3 fat is incorporated into cell membranes, helping to maintain their efficient functioning. Flaxseeds are a rich source of soluble fiber, which helps keep the bowel moving and well cleansed.

RECIPES fresh fruit salad (page 92)

grains and legumes

SOY BEANS *(Glycine max)*

★ VITAMINS A AND B-COMPLEX, FOLIC ACID; CALCIUM, MAGNESIUM; CARBOHYDRATE, FIBER, LECITHIN, PROTEIN

● ANTI-AGING; PREVENTS SUN SPOTS, AGE SPOTS, OSTEOPOROSIS

As women approach the menopause, their bodies produce less estrogen, and their skin loses some of its elasticity and appears drier. Soy contains large amounts of isoflavones, the plant form of this hormone, which help the skin retain moisture and firmness and reduce skin discolorations, such as age or sun spots.

RECIPES weekend omelet (page 93), mediterranean oven-roasted vegetable soup (page 94), vegetarian flan (page 99), lentil and red onion quiche (page 109), nutty oven-baked monkfish (page 111), Bramley apple and blackberry layer (page 113)

CHICKPEAS (GARBANZO BEANS) *(Cicer arietinum)*

★ CALCIUM, IRON, MAGNESIUM, PHOSPHORUS, POTASSIUM, SILICA; CARBOHYDRATE; PROTEIN

● GOOD FOR NAILS AND HAIR; PREVENT STRESS, DIGESTION, PIMPLES

Also called garbanzo beans, chickpeas have a nutty flavor and a firm texture and are used extensively in Middle Eastern, Indian, and Mediterranean cuisines. They are the main ingredient in falafel and hummus. Chickpeas contain silica, iron, and calcium, needed for strong, healthy hair and nails, and magnesium, which supports the nervous system and alleviates stress. They can aid a sluggish digestion, and so help prevent pimples around the mouth and chin.

RECIPES warm chickpea and tuna salad (page 105)

RED KIDNEY BEANS *(Phaseolus vulgaris)*

★ CALCIUM, IRON, MAGNESIUM, PHOSPHORUS, POTASSIUM; CARBOHYDRATE; FIBER; PROTEIN

● PREVENT DRY SKIN AND HAIR, BRITTLE NAILS, INSOMNIA, FATIGUE

Red kidney beans are a rich source of iron, required for oxygen transport in the blood and muscles. Lack of oxygen to the extremities can lead to dry skin and hair, pale or brittle nails, and fatigue. Kidney beans also contain magnesium, needed for healthy skin and nervous system, and to repair and maintain tissues.

RECIPES mushroom and bean soup (page 95)

LENTILS *(Lens culinaris)*

★ FOLIC ACID; CALCIUM, IRON, POTASSIUM; PROTEIN, CARBOHYDRATE

● STRENGTHEN TEETH, HAIR, BONES; AID DIGESTION, TREAT PIMPLES

Lentils are an ideal food for women of all ages, as they contain folic acid (vital for fetal development), calcium (to prevent osteoporosis), and iron (to combat anemia). Lentils also boast large amounts of fiber, which is required for a healthy digestive system. An irregular digestive system can lead to gray, sallow, or spotty skin.

RECIPES leek and lentil soup (page 96), stuffed bell peppers (page 99), lentil and red onion quiche (page 109)

RICE *(Oryza sativa)*

★ VITAMINS A AND B-COMPLEX; CARBOHYDRATE; FIBER; PROTEIN

● ANTI-AGING; PROMOTES SMOOTH SKIN, HAIR GROWTH, STRONG NAILS, PINK NAIL BED

Rice is not only nutritious, it has many skin-boosting benefits. It contains iron, needed for oxygen transport to the hair follicles, skin, and nail bed. It also contains the antioxidant vitamins A and B, which fight free-radical damage caused by cigarette smoke, pollution, and sunlight and so help the skin maintain its youthful appearance for longer. Choose brown, organic rice, as white rice loses most of its nutrients during processing. If you have an allergy or intolerance to cow's milk, rice milk is a healthy alternative.

RECIPES smoked haddock kedgeree with grilled tomatoes (page 93), steamed lemon grass chicken and rice rolls (page 98), sesame beef rice and paper rolls (page 99), vegetable rice paper rolls with chili dipping sauce (page 101), multicolored rice salad (page 105)

WHEAT *(Triticum sp.)*

★ VITAMINS A, B, AND E; PHYTOSTEROLS; POTASSIUM; CARBOHYDRATE; PROTEIN; FIBER

● GOOD FOR CLEAR EYES, STRONG BLOOD VESSELS, HEALTHY BOWELS; HELPS PREVENT INSOMNIA AND STRESS

Many people now follow a wheat-free diet, even though research has shown that only one percent of the population truly has an adverse reaction to this food. Nonetheless, many would benefit

from avoiding processed wheat, such as white bread, as this has
been stripped of its nutrients. In its organic, natural, nutrient-rich
state, wheat is full of fiber, helping to maintain an efficient digestive
system, thereby lowering the risk of colon cancer, and reducing
high blood pressure. Wholegrain wheat also contains B-complex
vitamins, which are necessary for a healthy nervous system.

*RECIPES smooth and sweet honey and berries (page 93), pea and
fava bean soup (page 94), pasta and yogurt dressing (page 111),
summer pudding (page 113)*

RYE *(Secale cereale)*

★ VITAMINS A AND B-COMPLEX; CALCIUM, IRON, POTASSIUM, SULFUR;
  CARBOHYDRATE, FIBER

● GOOD FOR ENERGY AND DIGESTION; PREVENTS PIMPLES, STRESS,
  FINE LINES, INSOMNIA

Rye is available flaked, cracked, or as a wholegrain or flour. Dark
and coarsely ground rye is called pumpernickel flour. If you suffer
from a wheat intolerance or allergy, try rye products instead. When
stressed, your body's stores of B-complex vitamins become
depleted, and you may suffer irritability, insomnia, and lethargy. The
B vitamins in rye help to maintain a healthy nervous system, as well
as aiding energy production and helping to rebuild tissue.

RECIPES tasty tuna snack (page 99)

BEANS *(Phaseolus sp.)*

★ CALCIUM, POTASSIUM, IRON, ZINC; FIBER, PROTEIN

● GOOD FOR WOUND HEALING; PREVENT ACNE, DRY SKIN, DIGESTIVE
  PROBLEMS, REDUCE HIGH CHOLESTEROL LEVELS

Beans are an excellent source of soluble fiber, which helps to lower
cholesterol levels. One study has shown that regular intake of
beans can reduce the risk of heart attack by almost 40 percent.
The insoluble fiber in beans and other legumes adds bulk to stools,
thereby promoting a healthy digestive system; it also helps to
protect the lining of the colon from cancer-forming agents and so
reduces the risk of colon cancer. Beans contain high levels of zinc,
which is one of the most skin-supportive vitamins. Zinc is
especially useful for those suffering from acne, as it promotes
wound healing and aids healthy skin growth. Zinc also improves
dry skin, and enhances the quality and thickness of hair.

*RECIPES pea and fava bean soup (page 94), vegetable and bean
soup (page 96), lima bean, tomato, and rocket salad (page 104),
warm chickpea and tuna salad (page 105)*

PEAS *(Pisum sativum sp.)*

★ VITAMIN C, FOLATE; CALCIUM, IRON, POTASSIUM, ZINC; PROTEIN,
  FIBER

● PROMOTE WOUND HEALING, AID DIGESTION, HELP PREVENT
  WHITE SPOTS, HEART DISEASE, INSOMNIA, THINNING HAIR,
  EXHAUSTION

In order to maintain a healthy body, it is important to obtain the
correct amount of carbohydrates, fat, and protein from your meals.
Peas are an excellent addition to the diet because they supply all
these nutrients in abundance. Peas are particularly rich in protein,
normally gained from meats or dairy foods, and so are especially
important for vegans and vegetarians. A lack of good-quality
protein in the diet can lead to thinning hair, slow wound healing,
and poor digestion.

Peas are digested slowly and only gradually absorbed into the
bloodstream. This is good news for people with diabetes (both
insulin- and non-insulin-dependant forms). By including peas and
other legumes (such as beans, lentils, and kidney beans) in the diet
on a regular basis, diabetics can help regulate their blood sugar
levels. Peas are high in fiber, which helps lower the levels of blood
fat and cholesterol and so reduces the risk of heart disease. Peas
are among the richest sources of vitamin B1. A lack of this vitamin
can cause extreme tiredness, anxiety, and loss of appetite. Black-
eyed peas contain folate (a form of folic acid), which is necessary
for strong, healthy nails and to help the body control stress levels.

RECIPES pea and fava bean soup (page 94)

oats

OATS TRULY ARE A "COMPLETE" FOOD, CONTAINING ALMOST THE
ENTIRE RANGE OF VITAL NUTRIENTS—INCLUDING PROTEIN, ESSENTIAL
FATTY ACIDS, FIBER, VITAMINS, AND MINERALS. OATS ARE NOT ONLY
BENEFICIAL FOR INTERNAL CONSUMPTION—THEIR TEXTURE MAKES
THEM AN IDEAL EXFOLIATING INGREDIENT IN MANY BEAUTY RECIPES.

History of oats

The history of oats is somewhat clouded because there are so many
different species and subspecies, which makes identification of
ancient samples very difficult. Probably the oldest oat grains yet
discovered were found in Egypt among remains dating from the 12th
Dynasty, around 2,000 BC, although there is no evidence of oats
being cultivated in Egypt during this time. The oldest known
cultivated oats were found in caves in Switzerland and are believed
to date from the Bronze Age. Since ancient times oats have been
used as feed grain for livestock, and as hay or silage. In Samuel
Johnson's famous dictionary, oats were defined as a food "eaten by
people in Scotland, but fit only for horses in England." The
Scotsman's retort to this is, "That's why England has such good
horses, and Scotland has such fine men!"

Health profile

For nutritional impact, oats are hard to beat. For example, they are
a prime source of the complex carbohydrates that help to sustain
energy. They contain about 50 percent more protein than bulgur
wheat and twice as much as brown rice. They offer impressive

levels of selenium, thiamine, phosphorus, and manganese, and respectable quantities of copper, folate (folic acid), vitamin E, and zinc. It is the high soluble-fiber content of oats that captures the attention of many nutritionists and has been credited with helping to lower blood cholesterol levels. Around 75 g of cooked oatmeal contains 4 g of fiber—16 percent of the total amount of fiber required in the daily diet. About half of that is soluble fiber.

A recent study also found that oats are ideal for warding off symptoms of seasonal affective disorder (SAD). SAD is caused mainly by low light levels during the winter months, when serotonin levels get depleted, which lowers mood, energy levels, and appetite. Eating oats (in the form of oatmeal, for example) every day is a great way to stay happy and healthy all winter long.

Beauty-boosting properties

Other than the numerous skin-boosting benefits gained from eating oats, this food has an overall relaxing effect on the nerves. When we are stressed we tend to frown, breathe incorrectly, and perhaps turn to caffeine drinks, alcohol, and other stimulants. Stress also floods the body with hormones that increase the heart rate, widen the blood vessels, and so increase the risk of skin disorders and broken veins. People who suffer chronic stress may find they suffer outbreaks of small pimples along the jawline. Oats contain vitamin E, which is good for maintaining firm, plump, and healthy skin. Lack of vitamin E may lead to thinning skin, which ages prematurely. Nails also need this vitamin to maintain their pale pink color and keep them looking healthy and strong.

inside out: recipe

DATE AND WALNUT BREAD

4½ lb/12 cups pitted dates, coarsely chopped	½ tsp baking soda
8 fl oz/1 cup boiling water	3 oz/½ cup firmly packed light brown sugar
4½ oz/1½ cups rolled oats	4 fl oz/½ cup mild molasses
3 oz/1 cup walnuts	2 tbsp extra-light olive oil
5 oz/1½ cups flour	1 large egg, plus 1 large egg white
1 tsp salt	7 oz low-fat cream cheese
1 tsp baking powder	

Preheat the oven to 350°F. Lightly oil two 8¼ x 4¼ in loaf pans. In a medium bowl, combine the dates and boiling water. Leave to stand. Bake the oats in a pan for 12 minutes or until crisp and golden brown. Bake the walnuts in a separate pan for 7 minutes or until lightly crisped. When cool to handle, coarsely chop the walnuts. Transfer the oats to a food processor and grind until finely ground. In a large bowl, stir together the flour, salt, baking powder, baking soda, and ground oats. Stir the brown sugar, molasses, oil, whole egg, and egg white into the dates. Make a well in the center of the dry ingredients. Stir in the date mixture and walnuts until moistened. Pour into the prepared pans. Bake for 55 minutes. Leave for 5 minutes, then tip out onto a rack to cool. Cut into slices and spread with cream cheese.

outside in: treatment

OATMEAL EXFOLIATOR

1½ oz/½ cup oats
1 tbsp honey
2 tbsp warm water
1 tsp jojoba or almond oil

Combine all the ingredients and apply to cleansed skin. Leave for 5 minutes and rinse well. Pat dry and apply moisturizer for your skin type.

BEAUTIFUL FOOD PROFILE

HEALTH COUNTER/100 g	CALORIES 375; CARBOHYDRATE 66 g; PROTEIN 11 g; FAT 9 g; SOLUBLE FIBER 4 g, INSOLUBLE FIBER 2 g
VITAMINS AND MINERALS	VITAMIN E; IRON, ZINC
GOOD FOR	STRONG NAILS AND HAIR, ECZEMA, PSORIASIS, ACNE, SUNBURN, THINNING SKIN, WHITE SPOTS, CRACKED LIPS, FLAKY SCALP, CONJUNCTIVITIS

fish, meat, and dairy products

SALMON *(Salmo salar)*

★ VITAMINS B12, D, AND E; EICOSAPENTANOIC ACID (EPA); IRON, CALCIUM; OMEGA-3 FAT, PROTEIN

● PREVENTS DRY, FLAKY, ITCHY SKIN, FINE LINES AND WRINKLES

Salmon is a powerful skin food, owing to the fact that it is a good source of eicosapentanoic acid (EPA), a nutrient that is converted in the body into chemicals called prostaglandins. These are produced in most tissues of the body. The prostaglandins made from EPA help to restrict inflammation, which can cause dry, flaky, itchy, sore, and broken skin. Salmon—and indeed all oily fish—help to keep the skin well hydrated, plumping out fine lines and preventing wrinkles. Salmon is also a good source of proteins that promote the production of collagen, a substance needed to keep the skin smooth and elastic, and which can decline with age.

RECIPE salmon steaks with sesame seed crusts (page 109)

ANCHOVIES *(Engraulis encrasicholus)*

★ VITAMINS B12 AND D; CALCIUM, IRON; DIMETHYLAMINOETHANOL (DME), PROTEIN

● GOOD FOR SKIN AND NAILS; HELP PREVENT ANEMIA

Anchovies are an excellent source of iron, so helping to prevent anemia, a common condition in women. Anemia can cause various symptoms including fatigue, lackluster skin, and small white marks on the nails. Anchovies also contain large amounts of the powerful antioxidant coenzyme Q-10 and are rich in a nutritional compound called dimethylaminoethanol (DME), which increases evenness of tone in the skin, so smoothing out irregularities such as small bumps and blotchiness. Anchovies (and herrings) are good sources of vitamin D, which is essential for the absorption of bone-strengthening calcium, and—along with iron, also found in anchovies—helps keep nails strong, shiny, and well-formed, especially important if you suffer from thin, brittle nails.

RECIPE warm chickpea and tuna salad (page 105)

TUNA *(Thunnus thynnus)*

★ VITAMINS B12 AND D; CALCIUM; PROTEIN

● ANTI-AGING, BOOSTS CIRCULATION, TREATS DRY SKIN, DRY AND SPLITTING NAILS, BRITTLE HAIR

Probably one of the most widely eaten forms of oily fish, tuna, whether canned or prepared fresh, is an excellent source of skin-boosting nutrients. It contains collagen, the "foundation" of the skin, giving it structure and keeping it smooth, firm, and elastic. As you age, your skin experiences a loss of collagen, and unless it is replaced this can lead to wrinkles, dryness, and sagging. Including oily fish such as tuna in the diet at least three times a week helps to prevent premature skin aging. Tuna is a very good source of vitamin D, which helps to strengthen the nail bed as well as enhancing the luster of hair. Tuna contains circulation-boosting nutrients, such as vitamin B12. This vitamin ensures a constant supply of blood to the extremities, so helping to give the nail bed a pink, rosy glow, and promoting healthy hair and nail growth.

RECIPES tasty tuna snack (page 99), warm chickpea and tuna salad (page 105)

SHRIMPS *(Leander serratus)*

★ VITAMIN E; CALCIUM, IODINE, IRON, MAGNESIUM, SELENIUM, ZINC; PROTEIN

● AID SPLITTING NAILS, DRY/OILY SKIN, ACNE, HAIR GROWTH

Shrimps are crammed full of anti-aging nutrients, helping to keep the skin healthy and smooth. For example, they are a good source of the antioxidant minerals zinc and selenium, which help to counteract the damaging effect of free radicals. Zinc is also vital for skin repair and renewal, as well as for the normal growth of hair and nails. Shrimps contain magnesium, which is important for bone strength and to keep muscles well toned.

RECIPE Thai sweet and sour soup (page 95), large shrimp and noodle soup (page 96), seafood pasta pesto (page 107)

SCALLOPS *(Pecten maximus)*

★ COPPER, MAGNESIUM, SELENIUM, ZINC; PROTEIN

● PROMOTE HAIR GROWTH, STRENGTHEN NAILS, HELP TREAT DRY/OILY SKIN AND ACNE

Scallops are wonder foods—high in protein, yet very low in fat. They contain significant amounts of omega-3 fat, which helps prevent heart disease and counteracts inflammation. They are also good sources of minerals including the antioxidants selenium and zinc. If you suffer from excessively dry or oily skin, or your skin breaks out in pimples on a regular basis, you could be deficient in zinc, which is vital for skin repair, as well as for normal hair and nail growth. The protein in scallops is important for the production of keratin, which helps nails grow and strengthen.

RECIPE *lime, tomato, and scallop salad (page 102)*

MUSSELS *(Unionidae)*

★ COPPER, MAGNESIUM, SELENIUM, ZINC; PROTEIN

● GOOD FOR HAIR, SKIN, NAILS, WOUND HEALING

Mussels contain magnesium, which helps ensure that cells have the energy they need to renew themselves. Healthy cells also need protection from free radicals, which can be caused by poor diet and external factors such as pollution and cigarette smoke. Mussels and other shellfish are a good source of selenium, an important antioxidant that is often deficient in the diet. Selenium combats free radicals, helping to maintain healthy skin and hair, as well as protecting the immune system. It also helps prevent brittle, flaking nails and dry skin and can aid in wound healing.

RECIPES *Thai sweet and sour soup (page 95), seafood pasta pesto (page 107), mussels in ginger and lemon grass broth (page 107)*

eggs

INTERNALLY AND EXTERNALLY, EGGS HAVE ANTI-AGING PROPERTIES. THEY CONTAIN PROTEIN, WHICH ENCOURAGES COLLAGEN FORMATION TO GIVE THE SKIN STRENGTH, SUPPLENESS, AND ELASTICITY, AND RETINOL, WHICH AIDS SKIN REGENERATION AND REDUCES WRINKLES.

History of eggs

The egg is, understandably, a symbol of fertility and renewal. In Celtic tradition spring was celebrated with eggs that were dyed red and eaten at a special feast. The shells were crushed to drive off winter. In Germany eggs were hung in evergreens to symbolize rebirth. In China eggs are linked to the fertility cycle; they are believed to prevent miscarriage, and are also given to pregnant women whose "lively" baby needs calming in the womb.

Health profile

Eggs are an important dietary source of vitamin D, needed for calcium absorption and to build and maintain strong bones. Vitamin D is made by the action of sunlight on the skin, but in northern climes many people do not get enough this way, particularly in winter, and so need to obtain it from the diet. Lack of vitamin D can cause rickets in children and weak bones in adults. At one time eggs were frowned upon because of their cholesterol content. But research shows that dietary cholesterol has little effect on blood cholesterol, and healthy people who eat eggs regularly (up to one egg a day) are at no greater risk of heart disease than egg avoiders. In fact, the vitamin E and selenium in eggs help protect blood vessels and reduce the risk of heart disease. Eggs contain vitamins B2, B3, B12, and folacin (a form of folic acid), which support the nervous system, and egg white contains an exemplary balance of amino acids—from which proteins are made.

Beauty-boosting properties

Eggs contain many skin-boosting vitamins and minerals, namely zinc, lysine, and vitamins A, E, and biotin. Zinc is excellent for problem skin. It helps reduce inflammatory processes within the body and aids healing. Zinc also enables the body to utilize vitamin A, needed for the growth and repair of wounds, to avoid acne, prevent white spots on the nails, and strengthen the hair.

Eggs contain biotin (sometimes known as "vitamin H"), a member of the vitamin B-complex, which is also synthesized by bacteria in the gut. A deficiency of biotin can cause dermatitis, hair loss, and brittle nails. Selenium, also present in eggs, supports the immune system, and protects the body against free-radical activity and pollution, and so helps to maintain healthy skin and hair.

Applied externally, the albumin in egg white can alleviate the appearance of fine lines, especially when used around the delicate eye area. As the albumin dries, it shrinks and contracts the skin, leaving the area smoother and plumper.

BEAUTIFUL FOOD PROFILE	
HEALTH COUNTER/100 g	CALORIES 148 g; PROTEIN 12.6 g; UNSATURATED FATS 7.7 g; SATURATED FAT 3.1 g
VITAMINS AND MINERALS	VITAMINS A, B2, B3, B12, D, AND E; CALCIUM, IRON, SELENIUM
GOOD FOR	THINNING NAILS, COLD SORES, SCALY SKIN, ABNORMALLY PALE SKIN, WHITE SPOTS, AND DRY, SPLITTING HAIR

inside out: recipe

ENERGY DRINK

You'll bound through the day—or at least until lunchtime—with this high-energy smoothie.

5 fl oz low-fat milk
1 egg (organic free-range if possible)
1 banana
2 tsp honey
nutmeg or cinnamon

Pour the milk into the blender, and add the egg, banana, and honey. Blend for around 30 seconds, or until all the ingredients are puréed. Pour into a tall glass and grate nutmeg or cinnamon on top.

outside in: treatment

HAIR CLEANSE

1 egg yolk (organic free-range if possible)
4 fl oz/½ cup natural yogurt
rind of 1 lemon

Mix all the ingredients together. Work the mixture through wet hair prior to shampooing. Not only will it cleanse your hair and prevent a build-up of hair products, but it also adds shine and manageability to dry hair. Rinse with cool water—this helps the hair strands to lie flat and adds shine to your locks.

BEEF

★ VITAMIN B12; IRON, SELENIUM, ZINC; MONOUNSATURATED FAT, POLYUNSATURATED FAT, SATURATED FAT, PROTEIN

● HELPS COMBAT FATIGUE, DRY HAIR, BRITTLE NAILS, HEART PALPITATIONS

There is much conflicting advice over whether meat should be a regular part of a healthy diet. I believe that the body functions at its best when it is fed the foods of our forefathers: vegetables, fruit, nuts, seeds, grains—and meat. All meat is packed with nutrients, including the antioxidant minerals zinc and selenium, which have many valuable properties, including helping to prevent premature skin aging. To avoid the potentially high fat content of some beef products, opt for low-fat cuts—organic if available. One of the main health-giving benefits of beef is its high iron content. Iron deficiency can manifest itself as dry, sallow skin; brittle, lifeless hair; lack of red color inside the lower eyelid; loss of appetite; and fatigue. Beef also contains vitamin B12, which offers numerous health benefits (see pork, below). B12 also aids in the absorption of iron, which, in meats, is present in the form of heme.

RECIPES sesame beef rice and paper rolls (page 99), beef and noodle salad with chili lemon grass dressing (page 102)

PORK

★ VITAMIN B12; IRON, SELENIUM, ZINC; MONOUNSATURATED FAT, POLYUNSATURATED FAT, SATURATED FAT; PROTEIN

● ANTI-AGING, GOOD FOR HEALTHY HAIR AND NAIL GROWTH

Pork isn't usually considered a healthy food, but if you choose lean, organic cuts, you'll obtain its many skin-boosting benefits without adding too many extra calories. Pork is a good source of minerals and vitamins, one of the most important being vitamin B12, necessary for the growth and repair of tissues, and the absorption of iron. Its health-giving properties seem endless. B12 helps prevent nerve damage by maintaining the fatty sheaths that cover and protect nerve endings, maintains fertility, and promotes normal development. It also boosts energy, improves memory, appetite, and digestion, and works with folic acid in regulating the formation of red blood cells. B12 is thought to play a vital role as an anti-aging nutrient. Many of its functions, such as promoting DNA synthesis, strengthening the immune system, and inhibiting inflammation, are fundamental to a healthy body, inside and out.

RECIPES pork fillets with date and hazelnut stuffing (page 106), barbecue pork san choy bau (page 108)

CHICKEN

★ VITAMIN B12; LYSINE; IRON, ZINC; UNSATURATED FAT, PROTEIN

● HELPS PREVENT CRACKED LIPS, COLD SORES, FINE WRINKLES

If you suffer from cold sores, consider including chicken in your diet at least three times a week. Chicken is rich in the amino acid lysine, which has been shown to help suppress the herpes simplex virus—the cause of cold sores. Cold sores tend to appear when the body is stressed or the immune system is run-down. Lysine, iron, zinc, and B12, all found in chicken, are important immune-system boosters. Lysine is also vital for the production of collagen, which is the foundation of youthful, unlined skin. Maintaining adequate levels of collagen helps to prevent the fine lines that can otherwise form around the mouth as we age as a result of losing fullness and moisture. Chickens are a good source of iron, which is needed for the formation of the red blood pigment hemoglobin, and so helps to promote the redness of the lips. Iron and vitamin B12 aid tissue repair and therefore help prevent cracked lips.

RECIPES large shrimp and noodle soup (page 96), spicy chicken salad in witlof (page 98), steamed lemon grass chicken and rice rolls (page 98), chicken salad with soy dressing (page 102), marinated chicken with prune salsa (page 106), chicken breast baked in olives, lemon, and capers (page 108), chicken and broccoli in mushroom sauce (page 110)

BUTTER

★ VITAMINS A, B1, B2, AND D; SATURATED FAT

● GOOD FOR SKIN RENEWAL, SKIN PROTECTION, STRONG BONES

Butter is high in saturated fat (hard animal fat) and calories, so should be used sparingly. However, in moderation butter is not harmful—as we are often led to believe—and provides important nutrients such as the fat-soluble vitamins A and D. Vitamin A in particular is crucial for healthy skin because it helps control the process of keratinization that builds new skin cells. It is also a powerful antioxidant that helps to protect the skin from sun damage (but you should still use skin protection!). Vitamin D aids the absorption of calcium in the gut and helps control its use in the body, and so is needed for healthy bones. Vitamin D is also produced in the body by the effect of sunlight on skin.

RECIPES weekend omelet (page 93), pumpkin soup (page 94), seafood pasta pesto (page 107), chicken and broccoli in mushroom sauce (page 110), mixed fall fruits with pancakes (page 112), Bramley apple and blackberry layer (page 113)

MILK AND CHEESE

★ VITAMINS A, B1, B2, AND D; CALCIUM; PROTEIN, MONOUNSATURATED FAT, POLYUNSATURATED FAT, SATURATED FAT

● BOOST IMMUNE SYSTEM; HELP PREVENT COLD SORES, SPLITTING NAILS, DRY HAIR, AND SORE, ITCHY EYES

Calcium, one of the most important nutrients found in dairy foods, is needed for a woman's overall health and well-being. Between the ages of 30 and 40, women should try to achieve their recommended daily intake (RDA) of calcium (around 700 mg) to ensure optimum development of bones, teeth, and other tissues. Dairy foods also contain the all-important vitamin D, which the body needs to absorb calcium in the diet. Milk and cheese provide vitamins B1 and B2, which help the body maximize the energy obtained from foods. B-complex vitamins help to prevent cracks and sores forming around the mouth, boost energy levels, and combat premenstrual syndrome. If you're feeling run-down, increase your intake of vitamin B-rich foods to strengthen your immune system and combat stress, which often shows up through spots, cold sores, and lank, dry hair. Milk and cheese are good sources of vitamin A (which in dairy products is called retinol), an essential skin nutrient that helps to promote wound healing and good skin hydration.

Just ¼–½ oz of hard cheese, eaten at the end of a meal, can help to reduce dental decay by protecting the tooth enamel from the acids formed when bacteria in the mouth break down food. This is because cheese is alkaline and so neutralizes mouth acidity by returning pH (acidity/alkalinity) levels to normal.

Some people are allergic to dairy products, or, more commonly, have a sensitivity to the sugar (lactose) found in milk. Allergies can affect the skin, digestive system, and even the respiratory system. Skin reactions may include an itchy, red rash (urticaria), eczema, darkened area around the eyes, and swollen lips, mouth, tongue, face, or throat. Lactose intolerance is caused by a lack of the enzyme lactase, needed to break down milk sugar. The symptoms of lactose intolerance are less severe than those of an allergy but usually include abdominal pain and bloating. If you have an intolerance to cow's milk, try goat's milk instead, as this is less likely to provoke a reaction. If you suffer from acne, try eliminating full-fat cow's milk from your diet or replacing it with goat's milk.

Fancy being Cleopatra for half an hour? Try a milk bath or treatment. It softens the skin wonderfully, and adds color and vitality to the cheeks.

RECIPES *weekend omelet (page 93), vegetarian flan (page 99), baby spinach, potato, and egg salad (page 103), baked feta and roasted tomato pasta salad (page 103), shredded beet and feta salad (page 105), lentil and red onion quiche (page 109).*
TREATMENTS *milk and tomato juice cleanser (page 116), family cleanser (page 117), face mask for normal skin (page 122)*

YOGURT

★ VITAMINS A, B1, B2, B3, AND D; CALCIUM, MAGNESIUM, PHOSPHORUS, POTASSIUM, ZINC; PROTEIN

● PROMOTES HEALTHY DIGESTION, HELPS PREVENT ACNE, OILY SKIN, PIMPLES, THRUSH, DRY SKIN, CRACKED LIPS, DULL AND LIFELESS HAIR, DIARRHEA, CONSTIPATION, IRRITABLE BOWEL SYNDROME (IBS)

The culinary uses of yogurt are numerous and, best of all, it offers many health benefits, both internally and externally. Internally, "live" or "bio" yogurt contains friendly bacteria that may help prevent diarrhea, constipation, and irritable bowel syndrome (IBS). The "probiotic" bacteria present in yogurt, such as *Lactobacillus*, boost the numbers of "friendly" bacteria that are present naturally in the gut and so help to prevent the proliferation of harmful bacteria, fungi, and other micro-organisms. Acupuncturists believe that the area around the mouth is represented in the digestive tract. Therefore, if there is a digestive blockage or other irregularity, this imbalance will show up on the face. Constipation, which can be a symptom of IBS, can lead to outbreaks of spots around the mouth and an unhealthy pallor.

Soy yogurt is packed with isoflavones, which makes this food a great anti-aging ingredient. Isoflavones are plant nutrients that are similar in structure to the human hormone estrogen, needed to maintain the production of lubricating oils and collagen, which declines with age. Oils and collagen ensure that the skin stays firm, moist, and supple and so keep sagging and wrinkles at bay. Externally, yogurt is an ideal ingredient to include in many face packs and is cheap and easy to use. It contains lactic acid, which acts as nature's exfoliant, removing flaky skin and dead cells. Regular exfoliation helps promote healthy-looking, glowing skin; you should exfoliate no more than twice a week though, or you may develop skin irritation.

RECIPES *fresh fruit salad (page 92), smooth and sweet honey and berries (page 93), strawberry spread (page 93), strawberry starter smoothie (page 114).* TREATMENTS *hair cleanse (page 55), berry bright (page 122), banana and cream anti-aging mask (page 122)*

herbs, spices, and condiments

ROSEMARY *(Rosmarinus officinalis)*

★ VITAMINS C AND E, FOLIC ACID; CAROTENES; IRON

● BOOSTS BLOOD CIRCULATION AND NERVOUS SYSTEM, HELPS
  COMBAT STRESS, HEART DISEASE, WRINKLES

This beautifully scented herb is excellent for really lifting your mood, so helping to relieve stress and anxiety. Uncontrolled stress raises blood pressure and heart rate, lowers immunity, and causes pimples and wrinkles. Relieve stress through exercise, meditation, and a healthy, balanced diet. The leaves of rosemary also stimulate the circulatory and nervous systems, allowing the body and mind to relax and function in a normal, healthy way.

RECIPES mediterranean oven-roasted vegetable soup (page 94), rosemary potatoes (page 97), oven-baked vegetable salad (page 105). *TREATMENTS* family cleanser (page 117), all-over body pamper (page 118), dry hair conditioner (page 120), essential oil leave-in conditioner (page 121)

CAMOMILE *(Matricaria chamomilas)*

★ VITAMINS C AND E, FOLIC ACID; CAROTENES; CALCIUM, IRON,
  MAGNESIUM

● HELPS PREVENT PALE SKIN, BRITTLE NAILS, DRY HAIR, STRESS,
  INSOMNIA, CONSTIPATION, INDIGESTION

This pretty, daisy-like flower is rich in calcium, magnesium, and iron, which are vital for healthy skin, working to repair and maintain cells. The iron present in camomile aids production of hemoglobin, the red pigment in blood cells, which transports oxygen to the tissues. This mineral also gives the cheeks a healthy glow, helps moisturize the hair roots, and increases blood flow to the nails. The oils in the flower—apigenin and azulene—calm the nervous system, relax the digestive tract, speed healing, and fight disease.

TREATMENTS cooling toner (page 117), all-over body pamper (page 118), essential oil leave-in conditioner (page 121), blonde moment (page 121)

FENNEL *(Foeniculum vulgare)*

★ VITAMINS C AND E, FOLIC ACID; CAROTENES; IRON

● AIDS DIGESTION, TREATS ACNE, HALITOSIS, CRAMPS

Fennel is mainly used as an aid to digestion, helping to counteract the effects of a poor diet—for example, one filled with sugars, caffeine, and fatty foods—that can lead to flatulence, cramps, nausea, and acne. A poor digestive system can cause bad breath, and many people advise chewing fennel seeds to mask halitosis.

TREATMENTS healing toner (page 125)

SAGE *(Salvia officinalis)*

★ VITAMINS C AND E, FOLIC ACID; CAROTENES; IRON

● AIDS DIGESTION, TREATS ACNE; FIGHTS CELLULITE

The Latin name for sage, *Salvia*, can be translated as "healing plant." Sage's medicinal and beauty benefits are numerous—for example, a tonic for the central nervous system. Cellulite, the orange-peel-like fatty deposits that can occur on the legs, thighs, and stomach, is believed to be caused by poor circulation and diet. Sage helps fight cellulite by improving the digestion, breaking down fats in the body, and boosting blood flow.

RECIPES mushroom and bean soup (page 95)

THYME *(Thymus vulgaris)*

★ VITAMINS C AND E, FOLIC ACID; CAROTENES; IRON

● ANTI-AGING; COMBATS HEADACHES, INSOMNIA, STRESS

Thyme has many skin-saving properties. Its antioxidant qualities are especially useful in the fight against aging. It is believed that thyme helps to stop the breakdown of the long-chain fatty acids present in the walls of cells. By helping these fats resist oxidation, thyme may protect the body in general, and the skin in particular, against the aging affects of pollution and excess sun. A cup of cold thyme tea is recommended for tension headaches.

RECIPE spinach salad with warm garlic dressing (page 107)

parsley

PARSLEY HAS MANY BEAUTY BENEFITS. PACKED FULL OF VITAMIN C,
IT IS AN IDEAL HERBAL HELPER FOR THE COMPLEXION, MAINTAINING
THE SKIN'S COLLAGEN STRUCTURE AND FIGHTING FREE RADICALS. AS
IT CAN BE ADDED TO MOST RECIPES, PARSLEY IS AN EASY-TO-USE
ANTI-AGING REMEDY—AND A NATURAL BREATH FRESHENER!

History of parsley

The culinary uses of parsley (*Petroselinum crispum*) have been
recorded as long ago as the third century BC. The Romans used it
as a flavoring and garnish and also hung it around their necks to
absorb noxious smells. It takes 11 lb of fresh parsley to make 1 lb
of the dried herb. Nevertheless, more people use dried parsley
than fresh as a garnish in soups, salads, and sauces.

Health profile

Parsley contains two types of unusual components that provide
unique health benefits—volatile oils and flavonoids. In studies on
animals, parsley's volatile oils—particularly myristicin—have been
shown to inhibit tumor formation, especially in the lungs. These oils
help neutralize particular carcinogens, including cigarette smoke
and pollution. The flavonoids in parsley, such as luteolin, are
powerful antioxidants that neutralize free radicals produced, for
example, by pollution, and so help prevent damage to cells. In
addition to its volatile oils and
flavonoids, parsley is an
excellent source of
three vital nutrients
that are important for
the prevention of many
diseases: vitamin C, beta-
carotene, and folic acid.
Vitamin C's antioxidant
properties also help
protect the body against free radicals. It is reported to act as an
anti-inflammatory agent to relieve the symptoms of osteoarthritis
and rheumatoid arthritis. And, as vitamin C is needed for the
healthy function of the immune system, it can also be helpful in
preventing recurrent ear infections and colds.

Parsley contains folate (the plant form of folic acid) and one of
the most important B vitamins, which carries out many tasks in the
body. One of its most important functions is in enhancing
cardiovascular health. Folic acid has a part in regulating cell division
and is therefore vitally important for preventing cancers, particularly
of the cervix and colon.

Beauty-boosting properties

Parsley contains many skin-friendly nutrients, including the crucial
B vitamins. These vitamins are needed for the repair and rebuilding
of tissue. A deficiency of B vitamins can lead to dry hair and skin,
and cracks or sores around the mouth. B vitamins also have anti-
aging properties. The folic acid in parsley helps keep skin tone
vibrant, as it plays a key role in the formation and
maturation of red blood cells. A pale, sallow complexion;
brittle, white-spotted nails; and dry hair may be signs of
folic acid-deficiency anemia.

Beta carotene is an extremely important anti-aging
nutrient. Free radical damage to the skin can lead to
wrinkles, dry, scaly skin, and loss of elasticity. Beta
carotene helps prevent free radical damage and also
encourages production of new skin cells. The vitamin
C in parsley helps to safeguard the collagen in the
skin, particularly around the mouth,
preventing dryness and premature
wrinkles. Parsley contains plant oils
and chlorophyll that neutralize
mouth odors and freshen breath.

BEAUTIFUL FOOD PROFILE	
HEALTH COUNTER/100 g	CALORIES 34; FIBER 0.9 g
VITAMINS AND MINERALS	VITAMINS A, B3, AND C, FOLATE; CALCIUM, IRON, MAGNESIUM, MANGANESE, ZINC
GOOD FOR	CRACKED LIPS, BRITTLE NAILS, WHITE SPOTS, LACKLUSTER HAIR, ANTI-AGING, FRESH BREATH

inside out: recipe

PARSLEY DIP

This refreshing summer dip is ideal for vegetarians. The combination of garlic, lemon juice, and yogurt provides large amounts of antioxidants and calcium—ideal for stronger, healthier nails.

2 red bell peppers	2 fl oz/¼ cup sesame oil
15 oz cottage cheese	2 fl oz/¼ cup lemon juice
1 oz/½ cup parsley, chopped	2 tsp soy sauce
1 clove garlic, minced	yogurt, as desired

Preheat the oven to 300°F. Cook the bell peppers until the skins are black. Remove from oven and cover with a towel. Allow to cool. Blend the cottage cheese, parsley, oil, and garlic. Season with lemon juice and soy sauce. Remove skins, tops, and seeds from the cooled bell peppers. Rinse with cold water. Mince and add to the dip. Stir in yogurt for a creamier texture.

outside in: treatment

PARSLEY AND MINT FACIAL RINSE

This refreshing facial rinse is a great way to bring a glow to your skin in the morning. The astringent qualities in the mint refresh and calm sensitive skin, while the parsley helps to tighten the pores.

½ oz/¼ cup fresh parsley
1 tsp dried mint leaves
8 fl oz boiling water

Add the parsley and mint leaves to the boiling water. Remove from the heat and leave for 30 minutes. Strain the solution through cheesecloth and pour into a bottle. Use as a facial rinse every time you wash. It's best to make up a fresh batch every 3–4 days.

BASIL *(Ocimum basilicum)*

★ VITAMINS C AND E, FOLIC ACID; CAROTENES; IRON

● RELIEVES MIGRAINE, STRESS, FLATULENCE, CRAMPS, NAUSEA, PREVENTS DRY SKIN AND BRITTLE NAILS

The fragrance of basil has a mood-enhancing effect. Being run-down or suffering from emotional stress or depression has a negative influence on the immune system, and this can lead to dry, scaly skin; unmanageable, coarse hair; and splitting nails. Basil can also relieve migraine and stomach cramps.

RECIPES mediterranean oven-roasted vegetable soup (page 94), bruschetta with olives and tomatoes (page 97), classic tomato sauce (page 101), baked feta and roasted tomato pasta salad (page 103), oven-baked vegetable salad (page 105), seafood pasta pesto (page 107), tofu risotto (page 110)

GINGER *(Zingiber officinale)*

★ ZINGERONE, SHOGAOL, ZINGIBERENE

● STRENGTHENS NAILS, HAIR GROWTH; RELIEVES NAUSEA, MORNING SICKNESS, TRAVEL SICKNESS

Ginger contains extracts called bilobides that improve the tone and elasticity of blood vessels and so promote healthy circulation and improved transport of vital nutrients around the body. This is important for the hands and feet, as poor circulation to the extremities can affect the strength and appearance of nails. Ginger also relieves nausea, especially travel and morning sickness.

RECIPES large shrimp and noodle soup (page 96), beef and noodle salad with chili lemon grass dressing (page 102), chicken salad with soy dressing (page 102), mussels in ginger and lemon grass broth (page 107), barbecue pork san choy bau (page 108), perfect start (page 114), happy and healthy (page 115), great start (page 115)

CINNAMON *(Cinnamomum zeylanicum blume)*

★ EUGENOL, CARVONE, LIMONENE, CUMINALDEHYDE

● WOUND HEALING; PROMOTES HAIR GROWTH; HELPS PREVENT DRY HAIR, BRITTLE NAILS, ACNE, BLEMISHES

Cinnamon helps to improve the tone and elasticity of blood vessels. This helps speed up the healing of wounds and skin complaints by improving circulation to the affected area.

RECIPES alpine muesli with red and green grapes (page 93).

TREATMENTS family cleanser (page 117)

CORIANDER *(Coriandrum sativum)*

★ COPPER, MANGANESE; PHYTONUTRIENTS, FLAVONOIDS; FIBER

● ANTI-AGING; PREVENTS BROKEN VEINS, BRUISING, BLEEDING GUMS

Coriander seed oil has myriad medicinal uses, for example as an antibacterial and a treatment for colic, neuralgia, and rheumatism. It contains chlorophyll, which helps neutralize odors—good news for those who suffer from bad breath. Many of the healing properties of coriander can be attributed to its exceptional phytonutrient content, especially flavonoids, which strengthen the capillaries in the skin and guard against free radicals, caused by ultraviolet rays, so protecting against sun damage. Flavonoids also strengthen collagen fibers, restoring skin flexibility and resilience.

RECIPES Thai sweet and sour soup (page 95), large shrimp and noodle soup (page 96), spicy chicken salad in witlof (page 98), lime, tomato, and scallop salad (page 102), marinated chicken with prune salsa (page 106), exotic kedgeree (page 107), rice jumble (page 109)

CARDAMOM *(Elettaria cardamomum)*

★ EUGENOL, CARVONE, LIMONENE, CUMINALDEHYDE

● ALLEVIATES INDIGESTION AND CRAMPS; HELPS PREVENT BLEMISHES, DRY HAIR, BRITTLE NAILS

Cardamom boasts "warming" properties, helping to increase circulation to the extremities. Therefore, it's an excellent herb to include in your diet if you suffer from brittle nails or have dry hair. Cardamom is also an excellent digestive aid, helping to relieve constipation, wind, and intestinal cramping. This also helps keep your skin clear and smooth, as any stomach complaints tend to reflect themselves as pimples around the mouth.

GARLIC *(Allium sativum)*

★ FOLATE; IRON, MAGNESIUM, SELENIUM, SODIUM, POTASSIUM, ZINC; ALLICIN

● BOOSTS CIRCULATION AND IMMUNITY, STRENGTHENS NAILS, TREATS PIMPLES AND BLEMISHES, WARTS, ATHLETE'S FOOT, FUNGAL INFECTIONS, THRUSH, HAY FEVER

Garlic has countless health-giving properties. Its main benefit is its ability to improve circulation, enhancing the flow of nutrients and oxygen to the fingers and toes. This ensures that the nails and nail beds remain strong and better able to resist infection, dryness, and splitting. Garlic boasts the antifungal chemical allicin, so those prone to thrush would do well to include garlic in their cooking several times a week. Garlic contains sulfurous compounds that help the body resist colds, flu, and other infections. These compounds also stimulate the liver, and act as a detoxifier, helping to rid the body of any toxins and so clear pimply, blemished skin. If you have a wart, try this folk remedy: rub the area with garlic and, if you desire, cover with a piece of garlic and hold in place overnight with sticking plaster. The wart should disappear within three days.

RECIPES pea and fava bean soup (page 94), mediterranean oven-roasted vegetable soup (page 94), pumpkin soup (page 94), leek and lentil soup (page 96), cashew stuffed potato boats (page 96), bruschetta with olives and tomatoes (page 97), stuffed bell peppers (page 99), classic tomato sauce (page 101), lima bean, tomato, and rocket salad (page 104)

NUTMEG (*Myristica fragrans*)

★ EUGENOL, CARVONE, LIMONENE, CUMINALDEHYDE

● GOOD FOR ECZEMA, DRY SKIN, POOR DIGESTION, PIMPLES

Nutmeg aids the digestion, which can benefit the complexion. A poor digestive system does not remove toxins efficiently and this can show up as sallow, pimply skin. Applied externally, nutmeg has a calming and healing effect on skin disorders such as eczema, thanks to its high oil content and restorative properties.

RECIPES smooth and sweet honey and berries (page 93), chicken and broccoli in mushroom sauce (page 110), nutty oven-baked monkfish (page 111), get up and glow (page 114)

CHILIES (*Capsicum anuum*)

★ VITAMIN C, FOLIC ACID; CAROTENES, CAPSAICIN; IRON, POTASSIUM

● BOOST CIRCULATION; HYDRATING; HELP FIGHT COLDS AND FLU

Chilies are packed full of stimulants—including the "hot" ingredient capsaicin—that increase blood flow, tone the nervous system, stimulate appetite, relieve indigestion, and encourage sweating. The potassium in chilies helps maintain a healthy fluid balance, thus keeping the skin hydrated, and helping to prevent wrinkles around the eyes and mouth. Chilies increase blood flow to the stomach lining, and so may help protect against stomach ulcers, and the damage caused by excessive alcohol intake. Chilies also boost the immune system, enabling the body to fight colds and other infections. Capsaicin is used medicinally in a cream as a topical (externally applied) painkiller for arthritis. Cayenne pepper is made from dried and ground chilies and so shares many of their medicinal properties.

RECIPES steamed lemon grass chicken and rice rolls (page 98), beef and noodle salad with chili lemon grass dressing (page 102), lime, tomato, and scallop salad (page 102)

HONEY

★ IRON, COPPER, SODIUM, POTASSIUM, PHOSPHORUS; PROTEIN; SUGARS

● AIDS WOUND HEALING, TREATS PIMPLES, ALLEVIATES COUGHS

Once regarded as the "nectar of the gods," natural honey contains phytochemicals that have important anti-inflammatory and antimicrobial properties. As a result, honey is increasingly being employed by therapists in the treatment of skin disorders (applied to wounds it speeds healing and alleviates infection) and in beauty spas to revitalize the skin. Because of its antibacterial properties honey is regarded as a highly efficient "zit-zapper." Apply a little at bedtime and blemishes vanish almost overnight.

RECIPES fresh fruit salad (page 92), smooth and sweet honey and berries (page 93), Thai sweet and sour soup (page 95), warm chickpea and tuna salad (page 105), mixed fall fruits with pancakes (page 112), Bramley apple and blackberry layer (page 113), get up and glow (page 114). TREATMENTS berry bright (page 122), banana and cream anti-aging mask (page 122)

✦saffron

SAFFRON IS THE WORLD'S MOST EXPENSIVE SPICE, YET THANKS TO ITS MANY CULINARY USES, ITS VARIED HEALTH-GIVING PROPERTIES, AND ITS REVITALIZING EFFECT ON THE HAIR, SKIN, AND NAILS, THIS AROMATIC ADDITIVE IS TRULY WORTH ITS WEIGHT IN GOLD.

History of saffron

Saffron is a product of the crocus flower (*Crocus sativas*) and not only adds a pungent and aromatic flavor to dishes, but also gives food a beautiful golden color. According to Greek myth, the handsome mortal Crocos fell in love with the beautiful nymph Smilax. But alas, his advances were rebuffed, and Crocos was turned into a beautiful purple flower. The crocus is native to Asia, where it has been cultivated for thousands of years for use in dyes, medicines, perfumes, and as a flavoring in foods and drinks.

Health profile

The antioxidant qualities of saffron, and indeed its less-expensive cousin, turmeric, are well-documented. The orange pigment in saffron, curcumin, is believed to have significant anti-inflammatory properties, helping to relieve muscle tension. As an antioxidant, curcumin is able to neutralize free radicals, chemicals that can travel through the body and cause damage to healthy cells and cell membranes. Free radicals may play a part in the painful joint damage and inflammation of arthritis. Saffron's (and turmeric's) combination of antioxidant and anti-inflammatory effects explains why many people with arthritis and other joint diseases often find relief when they use this spice regularly.

Beauty-boosting properties

The curcumin in saffron is believed to improve the function of the liver, which acts as a waste disposal for the body, ridding it of toxins. However, when the liver is overloaded with fatty foods or alcohol, it is unable to function efficiently. Owing to its antioxidant properties, saffron enables the liver to process and detoxify the system. A healthy liver is reflected in clear, vibrant skin and eyes, an unhealthy liver tends to cause pimples, sallow skin, and yellow or "cloudy" eyes.

Saffron also contains iron, which can be regarded as "food" for the hair, skin, and nails. Iron is an essential trace mineral needed for hemoglobin, the red pigment in blood cells, and myoglobin, a similar pigment that stores oxygen in muscle tissue. Proper functioning of the blood cells ensures that adequate levels of nutrients are transported to the extremities, helping to keep the hair, nails, and skin healthy. However, it seems that many women are lacking in iron, which not only affects their appearance but may also lead to iron-deficiency anemia, a condition that causes fatigue, loss of appetite, and headaches, among other symptoms.

The colorful dye present in saffron can be used as a natural colorant for graying hair or to add a reddish tinge to the hair. The essential oil also present in the spice coats the hair shaft, smoothing the hair and leaving a silky sheen.

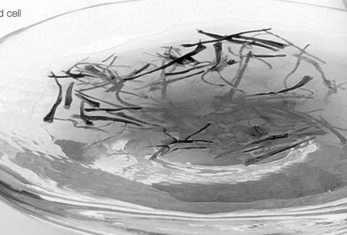

BEAUTIFUL FOOD PROFILE	
HEALTH COUNTER/100 g	CALORIES 34 g; FIBER 1.0 mg
VITAMINS AND MINERALS	VITAMIN B6; COPPER, IRON, MAGNESIUM, MANGANESE, POTASSIUM, ZINC
GOOD FOR	SKIN, HAIR, AND NAILS, LIVER FUNCTION, ANEMIA

inside out: recipe

MUSHROOM AND LEEKS WITH SAFFRON RICE

3 tsp water (for sauté)
1 tsp garlic, minced
7 oz/2 cups leeks, thinly sliced
16 fl oz/2 cups boiling water
¾ tsp salt
9 oz/1½ cups long-grain brown
  rice, rinsed and drained
8 oz button mushrooms, cut into
  ½-in slices

1 carrot diced
1 tsp whole fennel seeds
salt to taste
¼ tsp saffron threads
⅛ tsp ground pepper
2 tbsp fresh parsley minced
  for garnish

In a pressure cooker, sauté the garlic and leeks for 2–3 minutes. During this time, boil the water. Mix the salt into the water. Add the water to the cooker along with the remaining ingredients (except for the parsley). Cover, lock, and immediately bring to high pressure. Continue to heat for 25 minutes. Remove from the heat and cool for 10 minutes, after which release/open the cooker. Stir, garnish, and serve. Serves 4.

outside in: treatment

SEEING RED

Saffron adds a wonderful reddish luster to naturally dark or red hair.

1 oz saffron
20 fl oz/2½ cups water

Chop the saffron (finely if necessary) and add to a saucepan of water. Bring the water to the boil and allow to simmer for 30 minutes. If necessary, top up with extra water to make 12 fl oz/1½ cups. Cool, strain, and bottle. Keep in the refrigerator and use within a few days.

water

BEAUTY BENEFITS OF WATER

Water truly is nature's greatest beauty treatment—and best of all, it's free! While you can survive for up to a week without food, you could only survive for about two days without making up fluid lost from the body. Considering that the body is 75 percent water, it is surprising to think that you need to drink only around 3 pints of water every day to keep your body well supplied. Water is necessary for all bodily processes, and certainly plays a vital role in maintaining natural beauty. For example, you need water to flush toxins through your liver and kidneys, to help pump oxygen through your body, and to keep your skin smooth and supple.

Drinking water has both direct and indirect effects on the skin. Water is needed directly to plump up the skin, keeping it soft, smooth, and healthy. But for skin to function correctly, your internal organs must work at optimum levels, and this is where water plays such an integral part. For example, the blood circulation cannot deliver oxygen and nutrients to all parts of the body effectively and quickly if we do not maintain an adequate intake of water.

WATER AND THE LIVER

If you think of the liver as your very own cleansing system, it makes sense to take care of it. The liver is responsible for neutralizing the toxins and wastes produced in the body as a result of the breakdown of, for example, fatty foods and alcohol. If you've been eating unhealthy foods and drinking too much alcohol, you may

SEASONAL DEHYDRATION

During the colder months you may find that your skin is drier than usual. This is caused by central heating, the cold winter winds, and a drop in your daily water intake. Ensure that you are drinking at least 3½ pints of fluids every day, no matter how cold it is outside. You can achieve this quota through herbal drinks. Try green tea (packed full of antioxidants), peppermint tea (aids digestion), or honey and lemon tea (good for sore throats and to kick-start your digestive system).

feel lethargic and generally "under the weather." In part, this is because you have been putting your liver under too much pressure, and it is unable to continue processing toxins at its optimum rate. Drinking plenty of water supports the liver's cleansing function, by flushing out wastes before they accumulate.

WATER AND THE KIDNEYS

The kidneys play a similar role to that of the liver, filtering and neutralizing bodily wastes. They do this by removing waste products from the blood, diluting them with water, and flushing them out of the body. However, this delicate balance is easily upset. For example, a high salt intake in the diet encourages the kidneys to reabsorb too much water, which may lead to fluid retention and puffy-looking skin. Coffee and alcohol, on the other hand, act as diuretics, encouraging excess water loss via the urine, and this can lead to the opposite problem—dehydration.

TAP, DISTILLED, OR MINERAL?

There is much research and debate over which is the healthiest source of drinking water—tap, distilled, or mineral. Tap water is arguably the closest to being a "processed" source, as it will probably have had chlorine, fluoride, and aluminum sulfate added during purification. However, research shows that the chemicals added during this process provide few if any health benefits, and so I'd recommend using a water jug with a carbon filter, which removes any added chemicals but allows through the naturally occurring minerals that are beneficial to health.

Distilled water is certainly the purest form of water, devoid of any impurities and other negative elements such as lead, fluoride, chlorine, and pesticides. However, drinking only distilled water may mean that your body misses out on some of the important minerals present in other waters.

Many people today drink bottled water, assuming that they are providing their body with the healthiest form of fluid available. However, bottled water can come in many forms, variously labeled natural mineral water, mineral water, spring water, and table water. Some of these terms have no legal significance and do not necessarily mean that the water is free of impurities. Some may have been bottled from sources such as lakes, rivers, and even municipal water supplies. If you are unsure about which type to buy, look for "natural mineral water." This indicates that the water has not been processed in any way and is of a high standard.

WATER FOR HEALTH

If you regularly suffer from the "3pm slump," it is quite likely that you try to overcome this mid-afternoon spell of tiredness with caffeine or a sugary or fatty snack. This may revive you initially, but within an hour you will probably once again feel tired, and perhaps even headachy and even slightly nauseous. Instead of snacking, try drinking a large glass of water, or eating a juicy piece of fruit, such as an orange or apple, or some grapes. You'll immediately feel the benefits of rehydrating your body and mind and will be less likely to suffer another energy slump.

Regular exercise is good for you but rapidly increases water loss. It is possible to lose almost 2 pints of water during a hard workout, so ensure that you have a bottle of water nearby to keep your fluid levels topped up. Steam rooms and saunas are ideal for sweating out toxins, but they also promote increased moisture loss, so replenish the missing fluid at the first opportunity.

WATER FOR BEAUTY

The skin is the largest organ in the body, containing around 16 pints of water. When the epidermis—the layer of skin closest to the surface—is well hydrated, the cells are plump and smooth. If you have been neglecting your water intake, your skin will start to become dry and wrinkly, and to look older and feel tighter than usual. (Just think of an apple that has been left out in the sun. Its peel becomes dry, wrinkled, and discolored. So does your skin!)

Epidermal cell membranes are composed of essential fatty acids (EFAs)—such as linoleic acid and alpha-linolenic acid, and cholesterol. As EFAs cannot be made in the body, they must be obtained from food. When your skin is not receiving its required amount of EFAs (about 15 percent of your daily calorie intake), it rapidly loses water and becomes dry, flaky, and itchy. EFAs are found in oily fish such as salmon, herring, mackerel, and sardines, and from flaxseed oil and vegetable oils.

Naturally beautiful tip: Using an oil burner not only smells wonderful and helps to create a calming mood, it will help protect your skin from dehydration caused by central heating.

natural beauty
clinic

How you look speaks volumes about you: whether you're happy or sad, energized or tired, healthy or unwell, for example. Your exterior is like a movie trailer for your inner self—it gives everyone around you a preview of the whole story.

It may be possible to achieve smooth-looking skin and glossy hair through the use of cosmetics, but this is merely masking the problem temporarily. No matter how many products you use, nothing you apply to your skin will convincingly hide pimples, split ends, or ragged nails. In order to look fantastic, your skin, hair, nails—and your general health—need to be in tip-top condition. You not only have to feel wonderful, you also have to provide a strong, healthy foundation on which to build (or in this case, to apply your make-up!). Luckily, the skin is a living, breathing entity that responds quickly and relatively easily to the foods we feed it. Changing your diet to include healthy, nutritious foods will be reflected in your skin within a matter of days. Similarly, using food as ingredients in treatments gives quick results, too. This is because the skin, hair, and nails respond so well to natural products.

In this chapter you will find lists of ailments that may affect your skin, hair, and nails, along with suggestions for the appropriate dietary and beauty treatments for each problem. You'll also see some first-aid hints, and wise advice that has been passed down through the generations.

skin

STAR FOODS FOR SKIN: AVOCADO, BANANA, BERRIES, BROCCOLI, BRUSSELS SPROUTS, CABBAGE, CARROT, CAULIFLOWER, CITRUS FRUITS, DAIRY FOOD, EGGS, FISH, FLAXSEED OIL, GRAINS, MANGO, MEAT, NUTS, GRAPES, RICE, SEAFOOD, SEEDS, SOY, SWEET POTATO, OLIVE OIL, WHEAT GERM

The skin is one of the first things people notice about you. Whether you're glowing with health, or pale and (un)interesting, your skin says much about your physical and emotional state. The skin is the largest organ in the body, both by weight and by surface area. In adults, it accounts for 16 percent of total body weight. Skin acts as a barrier against the environment, prevents water loss, and helps regulate body temperature.

The skin is a barometer of overall health. When you are run-down or ill, it shows up in pimples, dryness, eczema (or dermatitis), and premature aging. Dry skin reflects deficiencies of essential fatty acids (EFAs) and vitamin E; sensitive skin is often owing to poor digestion; pimply skin indicates a diet high in fatty, processed food.

Your skin retains less moisture as you age, which means late nights and a poor diet show up more readily than when you were in your teens. So you need to pay close attention to what you put on your skin, and what you feed it. A good diet not only enhances the health of your skin, natural food products also protect it against external factors such as pollution, air-conditioning, central heating, sunlight, and cigarette smoke. The skin requires these protective nutrients in the diet, but food can also be applied topically (to the skin), where its healing agents have a direct effect.

SKIN LAYERS

Structurally, the skin is divided into two layers. The inner layer, the dermis, is composed of connective tissue, blood vessels, nerve endings, hair follicles, and sweat and oil glands. The outer layer, the epidermis, is the visible one and lies on top of the dermis. Its thickness varies with age, sex, and body area (the epidermis on the underside of the forearm is about five cell-layers thick, but on the sole of the foot it might be as much as 30 cell-layers deep). For the most part, the skin is impermeable to water, but it will absorb some moisture (this is why we wrinkle when we lie in the bath for too long!). The epidermis is renewed every 15–30 days. If the body is affected by psoriasis, the skin is renewed every 7–10 days.

ACNE

This condition (known medically as *acne vulgaris*) is an unsightly and uncomfortable skin condition. It mainly affects teenagers, but adults can also be afflicted. Acne is an inflammatory condition of the sebaceous (oil-producing) glands, especially of the face, neck, back, and chest. When excess sebum blocks the hair follicles and pores, bacteria builds up and pimples form. In teenagers this occurs mainly because androgens—hormones that control the sebaceous glands—are working overtime. The problem can also result from a hormonal imbalance, which is why some women may suffer an outbreak around the time of their period.

✔ Zinc is linked to skin health because it enhances immune function, reduces inflammation, and promotes healthy hormone levels. It is also vital for skin growth and repair and so helps heal acne outbreaks and prevents further eruptions. Zinc is found in cheese, fish, eggs, grains, meat, nuts, seafood, sweet potatoes, seaweed, and seeds. Most food sources of zinc also provide copper, which can be depleted by increased zinc consumption.

Vitamin B6 helps regulate hormone levels and control acne outbreaks triggered by puberty, the menstrual cycle, or menopause. B6 is found in sweet potatoes, chicken, rice, sunflower seeds, salmon, pork, and mango. Vitamin A aids skin healing and helps counteract inflammation. As vitamin A is derived from beta carotene, include sweet potatoes and carrots in your diet. Foods rich in essential fatty acids (EFAs) should be consumed for skin health as they help dilute the oily sebum that clogs pores, and are major liver-strengthening nutrients. The EFAs in flaxseed oil, tuna, and salmon have important skin-healing properties.

✗ Research into links between diet and acne has yielded mixed results. Too much processed and fast food cannot possibly be healthy, but some research suggests that it has no effect on acne. To be on the safe side, and to give your skin the best possible chance of healing and recovery, avoid foods that are high in sugar or difficult to digest. Dairy products may increase sebum production and trigger outbreaks, so try deleting these foods from your diet for at least one month to see if it makes any difference to your skin. To ensure you are receiving enough calcium in your diet, take a 600 mg supplement twice daily.

✚ Acne sufferers are often deficient in vitamins A, B1, and B2 and so may benefit from supplements. However, vitamin A supplements are not recommended if you are pregnant. If you are currently receiving medical treatment, seek your medical practitioner's advice before taking any nutrient supplements.

RECIPES *sweet potato soup (page 95), spicy chicken salad in witlof (page 98), steamed lemon grass chicken and rice rolls (page 98), mango, apple, and passion-fruit sorbet (page 112), strawberry starter smoothie (page 114).* TREATMENTS *pumpkin face mask (page 45), strawberry steam cleanser (page 117), face mask for normal skin (page 122), face mask for oily skin (page 122)*

AGING

The main cause of premature skin aging is overexposure to the sun (photoaging). A suntan may look "healthy" but it is actually visual evidence that the skin has been damaged. In fact, the sun causes more of the signs of aging than growing older itself! The sun emits two kinds of ultraviolet (UV) rays: UVA and UVB. These rays damage the skin in several ways (apart from sunburn, see page 76). Repeated exposure to UVB rays causes acute (short-term) damage to the epidermis and chronic (long-term) damage in the form of structural changes to deeper skin tissues. UVB rays are closely associated with skin cancer, especially in the epidermis.

UVA rays penetrate the skin more deeply than UVB rays. They have an effect on the deeper layers, where they alter the structure of the elastic fibers in the dermis. They also exacerbate damage caused by UVB rays, and so speed up the photoaging process. To help protect your skin from sun damage, it is important to use a sunscreen with a high sun protection factor (SPF—at least 15 plus) on your face and body. Strong sunshine also dehydrates the skin, and causes free radical damage. So you should include in your diet foods that help protect against these twin evils (see below).

Nicotine, especially combined with sun exposure, plays a role in premature skin aging, including facial wrinkles, by reducing the supply of oxygen and nutrients to the skin. The act of puckering the lips when smoking exacerbates wrinkles around the mouth. Smoking also produces free radicals that damage skin cells. This damage can be limited by antioxidants—free radical scavengers—

such as vitamin C. But levels of this vitamin are lower in smokers. If you smoke, or are regularly exposed to second-hand smoke, include vitamin C-rich foods in your diet to protect your skin.

✔ Carrots, squash, spinach, and broccoli all contain antioxidants to fight free radical damage. Maintain your moisture levels internally by eating foods rich in omega-3 essential fatty acids (EFAs), found in oily fish such as salmon, or in shellfish, and omega-6, found in nuts and seeds, sunflower oil, and wheat germ. These two EFAs combined help reduce the compounds that lead to inflammation. If left unchecked, inflammation inhibits normal cell renewal and accelerates free radical damage, leading to premature aging.

✘ Excess sugar intake causes cross-linkages to form between the collagen fibers in the skin. As a result, these fibers lose their strength and elasticity. This also encourages the appearance of brown discoloration marks and age spots. Sugar of all types should be avoided whenever possible. Avoid adding it to drinks and cooking and try not to eat anything that is very sweet or has a lot of pre-added sugar. You will need to be vigilant, as sugar is hidden in many processed foods and sauces—and even alcohol.

✚ Flavonoid supplements may improve skin flexibility and help slow the aging process. Coenzyme-Q10 supplements have an antioxidant function that guards against free radical damage.

RECIPES *beef and noodle salad with chili lemon grass dressing (page 102), Thai sweet and sour soup (page 95), pork fillets with date and hazelnut stuffing (page 106), mixed fall fruits with pancakes (page 112), boysenberry and apple muesli-style crumble (page 113).* TREATMENTS *everyday moisturizer (page 118), banana and cream anti-aging mask (page 122)*

DERMATITIS AND ECZEMA

Dermatitis and eczema are common skin conditions that cause flaking, redness, and irritation, especially on the hands, neck, and face. They tend to occur on areas of the skin where there are oil-producing sebaceous glands and/or hair follicles. The problem is exacerbated by stress, hormonal imbalance, or a build-up of toxins. Eczema can worsen if you scratch affected areas. Chronic eczema leads to patches of unsightly red, hardened skin. People who are susceptible to eczema often have a personal or family history of allergic reactions to foods, pollen, animal fur, or other substances. Many eczema sufferers have (or develop) hay fever or asthma, and their bodies often contain above-normal amounts of histamine, the chemical that triggers an allergic reaction in the skin. Foods containing beta carotene and vitamins C and E help calm the skin, reduce inflammation and itching, and counteract histamine.

✔ To help reduce dryness and itchiness, eat plenty of carrots, avocado, spinach, sweet potato, sunflower seeds, pine nuts, herring, and anchovies, which all contain beta carotene and vitamin E. Eczema sufferers may benefit from eating foods high in immune-boosting zinc, such as pumpkin seeds, beef, lamb, and sardines. Ensure you get enough histamine-fighting vitamin C, by eating kiwi fruit, green bell peppers, cabbage, and cauliflower.

✘ Try to identify foods that cause allergic reactions. Common culprits include milk, eggs, shellfish, wheat, chocolate, nuts, and strawberries. A food elimination diet may help determine what's bothering you. Simply avoid suspect foods for a while and then reintroduce them one by one to see if the problem returns.

✚ Eczema sufferers may need to try several supplements before they find one (or more, in combination) that works well for them.
Evening primrose oil (in capsules, gels, or liquid) contains essential fatty acids (EFAs) to relieve skin itchiness and inflammation.
Flaxseed oil contains omega-3 and omega-6 EFAs. Both help alleviate chronic allergic conditions, such as eczema.
Fish oil capsules help reduce the inflammation of eczema.
Vitamin A helps relieve skin dryness and itchiness. (Pregnant women, or women considering starting a family, should not exceed 5,000 iu (international units) of vitamin A per day.)
Vitamin C, a natural antihistamine, helps block the inflammatory response to allergens, such as pollen and pet dander, which can trigger the intensely itchy rashes associated with eczema.
Vitamin E is a potent antioxidant considered by many physicians and nutritionists to aid the treatment of eczema, possibly by enhancing the effects of vitamin A.
Zinc promotes healing and enhances immune-system functioning; it is also needed for the utilization of EFAs. If used for longer than a month, take copper supplements, too, as zinc supplements can deplete the body's own store of copper.
Grapeseed extract is rich in flavonoids, which can inhibit allergic responses, and so helps prevent or relieve itchy eczema flare-ups.

♥ If your eczema is made worse by stress, learn a relaxation technique, such as meditation (see page 128).

RECIPES carrot soup (page 94), multicolored rice salad (page 105), couscous medley (page 106), warm winter salad (page 106), happy and healthy (page 115). **TREATMENTS** *cooling toner (page 117), thirsty skin moisturizer (page 118)*

DRY SKIN

The sebaceous glands release an oily substance, sebum, to keep the skin lubricated, supple, and waterproof. Sebum, together with other natural oils, or lipids, and natural moisturizing factors (NMFs), forms a barrier called the hydro-lipid system. This barrier acts to keep foreign substances out and water in. In dry skin this barrier is no longer intact and skin quickly loses moisture. Dry skin tends to be flaky, slightly red, ultra-sensitive to soaps, cleansers, or detergents, and prone to itchiness or irritations.

✔ Eat foods rich in vitamin B, to help reduce skin dehydration. Vitamin E and B6 help neutralize the free radicals that cause skin sensitivity and dryness. Vitamin E also helps keep cell walls in optimum condition (necessary for the maintenance of healthy skin, nerves, muscles, blood cells, circulation, and heart). These vitamins can be found in wheat germ, cod, turkey, beef, bananas, Brussels sprouts, cabbage, and mango. Dry skin may indicate a lack of vitamin A, which is also vital for healthy skin cells. Good sources include butter, herring, anchovies, and avocado.

Dry skin may be due to a lack of fats and oils, especially in dieters. Fats and oils contain vitamin B5, which is necessary for smooth, well-hydrated skin. Eating foods such as milk, cheese, plain yogurt, and lettuce helps increase levels of B5.

✘ All skin types should avoid eating fried food. This contains free radicals that destroy vital enzymes in the body. Dry skin can be further exacerbated by excess alcohol and caffeine, as these have a diuretic effect, causing the skin to lose fluids and minerals.

♥ Avocado makes a great moisturizing face mask. Mash half an avocado with a tablespoon of plain bio-yogurt. Mix well and apply to cleansed skin. Leave for 10–15 minutes and rinse well.

RECIPES fresh fruit salad (page 92), weekend omelet (page 93), stuffed bell peppers (page 99), beef and noodle salad with chili lemon grass dressing (page 102), shredded beet and feta salad (page 105), couscous medley (page 106), mango, apple, and passion-fruit sorbet (page 112). **TREATMENTS** *return to youth (page 117), family cleanser (page 117), all-over body pamper (page 118), thirsty skin moisturizer (page 118)*

OILY SKIN

Oily skin occurs when the oil-secreting sebaceous glands produce more than is needed to lubricate the skin. This excess oil clogs the pores and also causes skin blemishes. Oily skin is often hereditary, but it can be affected by diet, hormone levels, and lifestyle.

Humidity and hot weather can stimulate the sebaceous glands into producing more oil than normal. Oily skin is more common in the teens, because of hormonal changes in adolescence, but it can occur at any age. Many people have skin that is oily in some areas and dry or normal in others, a condition called "combination" skin. Usually, the chin, forehead, nose, and the upper back tend to be the oiliest places. On the plus side, oily skin tends to age more slowly than dry skin, is less likely to show fine lines and wrinkles, and may not burn as easily as other skin types (although that's no reason not to take precautions!). Oily skin is not necessarily caused by oily food—the secret is to eat foods that produce "good" oils in the skin, to nourish and protect and aid detoxification.

✔ Flaxseed oils contain lots of essential fatty acids (EFAs) that help thin the oily sebum that can cause blocked pores. Toxins trapped in the body can also lead to blocked pores and blemishes. Omega-3 EFAs in the diet help to strengthen the liver and so support the detoxification process. Try including wheat germ, trout, and soy. Zinc is also needed to aid the healing process and may be helpful in reducing inflamed skin and balancing hormone levels. Zinc can be found in lamb, beef, oysters, turkey, and chicken.

✘ Although foods rich in EFAs are recommended, tuna, salmon, and walnuts also contain iodine, which is believed to aggravate the problem of oily skin and acne.

RECIPES *sesame beef rice and paper rolls (page 99), chicken salad with soy dressing (page 102), beef and noodle salad with chili lemon grass dressing (page 102), chicken breast baked in olives, lemon, and capers (page 108).* TREATMENTS *cool as a cucumber (page 117), face mask for oily skin (page 122)*

SENSITIVE SKIN

Sensitive skin tends to appear as stinging, itching, dry, or red patches that can appear all over the body, not just the face. Owing to the vast amount of pollutants and irritants we are exposed to each day, more women than ever suffer from sensitive skin. This condition is not necessarily caused by an allergy or an intolerance to a skin product. In fact, most skin irritations are caused by dehydration, so aim to drink plenty of water on a regular basis. A family history of eczema, hay fever, or asthma, or having a fair complexion or small sebaceous glands and pores, may increase your chances of having sensitive skin. Emotional triggers, such as

DAILY EATING PLAN FOR DRY SKIN

Dry skin lacks the natural oils that keep the skin smooth and supple. The following recipes contain foods that are rich in the vitamins and minerals that help replace the skin's natural oils; encourage the formation of healthy, smooth skin; and neutralize free radicals, which cause skin sensitivity, dryness, and premature aging.

BREAKFASTS

alpine muesli with red and green grapes (page 93), weekend omelet (page 93)

LUNCHES

stuffed bell peppers (page 99), shredded beet and feta salad (page 105)

DINNERS

beef and noodle salad with chili lemon grass dressing (page 102), couscous medley (page 106)

DESSERTS

fresh fruit salad (page 92), mango, apple, and passion-fruit sorbet (page 112)—pictured left

stress, and lack of exercise, may also contribute to the problem. Eat plenty of fruits and vegetables with a high water content to help maintain a healthy level of skin moisture.

✔ By drinking at least 3 pints of water a day you can help prevent dehydration—a major cause of sensitive skin. Include essential fatty acids (EFAs) in your diet, especially omega-3, as these help reduce skin inflammation and maintain skin moisture. Good sources of EFAs include extra virgin olive oil, sunflower and pumpkin seeds, brazil nuts, and almonds.

✘ Try to reduce your intake of artificial sweeteners and soft drinks, as these foods place extra stress on the nervous system. This, in turn, can exacerbate skin irritation. *Note: some foods, such as tomatoes, strawberries, seafood, or wheat can cause sensitive skin. If you find that eating these foods causes sensitivity problems, check with your doctor in case you have a food allergy.*

♥ Always test a new product on a patch of hidden skin, such as your inner elbow, before applying it to your face. The skin on the elbow is very similar to the skin on your face—but it won't be as visible if the product causes a rash.

RECIPES *strawberry spread (page 93), baby spinach and radicchio salad (page 97), rice jumble (page 109), nutty oven-baked monkfish (page 111).* **TREATMENTS** *cooling toner (page 117), mid-week scrub (page 119), dandruff elixir (page 120)*

WARTS

Warts are skin growths caused by a viral infection. Most are harmless and only mildly contagious. There are several types: *Common warts* can appear on any part of the body but especially on the hands, fingers, face, and neck. They can spread from one location to another (for example, from finger to finger). *Plantar warts* appear on the soles of the feet, either singly or in clusters. They tend to be hard and rough and can be painful. *Genital/anal warts* are sexually transmitted, unsightly, and pose a danger to health. They must be professionally treated, as they are associated with cancer of the cervix.

The quickest and most effective form of wart removal is through cosmetic surgery or medication. However, raw garlic is a common folk remedy, said to remove warts when applied directly. The powerful antiviral and antibacterial properties of garlic can also be obtained by including it in your diet on a regular basis.

✔ Warts are more likely to occur when the immune system is suppressed. Eating foods that are rich in vitamin A—a terrific

RECIPE FOR TREATING ACNE

This smoothie is packed with goodies to help combat acne and other blemishes. Banana contains Vitamin B6 and zinc, and has antibacterial properties—all of which help to control acne and promote healthy skin. Mango is antioxidant and detoxifying, and contains the skin-healing vitamin A.

CREAMY MANGO SMOOTHIE

1 mango

1 banana

wedge of fresh coconut

1 orange (freshly squeezed)

Blend the mango, banana, and coconut. Add the orange juice, mix well, and serve.

immune-strengthener—may help resist further outbreaks and also aid in the maintenance of healthy skin. Foods containing vitamin A include liver, butter, egg yolk, cream cheese, herrings, milk, and mackerel. Vitamin C also boosts the immune system and helps to strengthen cell walls. Foods rich in this vitamin, such as oranges, papaya, guava, green bell peppers, broccoli, strawberries, and kiwi fruit, help fight warts when eaten, and when used as a topical skin treatment.

✘ As warts tend to emerge when your immune system is below par, it is important to avoid anything that puts a strain on your health. Try to avoid or cut back on caffeine, nicotine, and alcohol—you'll not only look better, but as your immune system improves, you'll find that you have more energy as well.

♥ There is a wide range of supplements, oils, and tinctures that strengthen the skin and help combat skin infections such as warts. *Garlic oil* contains a potent substance called allicin that blocks the key enzymes that allow bacteria and viruses to invade tissues. *Tea tree oil* blends with natural oils and changes the chemistry of the skin, making it less welcoming to invading organisms and so reducing the risk of infection. Tea tree oil also promotes healing, and reduces the likelihood of scarring. *Goldenseal tincture* contains medicinal compounds, including the alkaloid berberine, with antibiotic and immune-boosting properties. *Aloe vera gel* has antiviral, antibacterial, and antifungal properties.

Pau d'arco tincture, derived from the inner bark of an evergreen tree, contains napthoquinones—powerful antiviral compounds—that, when applied directly, may help fight the wart and encourage skin healing.

RECIPES *spinach salad with warm garlic dressing (page 107), tofu risotto (page 110), chicken and broccoli in mushroom sauce (page 110), apple and almond fruit fool (page 113)*

PSORIASIS

Psoriasis is a chronic skin condition characterized by raised red patches, typically covered with silver or whitish skin flakes or scales. This non-contagious disease most often develops between the ages of 10 and 30, although people of any age can get it. The most common sites are the scalp, elbows, lower back, buttocks, and knees. Psoriasis can also affect the toenails and fingernails, leaving them yellowed and pitted. Psoriasis occurs when skin cells proliferate. New skin cells form in the lower layers of the skin and normally take about 28 days to rise through to the surface, where they are shed. In psoriasis, this life cycle lasts around eight days. New cells accumulate too quickly to mature and so cannot slough off. The skin becomes red and inflamed, with overlapping patches of white scales. Foods rich in antioxidants help protect the cells.

✔ Carrots, tomatoes, blueberries, strawberries, and raspberries all contain antioxidants that may help to prevent recurrent outbreaks. Eating oily fish such as cod or herring at least three times a week or taking 2–5 g of fish oil can help calm inflamed skin during an attack. Foods containing vitamin A can help regulate skin development and so reduce the number of attacks. Butter, whole milk, and herring all contain vitamin A.

✚ The following supplements may benefit psoriasis sufferers: *Grapeseed* extract has antioxidant properties and so can guard against damage to various types of cells, including skin cells. *Borage oil* has similar protective antioxidant benefits. *Milk thistle* can be useful for enhancing normal liver function, which is often beneficial for people with psoriasis. This herb also reduces leukotriene production in the white blood cells, which in turn helps slow the overactive life cycle of psoriatic skin.

❗ Researchers have found that smokers are more likely to have the condition. In particular, smokers with a 20 (or more) cigarettes-a-day habit had twice the risk of non-smokers, with female smokers more at risk than male smokers. According to researchers, as many as one in four cases of psoriasis may be smoking-related.

RECIPE FOR TREATING ECZEMA AND DERMATITIS

To help the skin retain moisture, you should include essential fatty acids (EFAs) in your diet. By plumping up the skin with moisture, you will help to combat the dryness caused by conditions such as eczema or dermatitis. There has been some research that suggests people with eczema may have an inability to process EFAs. A lack of EFAs may result in a deficiency of gamma-linolenic acid (GLA). Speak to your nutritionist or doctor about supplementing your diet with GLA, for example, with evening primrose oil. The following recipe contains EFAs.

SUNDRIED TOMATOES AND QUINOA

1 oz/⅓ cup sundried tomatoes (not oil-packed)

8 fl oz/1 cup boiling water

2 tbsp olive oil

1 medium red onion, finely chopped

2 cloves garlic, minced

26 oz/8 cups shredded Swiss chard

½ tsp salt

11 oz/2 cups quinoa, rinsed and drained

½ tsp pepper

3 oz/½ cup salted, dry-roasted sunflower seeds

2 oz/⅓ cup golden raisins

1 oz/⅓ cup grated Parmesan cheese

In a small bowl, combine the sundried tomatoes and boiling water. Let stand until the tomatoes are softened. When softened, thinly slice. In a large non-stick skillet, heat 1 tablespoon of oil over a medium heat. Add the onion and garlic. Cook, stirring frequently, for 5 minutes or until the onion is lightly browned. Add the Swiss chard, sprinkle with ¼ teaspoon of salt, and cook, stirring frequently, for 5–7 minutes until the chard is tender. Meanwhile, in a large non-stick skillet, heat the remaining 1 tablespoon of oil over a medium heat. Add the drained quinoa and cook, stirring constantly, for 5 minutes or until lightly golden. Add 32 fl oz/4 cups water, pepper, and remaining ¼ teaspoon of salt and bring to the boil. Reduce to a simmer, cover, and cook for 12–15 minutes or until quinoa is tender. Transfer mixture to a large bowl. Stir in sunflower seeds, raisins, Parmesan, Swiss chard mixture, and sundried tomatoes. Toss with a fork to combine. Serves 4.

RECIPES smoked haddock kedgeree with grilled tomatoes (page 93), tofu vegetable salad (page 102), lime, tomato, and scallop salad (page 102), summer pudding (page 113), strawberry starter smoothie (page 114), perfect skin (page 115). TREATMENTS cooling toner (page 117), mid-week scrub (page 119), dandruff elixir (page 120)

SUNBURN

Both types of ultraviolet (UV) radiation—UVA and UVB—can cause the reddening, inflammation, and pain of sunburn. Symptoms of sunburn can appear gradually, reaching their peak up to 24 hours after sun exposure. The intensity of a burn ranges from mild or moderate, to severe, in extreme cases. UV rays penetrate deeply into the dermis, the underlying skin layer, causing cell damage that may, in later years, lead to skin cancer. People with fair skin, blue eyes, and blond or red hair are most vulnerable to sunburn, but even those with darker complexions can be damaged by the sun's

harmful rays. All sunburn contributes to premature wrinkling and leathering of the skin, and age spots (see page 71). To reduce redness and help prevent blistering, rub fresh tomato over the sunburned area. Be sure to drink plenty of water and eat foods with a high water content. By keeping your system fully hydrated, you are less likely to suffer sunstroke, and your skin will be able to plump out the cells that have been dried out by the sun.

✔ To help safeguard the skin against the damaging effects of sunburn, include foods that are high in vitamin C, such as broccoli, green bell peppers, papaya, strawberries, kiwi fruit, and oranges, in your daily diet, especially when you are venturing into the sunshine. Vitamin C is essential for the production and maintenance of healthy collagen, which is the most important structural component of the skin, giving it strength, suppleness, and elasticity. It also has important antioxidant properties, helping to neutralize the triggers that cause aging and cancerous changes in the skin. Eating foods

INSECT BITES AND STINGS – PREVENTION AND TREATMENT

Some people can suffer a severe allergic reaction to bites and stings—swelling of the eyes, mouth, and throat and loss of consciousness. This requires immediate emergency medical aid. Otherwise, apply ice to the area to reduce inflammation and swelling. Native North Americans use basil to relieve insect stings. Pineapple contains bromelain, which helps reduce inflammation. If you are sensitive to pineapple, try bromelain supplements. For bee stings,

the vitamin C in green bell peppers, broccoli, papaya, oranges, and cauliflower may reduce swelling. Lavender oil is soothing and has antiseptic properties that help prevent infection. Tea tree oil fights infection and may prevent scarring. It blends well with other oils, which makes it a particularly effective topical treatment. Aloe vera gel contains active ingredients that relieve pain and itching and reduce swelling. Calendula cream has both anti-inflammatory and antiseptic properties. Quercetin is a plant flavonoid with anti-inflammatory and allergy-suppressing effects. It should be taken with vitamin C.

PREVENTION

Research in Japan has found that people who include lactic acid (present in most dairy foods) in their diet were less likely to be stung. At barbecues and other outdoor events, use insect-repellent candles. These usually contain citronella, an extract of the lemon-scented plant cymbopogon, grown in Asia. Citronella is the active ingredient in some anti-insect products applied to skin and clothing.

RECIPES rice jumble (page 109), chicken and broccoli in mushroom sauce (page 110), mixed vegetable skewers (page 111)—pictured, passion-fruit pineapple sorbet with mint sauce (page 113), hard as nails (page 114)

rich in vitamin E, such as sunflower seeds, sweet potato, avocado, and spinach, helps to maintain healthy skin, and offers some protection for the skin against the sun's damaging rays. If you have suffered sunburn, vitamin E aids cell repair and renewal.

✘ If you are planning to spend the day in the sun, it's important to realize the effect alcohol can have, not just on your brain, but also on your skin. Alcohol has an extremely dehydrating effect on your body in general, and your skin in particular. If you are being active in the sunshine, aim to increase your water intake by at least 2 pints over your normal level to stay fully hydrated.

✚ For an effective remedy for sunburn, add 10 drops of camomile oil or lavender oil to a cool bath and soak for 30 minutes. These oils contain calming properties to help relieve the stinging sensation of burned skin. Apply aloe vera gel to soothe irritation, speed up skin repair, and relieve the itching that often accompanies healing.

♥ It is vitally important that you choose the right sunscreen for your skin. Sun protection factor (SPF) ratings range from 2 to 60. The numbers indicate the product's ability to shield you from UV rays. If you normally burn in 30 minutes, SPF 15 is designed to protect you for about 450 minutes (15 X 30 = 450), or more than 7 hours. Most people should start with an SPF of at least 15, although susceptible individuals—blond/red-haired, fair skinned—and particularly children may need an SPF of 30 for better protection. Remember to reapply sunscreen regularly, especially after bathing—even if you are using waterproof sunscreen.

❗ If you get sunburned, rub tomatoes or papaya over the affected area. This will help reduce redness and promote healing.

RECIPES fresh fruit salad (page 92), sweet potato soup (page 95), steamed lemon grass chicken and rice rolls (page 98), stuffed bell peppers (page 99), vegetable rice paper rolls with chili dipping sauce (page 101), skin healer (page 114). TREATMENTS cooling toner (page 117), everyday moisturizer (page 118)

VARICOSE VEINS

Varicose veins are purplish, swollen blood vessels that are visible just under the surface of the skin. In healthy veins, there are special valves that open and shut like doors as blood passes through to keep the blood moving in one direction and prevent backflow. However, with age and when under particular strain, for example during pregnancy, the valves become weakened or damaged and fail to shut completely. As a result, blood can seep backward and pool, causing the vein to bulge. This is a varicose vein. At best, the

MANAGING CELLULITE

The "orange peel" look of cellulite affects as many as 90 percent of women, yet it is regarded with horror, and many people spend a great deal of money trying to get rid of it. Although cellulite isn't the same as fat, exercising and minimizing fat build-up is important. Exercise—at least three times a week—to stimulate lymph flow and blood circulation. Avoid foods containing additives, chemicals, sugar, and animal fats. Eat lots of fresh, colorful fruits and vegetables, such as blackberries, bell peppers, kiwi fruit, broccoli, citrus fruits, tomatoes, blackcurrants, strawberries, red grapes, and buckwheat. Take a supplement of gotu kola (30 mg three times daily) and skin brush toward your heart to stimulate circulation.

condition can be uncomfortable, and it may become painful if the veins get inflamed. Sometimes the skin over the veins may be itchy and scaly, the ankles may swell and there may be a heavy or aching feeling in the legs, especially after long periods on the feet.

✔ Vitamin C helps to strengthen the walls of the arteries, veins, and capillaries. Flavonoids, found in apricots, lemons, and broccoli, help to prevent vitamin C being destroyed. Vitamin E boosts blood circulation, fortifies blood vessel walls, and so helps prevent varicose veins forming. It works well in combination with vitamin C. To make sure you obtain this vitamin, include almonds, hazelnuts, pine nuts, muesli, sweet potato, and spinach in your diet.

✚ Supplements may help prevent or alleviate varicose veins. *Gotu kola (Centella asiatica)* is a valuable herb for varicose veins, because it tones the connective tissue around the veins, keeps the veins flexible, and encourages blood flow.

Bilberry is rich in antioxidants to strengthen capillaries and improve blood flow. It is a good companion to gotu kola, and these two herbs are often sold together in a combination product.

Horse chestnut seed extract reduces fluid retention, swelling, and inflammation and can be used along with gotu kola and bilberry.

Butcher's broom is a herb that is frequently combined with horse chestnut to strengthen the walls of blood vessels.

RECIPES alpine muesli with red and green grapes (page 93), baby spinach and radicchio salad (page 97), Italian salad (page 104), pork fillets with date and hazelnut stuffing (page 106), lemon and parsley fried fish (page 108), chicken and broccoli in mushroom sauce (page 110), apple and almond fruit fool (page 113)

hair

STAR FOODS FOR HAIR: APRICOTS, BEEF, BREWER'S YEAST, CANTALOUPE, COD, DAIRY FOOD, EGGS, GREEN LEAFY VEGETABLES, HADDOCK, LAMB, LIVER, MUESLI, MUSSELS, NUTS, OATS, OYSTERS, PORK, PUMPKIN SEEDS, SARDINES, SEAWEED, SEEDS, SOY, WHEAT GERM, YOGURT

Your hair is a daily barometer of your overall physical condition. It also speaks volumes about your personality and mood. When you're stressed, deficient in nutrients, or have a hormonal imbalance, it is reflected in your hair, which may become lifeless, dry, brittle, or just generally unmanageable. The state of your hair can even affect your emotions, hence the term "bad hair day!"

Even though hair isn't living tissue—it is made of keratin, the same fibrous protein found in nails—a constant supply of nutrient-rich blood is needed to nourish the hair follicles in the scalp from which each hair grows. Food is just as important for healthy hair as for overall health. To ensure you have healthy, shiny hair, your diet should contain plenty of green leafy vegetables, such as lettuce and Brussels sprouts, milk, fruit, wheat germ, and soy.

SLOW HAIR GROWTH

On average, hair grows 1 in every two months and sheds up to 100 of its 100,000 hairs every day. Hair growth can vary according to the weather (hair grows faster in the sunshine). Discarded strands are usually quickly replaced, but if your hair growth seems slow, it may be worth looking at your diet and lifestyle to ensure that you're getting all the nutrients you need.

✔ A diet high in all the vital nutrients, especially iodine, beta carotene, and protein, is necessary for shiny, healthy hair. Iodine is needed for production of the thyroid hormone thyroxin, which prompts normal hair growth, and is found in seafood such as cod, haddock, seaweed, and mussels. Beta carotene is converted into vitamin A, which the body needs to maintain strong, healthy hair. Beta carotene is found in green and yellow vegetables and fruit, including cantaloupe and apricots. As hair is made of protein, it needs foods such as meat, eggs, cheese, seeds, and nuts.

✘ Sugar, soft drinks, and fast foods do not contribute to the growth and health of the hair, and so should be eliminated from the diet. Caffeine, alcohol, and smoking rob the body of hair-boosting nutrients. Nicotine, in particular, destroys vitamin C.

✚ A selenium supplement delivers this nutrient to the hair roots and promotes stronger, healthier hair, but do not exceed 200 mcg of this mineral a day, as higher amounts may be toxic.

♥ Treatments that contain egg, mayonnaise, lemon juice, and beer can help to keep hair strong and shiny.

♥ Massage your scalp weekly to stimulate blood flow and relieve stress. When stimulated, hair follicles respond with faster growth.

❗ Need an excuse to get some extra shuteye? Research shows that around 7–9 hours of sleep per night speeds up hair growth.

RECIPES oatmeal with prunes and apricots (page 92), oatmeal with mixed fruit (page 93), Italian salad (page 104), mussels in ginger and lemon grass broth (page 107), rice jumble (page 109), chicken and broccoli in mushroom sauce (page 110), nutty oven-baked monkfish (page 111). TREATMENT lavender shampoo (page 120)

DRY AND BRITTLE HAIR

Dry, brittle hair is unattractive and can be a sign of a poor diet. For example, when protein intake is inadequate, the hair can become very fine, leading to hair breakage, split ends, and even hair loss. Studies have also shown that a gap of more than four hours between meals can adversely affect hair formation. Once hair splits there is little you can do, other than have it cut. But before this happens, dry and brittle hair will respond to external treatment.

✔ Zinc is an essential element required for a number of the body's biochemical processes. Zinc deficiency may be caused by poor diet, absorption problems of the bowel, excessive alcohol, or diuretics and can result in dry, brittle hair and hair loss. Increase your zinc levels by enjoying oysters, wheat germ, pumpkin seeds, roast beef, lamb, pork, and sardines. Silica has been shown to help retain moisture in the hair shaft, thereby reducing dryness and brittleness. Eat oats and muesli to increase your silica intake.

✘ Foods high in fat or sugar rob your body of precious minerals and moisture. Alcohol, caffeine, and nicotine also reduce fluid levels in the body, which can lead to dry hair.

✤ Taking 200 iu (international units) of vitamin E each day can help you overcome dry and brittle hair. It's important to check with your doctor before you begin any supplement program.

♥ Rinsing your hair with lemon juice helps unblock the follicles and allows moisture to reach the hair shaft. Apply once after shampooing and conditioning and pat your hair dry. A mixture of banana and olive oil, applied once a week, nourishes hair roots.

♥ Take a tip from hairdressers and keep your hairdryer on "cool" so that you do not over-dry the hair. As soon as one section of hair is dry, go on to the next. Over-drying brittle hair will make it worse.

RECIPES oatmeal with prunes and apricots (page 92), oatmeal with mixed fruit (page 93), alpine muesli with red and green grapes (page 93), sesame beef rice and paper rolls (page 99), couscous medley (page 106), an apple a day (page 115). *TREATMENTS* dry hair conditioner (page 120), essential oil leave-in conditioner (page 121), banana hair mask (page 123), hot hair mask (page 123)

DULL, LIFELESS HAIR

Dull and lifeless hair seems impossible to style or handle. Hair shines if it has a smooth surface. The outer layer of hair is called the cuticle and is made up of cells that overlap like roof tiles. Damaged or raised cuticles do not reflect light well, so use conditioner after shampooing to protect and smooth the hair cuticle. Some experts say that blasting your hair with cold water after you have washed it also encourages the cuticles to lie flat and therefore reflect the light better to give a lustrous shine.

✔ A diet lacking in essential fatty acids (EFAs) can lead to dull, lifeless hair. EFAs are found in salmon, mackerel, evening primrose oil, sunflower and sesame seeds, and flaxseeds. Dehydration also contributes to lifeless hair, so drink at least 3 pints of water a day. Keep a glass handy and fill up when you take a break.

✘ A high-fat diet of processed foods or ready-made meals can lead to lifeless hair. Replace these with fresh fruit and vegetables, legumes, and low-fat versions of your favorite foods.

♥ Rinsing your hair with vinegar helps remove the build-up of any hair products that may be making your hair appear lifeless, restoring the natural pH balance of your hair and scalp. Add 1 tsp of vinegar to a cup of warm water and apply after shampooing. Leave the mixture on your hair and dry and style as normal.

RECIPES tasty tuna snack (page 99), warm chickpea and tuna salad (page 105), salmon steaks with sesame seed crusts (page 109), pasta and yogurt dressing (page 111), strawberry starter smoothie (page 114), an apple a day (page 115). *TREATMENT* essential oil leave-in conditioner (page 121)

GREASY HAIR

Greasy hair is caused by overactive sebaceous glands. Avoid washing it daily, as this can stimulate already-overactive glands and aggravate the problem. Washing every other day is sufficient.

✔ Vitamin B2 helps rebalance the sebaceous glands and reduce oil production. Foods containing vitamin B2 include brewer's yeast, natural yogurt, cheese, eggs, liver, spinach, Brussels sprouts, and other green leafy vegetables.

✘ Avoid oily, fatty, and processed foods, which may exacerbate the problem. Try cutting out milk from your diet, as some people find that this helps reduce the amount of oil their body produces.

♥ If you are prone to pimples, keep styling products such as gels, mousses, or hairsprays away from your forehead. These products often contain ingredients that clog pores and can cause pimples.

♥ Dry shampoos are an effective way of removing oil between wet shampoos, without over-stimulating the sebaceous glands. Do not use very hot water when shampooing. Avoid brushing your hair too often or too vigorously. Brush gently along the length of the hair shaft to distribute the oil evenly. Oily hair benefits from vinegar or lemon rinses. These close the hair cuticles, remove excess oil, and leave hair shining and manageable.

❗ Anything that affects hormone levels (such as stress, or use of contraceptive pills) may cause oily hair. Check with your doctor regarding your choice of pill if you have excessively oily hair.

RECIPES strawberry spread (page 93), mushroom and bean soup (page 95), fresh fruit with maple-vanilla yogurt dip (page 98), tofu vegetable salad (page 102), spinach salad with warm garlic dressing (page 107), nutty oven-baked monkfish (page 111). *TREATMENT* conditioner for oily hair (page 120)

DANDRUFF

Dandruff is an embarrassing problem that occurs when the scalp sheds clumps or scales of dead skin (epidermal) cells. Dandruff appears as dry, white, or grayish flakes and small, irritating, unsightly patches, especially on top of the head. These flakes are highly visible, especially when they cover the shoulders. Dandruff also causes itching and soreness and the scalp can feel tight.

Scalp cells have a life cycle of about one month. Cells form in the deepest layer of the epidermis and slowly get pushed to the

ITCHY SCALP

Itchy scalp can be caused by allergy, poor diet, stress, smoking, excess alcohol, air-conditioning, central heating, and pollution. A healthy scalp needs a balanced diet low in saturated fat and sugar and high in moisture-retaining foods, such as watermelon, apple, broccoli, cabbage, cucumbers, carrots, lettuce, and green bell peppers. Other scalp-hydrating nutrients include omega-3 and omega-6 essential fatty acids (EFAs), found in salmon, tuna, and seeds. Try to drink at least 3 pints of water daily.

Oily foods such as olive oil, avocados, or bananas help soothe and nourish the area, when applied directly. Jojoba and almond oil are soothing and hydrating for the scalp. It's vital to protect your scalp from the sun; wear a hat in hot sun, apply sunscreen lotion to your hair parting, and use hair products that contain sunscreen.

RECIPES carrot soup (page 94), black-eyed peas and walnut spread (page 98), salmon steaks with sesame seed crusts (page 109), perfect start (page 114), perfect skin (page 115).
TREATMENT hot hair mask (page 123), banana hair mask (page 123)

surface, where they're shed. This process is usually unnoticed, but sometimes turnover is so rapid that clumps of dead cells appear as visible flakes—dandruff. Dandruff does not cause baldness but chronic dandruff may be associated with some general hair loss.

✔ Deficiencies of B-complex vitamins, essential fatty acids (EFAs), and selenium have been linked to dandruff. Eating foods such as avocado, apples, sesame seeds, bananas, beef, cod, mango, and eggs, which all contain B vitamins, helps prevent dandruff, as these foods reduce stress levels, which contributes to the condition. EFAs help to keep the scalp hydrated—enjoy salmon, mackerel, tuna, and sunflower and sesame seeds.

✘ Dandruff can be triggered by trauma, illness, overactive oil glands, food allergies, stress, excessive perspiration, hormonal imbalances, and excess consumption of sugar and starchy foods.

✚ Flaxseed oil contains omega-3 fatty acids that make hair more glossy and healthy looking. It may soothe the itching and flaking of dandruff, and help rid the scalp of psoriasis and eczema.

♥ Adding vinegar to a treatment or as a rinse helps neutralize any pH imbalance. Lemon juice helps exfoliate the scalp, thereby removing excess skin flakes. Treatment: 1 teaspoon of lemon juice,

1 teaspoon of vinegar. Mix the ingredients well. Wet the hair, then pour the mixture onto your head and massage lightly into your scalp. Rinse well and shampoo as normal. You may also like to try a rosemary or thyme infusion: steep 1 tablespoon of the dried ingredient in a cup of boiling water for 10 minutes, then rinse the hair with the infusion.

RECIPES tasty tuna snack (page 99), sesame beef rice and paper rolls (page 99), shredded beet and feta salad (page 105), apple, vegetable, and quorn curry (page 108), salmon steaks with sesame seed crusts (page 109), pasta and yogurt dressing (page 111), mango, apple, and passion-fruit sorbet (page 112)

HAIR LOSS

When you are in good health, you shed around 100 hairs a day—normally too few to notice. But if you shed more than this, or your hair starts falling out in clumps, it can indicate a nutritional deficiency due to poor diet, hormonal imbalance, over exposure to cosmetics or environmental chemicals, age-related hair loss, stress, anxiety, or tension. Whether stress or shock can cause severe hair loss (known as *alopecia areata*) is not known.

✔ Iron is a very important nutrient to include in your daily diet, as it helps prevent anemia, a cause of hair loss or thinning hair. Include servings of red meat, oily fish, dark poultry meat, legumes, and sunflower and sesame seeds in your daily diet. Protein-rich foods help to nourish the hair follicles and encourage hair growth. Include eggs, cheese, and chicken as part of a healthy hair diet. Silica, a mineral found in potato skin, green and red bell peppers, cucumbers, and bean sprouts, may also help to prevent hair loss.

✘ A high-fat diet full of processed snacks and fast foods does not contain the full range of nutrients and vitamins your hair requires and this can exacerbate hair loss.

♥ Olive oil helps stimulate hair growth. Apply a hot oil treatment to your scalp and give yourself a relaxing head massage every week. Treatment: mix together 1 1/2 oz avocado, 1 1/2 oz olive oil and apply to clean, damp hair. Cover with a plastic shower cap and heated towel. Leave for two hours. Rinse and wash as usual.

♥ If your hair is thinning, it may be a good idea to have it cut into a shorter style, to make the most of the volume you have.

RECIPES mediterranean oven-roasted vegetable soup (page 94), stuffed bell peppers (page 99), vegetable rice paper rolls with chili dipping sauce (page 101), chicken salad with soy dressing (page 102), warm chickpea and tuna salad (page 105)

GRAYING HAIR

Gray hair is a familiar sign of aging. The age when graying starts depends on your genetic inheritance, but around 50 percent of Caucasians find that half their hair has turned gray by the age of 50. Loss of hair color is due to a gradual decline in the production of a pigment, melanin, in the hair bulb. If you look at individual hairs on a graying head you will see a full color range, from the original shade to white—all along each hair, and from one hair to another. The first gray hairs usually appear near the temples. Then the grayness spreads to the crown, and later to the back of the head.

Apparent rapid graying may be due to the selective shedding of pigmented hair in a person who already has some gray hairs, which are retained. This kind of shedding usually takes several months. But it can occur in a few days, when the effects are dramatic, as the person's gray hairs would not have been so obvious until the darker hairs were lost. Loss of hair color before the age of 35 is termed premature graying. Excessive intake of tea, coffee, alcohol, meat, and fried, oily, greasy, spicy, sour, and acidic foods, can reduce the moisture and nutrients reaching the hair follicles and may lead to premature graying.

✔ A drop in melanin production may be caused by a lack of the mineral copper. Eat foods such as crab, oysters, sunflower seeds, cashews, and almonds, which have significant amounts of copper.

✘ Avoid foods loaded with artificial colors and preservatives, as these put a strain on your digestive system that can lead to dry, brittle hair and a dehydrated scalp. Too many carbohydrates, such as pasta and bread, can diminish levels of antioxidants in your body that are needed to neutralize free radicals.

♥ Instead of reaching for a packet of hair dye, try some natural applications. Sage or tea will temporarily coat the hair shaft, hiding the gray. Gray hair tends to be coarse and wiry, owing to a lack of moisture. Apply a hair mask once a week. Olive oil, avocado, or banana are excellent nourishing masks.

❗ Hair cannot really turn white "overnight"—this is an urban myth. Hairs grow with the pigment already inside them. As hair is dead, there is no process by which the melanin throughout a hair can be destroyed rapidly by natural causes, rather than chemicals (although it may be bleached by sunlight over many years).

RECIPES vegetable rice paper rolls with chili dipping sauce (page 101), lime, tomato, and scallop salad (page 102), lima bean, tomato, and rocket salad (page 104), salmon steaks with sesame seed crusts (page 109), strawberry starter smoothie (page 114)

DAILY EATING PLAN FOR GRAY HAIR

The rapid graying that occurs when pigmented hair falls out to reveal underlying gray hairs can be delayed by keeping your hair as healthy as possible. If you are going prematurely gray, drink plenty of water and fruit and vegetable juices. Fresh juice is full of antioxidants that help detoxify the body and protect the pigmented hairs that remain, and so delay the onset of premature graying.

BREAKFASTS

oatmeal with prunes and apricots (page 92), strawberry starter smoothie (page 114)

LUNCH

chicken salad with soy dressing (page 102) with a wide variety of vegetables

DINNER

vegetable and bean soup (page 96) with wholewheat pita bread

DESSERT

fresh fruit salad (page 92) and natural yogurt—pictured above

MORE RECIPES vegetable rice paper rolls with chili dipping sauce (page 101), lime, tomato, and scallop salad (page 102), lima bean, tomato, and rocket salad (page 104), exotic kedgeree (page 107), salmon steaks with sesame seed crusts (page 109), strawberry starter smoothie (page 114)

nails

STAR FOODS FOR NAILS: ASPARAGUS, BEEF, BELL PEPPERS, BLACK-EYED PEAS, CARROTS, CAULIFLOWER, CORN, DUCK, EGGS, GARLIC, LAMB, LEEKS, MILK, MUESLI, OILY FISH, ONIONS, OYSTERS, PAPAYA, PORK, PUMPKIN, SOY, SPINACH, SWEET POTATO, YEAST EXTRACT, ZUCCHINI

Nails comprise a hard nail plate and an underlying nail bed. Nail itself is made of the fibrous protein keratin, one of the toughest tissues in the body. Nonetheless, nails are vulnerable to damage from infections, skin irritations, allergies, and household chemicals, leaving them weak and brittle. Other common problems include injury, which if severe may cause the loss of the nail, and ingrown toenail, which occurs when the sides or corners of the nail dig into the soft surrounding tissue, causing inflammation and pain. Minor injuries disappear once the nail grows out. Nail grows at the rate of about 0.1 mm per day, and so it takes about six months to grow new nail from cuticle to tip. Ingrown toenail requires specialist care.

Nutrition plays an essential role in nail growth and health. Dietary deficiencies, and conditions such as anemia, are reflected in the appearance of the nails. Eating a balanced diet of fruits, vegetables, legumes (peas and beans), and whole grains keeps your system healthy and helps prevent nail problems.

BRITTLE NAILS

If you suffer from brittle or weak nails that split and tear easily, it's important to protect your hands from chemicals such as harsh detergents. Too much exposure to water can also damage nails. Water makes them swell and then shrink, resulting in loose, brittle nails. A lack of protein, or of vitamins A or D, in the diet can also cause nails to become brittle and vulnerable to damage. Some nutrients are particularly important for strong nails, including biotin, found in corn, soy beans, cauliflower, and egg yolk; and calcium, found in dairy products (where possible choose low-fat types). Oily fish are rich in omega-3 essential fatty acids (EFAs), which improve blood flow to the fingers and toes, ensuring nutrients and oxygen reach the nail bed to encourage the growth of strong, healthy nails.

✔ A lack of iron can lead to thin, brittle nails. Iron is not only important for the blood, it also helps the body absorb calcium. Iron is found in fish such as herrings and sardines, meat, muesli, eggs, and milk. You may find that your nails become brittle and dry when you are stressed. This is because stress robs the body of essential B vitamins, which are important for nail growth and repair. Eat spinach, Brussels sprouts, muesli, black-eyed peas, and asparagus for a healthy intake of B vitamins. Brittle nails may be caused by lack of moisture to the nail bed, so foods with a high moisture content are recommended. A large bell pepper contains around a glass of water, and so is an ideal food for healthy nails.

✗ Avoid over-indulging in high-fat foods, as these lack important nutrients and may make it more difficult for your body to utilize useful vitamins and minerals. Sugar wreaks havoc with hydration levels, so try to limit the amount of sugary food in your diet.

✚ Biotin is part of the vitamin B-complex group and is absorbed into the nail matrix, where nail cells are formed. A daily dosage of 2,500 mcg is recommended as a supplement.

♥ When you next apply an olive oil treatment to your hair and scalp, use any leftovers on your hands and nails, paying particular attention to the cuticles.

♥ Chemicals in nail polish, nail polish remover, and cuticle remover can dry and damage nails. Some health food stores and drug stores stock non-acetone nail polish remover that is kinder to the nails.

RECIPES baby spinach and radicchio salad (page 97), black-eyed peas and walnut spread (page 98), lime, tomato, and scallop salad (page 102), oven-baked vegetable salad (page 105), multicolored rice salad (page 105), lentil and red onion quiche (page 109)

NAIL INFECTIONS

About half of all nail problems are due to fungal infection. Moist environments, such as sweaty shoes and socks, make ideal breeding grounds for fungi, especially if they can get a "toehold" in small fissures, or breaks. High-impact exercise such as jogging can cause skin damage, leaving runners and other athletes especially prone to fungal nail infections. Typically, a fungus first appears as a small yellow or white spot that slowly spreads over the entire nail. The nail may turn yellow, brown, black, or gray and then gradually thicken and become so brittle that it may split. If left untreated, the nail may separate from the underlying nail bed. Fungal infection requires specialist treatment and prescription medication. Athlete's foot is an itchy fungal infection that usually develops between the toes and sometimes spreads to the nails. To prevent athlete's foot, always dry your feet thoroughly after showering, especially in communal changing areas. If you are prone to fungal foot infections, use an antifungal powder, cream, or spray regularly.

✔ To help your body fight fungal infection, load up on immune-boosting foods. Garlic, onions, leeks, and scallions contain allicin, a plant nutrient with antifungal properties.

♥ Tea tree oil or garlic oil can help control fungal infections.

RECIPES *mediterranean oven-roasted vegetable soup (page 94), pumpkin soup (page 94), mushroom and bean soup (page 95), leek and lentil soup (page 96), large shrimp and noodle soup (page 96), chicken salad with soy dressing (page 102)*

VERTICAL RIDGES

Vertical ridges can look unsightly and may lead to other problems, such as brittle, flaking nails. Pronounced ridges in the nails can often be traced to a deficiency of B vitamins, as these are needed by the nail matrix, where nail cells are generated. Stress can deplete stores of vitamin B. Vitamin A boosts immunity to infection and is essential for the maintenance and repair of nail tissue. A deficiency of vitamin A can also lead to ridged nails.

✔ To ensure that your nails are strong and smooth, include vitamin A-rich foods in your diet, such as oily fish, bell peppers, zucchini, asparagus, carrots, garlic, papaya, pumpkin, spinach, and sweet potato. If you are stressed, then increasing your daily intake of vitamin B12 will help to calm the nervous system. Vitamin B12 is found in pork, eggs, beef, muesli, duck, and yeast extract. As vitamin B12 is not found in fruit and vegetables, vegetarians and vegans may need to take a supplement to avoid a deficiency.

✘ Any foods that place a strain on the nervous system, such as coffee, nicotine, or alcohol, will rob the body of vitamin B12.

RECIPES *healthy fry-up (page 92), weekend omelet (page 93), beef and noodle salad with chili lemon grass dressing (page 102), warm chickpea and tuna salad (page 105), pork fillets with date and hazelnut stuffing (page 106)*

WHITE SPOTS

White spots on the nail can be a sign of zinc deficiency. Along with iron, zinc is needed to make hemoglobin, which gives the nail bed a healthy pink color. Calcium deficiency is another cause.

✔ To rebalance any zinc deficiencies, include oysters, pumpkin seeds, roast beef, lean roast lamb, pork, and sardines in your diet.

RECIPES *strawberry spread (page 93), beef and noodle salad with chili lemon grass dressing (page 102), couscous medley (page 106), barbecue pork san choy bau (page 108), lentil and red onion quiche (page 109)*

DAILY EATING PLAN FOR VERTICAL RIDGES

B-complex vitamins (especially B12) and vitamin A are necessary for healthy nails. A deficiency can lead to vertical ridges. Stress depletes the body of B vitamins, while the modern diet is often lacking in vitamin A. This nail-friendly diet can help restore these nutrients.

BREAKFAST

alpine muesli with red and green grapes (page 93)

LUNCH

chicken and broccoli in mushroom sauce (page 110)

DINNER

sweet potato soup (page 95)—pictured left

DESSERT

apple and almond fruit fool (page 113)

lips and teeth

STAR FOODS FOR LIPS: APPLE, ARTICHOKE, CAMOMILE, CARROT, CAULIFLOWER, CELERY, CHERVIL, CHESTNUT, CHICKPEAS, CHICKEN, CLOVE, CORN, DUCK, ENDIVE, GARLIC, GREEN BEANS, GREEN BELL PEPPER, KIWI FRUIT, LAVENDER, LEEK, LEMON BALM, LETTUCE, MINT, MUSSELS, OLIVES, ORANGE, PEAS, PAPAYA, PARSNIP, PINEAPPLE, PORK, POTATO, SHRIMPS, SOY, STRAWBERRY, SALMON, TUNA, TURKEY, WALNUT, WATERCRESS

Our mouths are our most sensual, expressive feature and the lips, like the hair, are an accurate indicator of internal health. If you are dehydrated, your lips may be dry and cracked. If your immune system is flagging, you may be more susceptible to cold sores or split corners. Lips are covered on the outside by a thin layer of skin and on the inside by virtually transparent mucous membranes and so are very easily damaged. Unlike other areas of skin, they do not have the pigment melanin to protect them.

The lips are made up of three regions. First, there is a relatively thin epidermis covering the outer area. Second, there is the vermillion zone, where the skin is so thin the blood vessels are visible (hence the red color). This is made of the same mucous membrane as in the lining of the mouth. Third, there is the tissue that fills the lips, composed mostly of collagen.

The lips are delicate and packed with blood vessels, and so are vulnerable to injury and bleed readily when damaged. They are also filled with nerve endings, and therefore very sensitive. The lips have no sweat or oil glands, which leaves them prone to dryness, cracking, and cold sores. A well-balanced diet maintains a healthy immune system and so is an important part of mouth care.

A tooth is like an iceberg—only a portion is visible and most lies beneath the surface. Your pearly whites not only give you your smile, but extend into your gums and then beyond the gums into the jaw. A tooth seems solid but is actually a multi-layered structure full of nerves and blood vessels. It is surrounded and supported by the delicate tissue of the gums. Poor oral hygiene and nutrition contributes to periodontal (gum) disease, which puts teeth at risk. The moment you start eating, bacteria in the mouth act on the food to produce acidic secretions. Unless neutralized or removed, the acid starts a process that leads to cavities.

Like the rest of the body, your mouth depends on good nutrition to stay healthy. Poor nutrition can lead to premature tooth loss and bad breath. Many nutritional problems affect the mouth before the rest of the body. This is because the cells in the lining of the mouth—the oral mucosa—are constantly being destroyed and replaced. A new group of cells can take the place of old cells in as little as three to seven days.

BAD BREATH

Bad breath, or halitosis, can be caused by certain foods, or the breakdown of food particles by the bacteria that inhabit the mouth. Almost everyone has experienced the bad breath caused by eating certain foods. The culprits are pungent sulfur compounds found in foods such as garlic and cabbage. Contrary to popular belief, sulfur compounds do not cause bad breath as a result of working their way back up into the mouth from the stomach. Rather, these compounds are absorbed by the digestive system, where they move into the bloodstream and are carried to the lungs. Here the sulfur compounds are expelled from the body in the air we exhale. Sulfur compounds are also excreted in the sweat and in urine for hours—or even days—after being eaten.

✔ Bad breath can be due to a lack of saliva. You can increase your saliva flow by drinking more water—this will also help wash away any lingering food particles or bacteria. Herbs such as parsley, cardamom, aniseed, coriander, and fennel seeds are natural breath fresheners. They contain chlorophyll, the green pigment in plants, which helps to eliminate odors. Parsley also contains essential oils that are released when the herb is chewed after a meal and can help to freshen the breath.

✘ Avoid foods such as cabbage and onions if bad breath is a chronic problem. Foods such as red meat that can take a long time to digest may also contribute to bad breath.

♥ Place a drop of lemon juice on the tip of your tongue to stimulate saliva flow. The natural astringent present in lemons will also neutralize odors.

RECIPES smoked haddock kedgeree with grilled tomatoes (page 93), black-eyed peas and walnut spread (page 98), lemon parsley-dill marinade (page 101), baked fillet of sole (page 107), rice jumble (page 109), fish in sleeping bags (page 110)

TOOTH DECAY

Tooth decay is destruction of the tooth enamel. It occurs when food residues containing sugar and starches, such as sugary drinks, sweets, and biscuits, are left in contact with the teeth for long periods. Mouth bacteria thrive on these foods, producing acids that, over time, damage the enamel, causing decay. The longer food remains in contact with the tooth, the more acid is produced. So sticky, sugary snacks, and foods such as potato chips that pack into crevices, are the worst offenders. The molars, and other teeth with lots of nooks and crannies, are more likely to trap food and so are more susceptible to decay. Some foods protect teeth because they neutralize acids, increase the flow of saliva, and replace the minerals needed for healthy teeth.

✔ *Chicken, dairy foods and nuts* counteract acidity and provide calcium and phosphorus—important tooth minerals. A small piece of hard cheese eaten at the end of a meal helps in a simple way to buffer the acids produced by sugary desserts.

Apples and pears have a high water content that dilutes the sugars in the mouth. They also help stimulate the flow of saliva, which contains antibacterial factors and so helps protect against decay.

TOP TIPS FOR PERFECT TEETH

A good oral hygiene routine helps avoid the plaque build-up that is the main cause of gum disease and tooth decay. In addition, have lots of sugar-free drinks (pure water is ideal!) between meals to flush away the acids produced by bacteria in the mouth.

- Brush at least twice a day with a fluoride toothpaste.
- Clean between your teeth daily with dental floss or dental tape.
- Eat a nutritious diet; end meals with a small piece of cheese.
- Avoid sugary snacks, candy, and drinks.
- Check with your dentist about use of fluoride supplements, which strengthen your teeth, and about the use of dental sealants (a plastic protective coating) applied to the chewing surfaces of the back teeth to protect them from decay.
- Visit your dentist regularly for a dental check-up and cleansing.

Milky tea contains fluoride, to strengthen tooth enamel, and minerals to help resist decay and strengthen the teeth. The water helps flush away food debris and dilute the sugar acids.

✘ *Carbohydrates*—all types—eventually break down into simple sugars, such as glucose, fructose, and maltose. Some foods, called "fermentable carbohydrates," are broken down in the mouth. Others are broken down further along the digestive tract. The fermentable carbohydrates pose the greatest risk to teeth, as they release sugars that bacteria can act upon. These include not only obvious sugary foods, such as cookies, cakes, soft drinks, and candy, but also less obvious ones such as bread, crackers, bananas, and breakfast cereals.

Tomatoes, oranges, lemons, and other very acidic foods may contribute to tooth demineralization. The effects of acid exposure are cumulative, so every bit counts. Since these are healthy foods, try to eat them as part of a meal or follow them with one of the anticariogenic (anti-decay) foods, such as cheese or milk.

Soft drinks, sweetened beverages, and sugar snacks, when consumed regularly throughout the day, provide a constant source of sugar for mouth bacteria. Since acid damage is cumulative, this means decay is more likely. Studies have shown that those who eat sweet foods as snacks have a higher incidence of decay than those who eat the same amount of sweet foods with their meals.

♥ Chewing sugar-free gum containing xylitol helps reduce the risk of cavities. It not only removes food stuck between the teeth, but also increases saliva flow to help buffer the bacterial acids.

RECIPES oatmeal with mixed fruit (page 93), alpine muesli with red and green grapes (page 93), chicken and broccoli in mushroom sauce (page 110)

STAINED TEETH

Teeth were never meant to be pure white. Their natural color is actually a light yellow or light yellow-red. However, as teeth darken with age, it's no wonder that we hanker for a "whiter-than-white" smile. Our teeth are constantly bombarded with food dyes, hot and cold and acidic foods, nicotine, caffeine, and alcohol. Over time, these elements affect tooth enamel, much as constant use dulls a porcelain plate. As we age, the surface enamel cracks and erodes, exposing the soft dentine inside, which absorbs food color. Stains also latch onto the plaque and tartar that builds up on the tooth surface and in the nooks and crannies. Eating foods that help to eliminate bacteria can help you keep your sunny smile.

✔ *Cranberries, blueberries, and raspberries* contain anthocyanins, which reduce bacteria numbers in the mouth. The fewer bacteria present, the lower the risk of gum disease and enamel erosion.

✗ Sugary foods, caffeine, nicotine, and colored foods all dye and stain the porcelain of your teeth. Try to limit their consumption.

♥ After every meal, have a drink of water to rinse away any lingering food residues.

❗ Polish with baking soda. Mix baking soda with a little hydrogen peroxide to a toothpaste-like consistency, then brush stains away. Take care not to use too much peroxide, as it can cause burning.

RECIPES oatmeal with mixed fruit (page 93), smooth and sweet honey and berries (page 93), strawberry spread (page 93), strawberry starter smoothie (page 114)

CRACKED CORNERS

During colder weather the lips can suffer from cracked corners. These can be painful and may take time to heal as the wound reopens every time you move your mouth. Cracked corners are more likely if there is a deficiency of zinc and vitamin B in your diet, as both are necessary for a healthy immune system and for the repair of damaged tissues. Signs of a flagging immune system include cracking in the mouth corners, pimples, and lack of energy.

✔ Bran flakes, chicken, avocado, soy beans, cottage cheese, eggs, and beef are good sources of B vitamins. Pumpkin seeds, beef, wheat germ, and sardines are rich in zinc.

✗ To maintain a healthy immune system, and smooth, kissable lips, avoid over-processed, fast foods. If you already suffer from cracked corners, spicy or salty foods may exacerbate the problem.

♥ Tea tree oil helps to heal cracked corners. Apply to the affected area at least twice a day, using a clean Q-Tip.

RECIPES spicy chicken salad in witlof (page 98), sesame beef rice and paper rolls (page 99), shredded beet and feta salad (page 105), couscous medley (page 106), rice jumble (page 109)

DRY, CHAPPED LIPS

Millions of us suffer from dry, chapped lips each winter. Why is this? The answer is that lips do not have the same protective outer layer—the *stratum corneum*—found in other areas of skin. Nor do lips have the same complement of oil and sweat glands. Their only source of moisture is saliva inside the mouth, which you apply when you lick your lips. Harsh winter wind and cold, and dry air—indoors and out—make lips vulnerable to chapping.

DIET PLAN FOR COLD SORES

If you've woken up and felt a familiar cold-sore tingle, or you're already suffering, try the dishes in this diet plan to boost your immune system and help fight the infection.

BREAKFAST

strawberry starter smoothie (page 114)

LUNCHES

large shrimp and noodle soup (page 96), lime, tomato, and scallop salad (page 102)—pictured

DINNERS

beef and noodle salad with chili lemon grass dressing (page 102), tofu vegetable salad (page 102)

DESSERT

summer pudding (page 113)

Make your own lip balm treatment to soothe susceptible lips; mix 1 tablespoon of vaseline with 3 drops of peppermint oil, and apply.

✔ Bran flakes, chicken, avocado, soy beans, cottage cheese, eggs, and beef are rich in vitamin B2, which helps to maintain a healthy mouth and lips. Lips are less likely to dry out if they are healthy and well-nourished. Pumpkin seeds, wheat germ, roast beef, and sardines are rich in zinc, which supports the immune system and aids tissue repair. Iron helps to transport oxygen around the body, thus nourishing and moisturizing chapped, dry lips. Iron-rich foods include sesame seeds, sardines, dried apricots, rump steak, tuna, and lamb.

✘ Fast foods, sugary snacks, caffeine, and nicotine all stress the immune system and contribute to dry, chapped lips.

♥ If you suffer from chapped lips, apply plenty of Vaseline or beeswax to your lips before bedtime or 15 minutes before having a shower. Then, using a toothbrush or facecloth, rub at the Vaseline. This helps to exfoliate dead skin cells without causing harm to the sensitive skin of the lips.

RECIPES *strawberry spread (page 93), steamed lemon grass chicken and rice rolls (page 98), shredded beet and feta salad (page 105), rice jumble (page 109), lentil and red onion quiche (page 109), an apple a day (page 115)*

COLD SORES

Cold sores are a painful condition caused by the *herpes simplex* type 1 virus (HSV-1). Once contracted, the virus lies dormant and then becomes reactivated when the immune system is weakened, for example, when you are run-down, stressed, fatigued, or anxious. Outbreaks can also be triggered by poor diet, and some women suffer an attack at the time of their period. Cold sores may appear anywhere on the body but most often occur on and around the lips, inside the mouth, and around the nostrils. The first sign is a tingling. Blisters form, then burst two to four days later. A crust develops and eventually falls off, revealing new skin underneath. Cold sores usually heal completely within 14 days. The virus can be spread by touch, so it's important not to kiss anyone if you have a cold sore. Some people find exposure to sunlight or wind, or hot or cold weather, can trigger a reaction. Chocolate and nuts, which contain the amino acid arginine, can encourage flare-ups. A diet full of fresh fruit and vegetables helps you maintain a healthy immune system, which will resist the virus.

✔ Broccoli, carrots, blueberries, pomegranate, limes, soy beans, and lemons all contain flavonoids, which, with vitamin C, are powerful antioxidants that strengthen the immune system, helping it to fight the cold sore virus. Good sources of vitamin C include strawberries, blueberries, and kiwi fruit. The mineral lysine has also been shown to help suppress the growth of the virus and so help prevent new cold sores forming. Clinical studies suggest that zinc helps prevent the herpes virus multiplying. Chicken, turkey, and beef are all good sources of zinc.

✘ High levels of the amino acid arginine allow the cold sore virus to thrive; arginine is present in large amounts in chocolate, nuts, wholegrain cereals, and gelatine.

♥ Wrap ice in a moist cloth and apply to the cold sore for a few minutes. This reduces swelling, eases pain, and encourages healing. Lemon and lime juice contain a natural antiseptic and can be applied to cold sores to stop the spread of infection and speed healing. Apply at the first "tingle" and regularly reapply.

♥ Keep lips moisturized at all times by using a lip balm, as dry, chapped, or cracked lips can be more susceptible to an outbreak. If you are prone to cold sore outbreaks, always apply sunscreen lip balm (SPF 15 or higher) to your lips before going out into the sun.

♥ Yoga, meditation, and other mind-body techniques help relieve stress, a possible cold sore trigger.

! To avoid spreading the virus, do not pick or squeeze a cold sore blister, or scab, and don't share personal items such as drinking glasses, toothbrushes, razors, or towels with other people.

✚ *Lysine*, taken orally at the first sign of a cold sore, inhibits the cold sore virus. You should see results in two or three days. Lysine cream, applied directly, promotes healing, and a low-maintenance dose may prevent recurrences.

✚ *Vitamin C and flavonoids* in a combined supplement promote healing and boost antiviral immune cells. Consider a short course of high-dose vitamin A, well known for its antiviral properties. In liquid form, vitamin A can be taken orally or applied directly to the cold sore. (High-dose vitamin A is not safe for pregnant women.)

✚ *Echinacea*, taken regularly, may help if you believe a weakened immune system is contributing to your frequent outbreaks of cold sores. Herbalists also recommend applying liquid extract of echinacea directly to cold sores to speed healing.

! Visit your doctor if a cold sore lasts longer than two weeks or if your eyes become sensitive to light during or after an outbreak.

RECIPES *fresh fruit salad (page 92), beef and noodle salad with chili lemon grass dressing (page 102), lime, tomato, and scallop salad (page 102), summer pudding (page 113), perfect start (page 114), skin healer (page 114)*

eyes

STAR FOODS FOR EYES: ANCHOVIES, BELL PEPPERS, BLUEBERRIES, BROCCOLI, BROWN PASTA, BROWN RICE, BUTTER, EGGS, GRAPES, HERRINGS, KIWI FRUIT, MACKEREL, MILK, OATS, ORANGES, PAPAYA, PEACHES, RASPBERRIES, SPINACH, STRAWBERRIES, TOMATOES, WHOLEGRAIN CEREALS

The eyes are not only the windows of the soul, they also reveal a lot about your health. Clear, sparkling eyes indicate good health; dry, gritty, or bloodshot eyes suggest illness, or problems related to lifestyle or diet that need to be addressed. Tear ducts around the eyes produce a special lubricating fluid that is smeared over the eyes every time we blink. This fluid prevents the eye drying out and also contains an antibacterial agent to resist infection. The white of the eye, or sclera, contains tiny blood vessels, or capillaries, that keep the eye surface supplied with nutrients. These vessels are so tiny they are normally invisible. They become apparent only when inflamed, causing the eyes to look "bloodshot." A balanced diet can keep the eyes looking healthy and—even more importantly—help safeguard vision. A poor diet, and lifestyle factors such as late nights, dusty or smoky atmospheres, and long periods spent staring at a computer screen, can cause dry and irritated eyes.

Some nutrients are vital for healthy eyes and good vision. Vitamin A maintains healthy cells in various structures of the eye, especially the retina (the light-sensitive layer at the back of the eye). It is required for the pigment that helps convert light into nerve signals and, in particular, enables us to see in the dark. Bilberry can improve poor night vision. It is sometimes used to help prevent eye diseases such as macular degeneration, diabetic retinopathy, and cataracts. The standard dose is 120 to 240 mg twice daily.

BLOODSHOT EYES

Bloodshot eyes can be caused by tiredness, eye strain, allergies, and dusty, polluted atmospheres. Healthy eyes need a good blood supply with plenty of iron to transport oxygen, so it's important to include lots of iron-rich foods in your diet. People who suffer from constipation may find that straining increases the pressure in blood vessels throughout the body, including the eye capillaries. Enlarged capillaries can burst, leading to bloodshot eyes. Eating a fiber-rich diet will help prevent constipation and it's consequent problems.

✔ Foods rich in iron include sesame seeds, sardines, dried

apricots, tuna, and bran. Prevent constipation by increasing your intake of fiber: try sprinkling bran over your morning cereal or fruit salad, and by eating more wholewheat bread, wholegrain cereals, brown pasta, oats, and brown rice. To strengthen the collagen in the walls of the eye capillaries, eat more fruits rich in vitamin C and flavonoids. Good sources include grapes, blueberries, strawberries, and raspberries—all delicious in a smoothie.

● Anything that restricts blood flow to the eyes should be avoided. Alcohol and caffeine rob the body of vitamin B12, necessary for healthy nerve function in the eyes. Cigarette smoke, whether received passively or by active inhalation, irritates and inflames the eyes. A good reason to quit, if you smoke, and to avoid smokers.

✚ Research has shown that grapeseed extract, which is rich in chemicals called anthocyanins, can help to improve circulation in the tiny blood capillaries found throughout the body, and especially in the eyes. This ensures the eyes are kept well supplied with oxygen and nutrients. Anthocyanins also strengthen the capillary walls, helping to prevent the eyes becoming bloodshot.

✚ Eyebright is a herb that has been used for centuries to treat eye irritations and itching caused by hayfever, allergies, and infections. The plant even looks as if it has bloodshot eyes, as it has red spots on its white or purple flowers. Its use is also recommended to alleviate the symptoms of conjunctivitis, and to maintain good vision. Eyebright is available in supplements, and as a tea that can also be used to alleviate nasal congestion and coughs.

♥ You've just rushed home from work and you've only got half an hour to look ravishing for a party. But your eyes look like a road map. Try this five-minute eye treatment to calm reddened eyes and soothe surrounding inflammation. Cleanse your eyelids of make-up, using cotton balls and warm water. Place two slices of cucumber over your eyes and lie down in a darkened room for five minutes (or 15 minutes, if you've time). Relax and breathe deeply. Imagine your cares leave you on the out-breath and fresh, clean air enters on the in-breath. Now splash your face with lukewarm water.

RECIPES sesame beef rice and paper rolls (page 99), multicolored rice salad (page 105), salmon steaks with sesame seed crusts (page 109), tofu risotto (page 110)

DARK CIRCLES

Dark circles under your eyes usually indicate lack of sleep. However, acupressure practitioners believe the eye area represents the kidneys, and therefore dark circles signify poor kidney function. Rich, fatty, and processed foods are difficult to digest and create high levels of toxins that the kidneys must deal with. Drinking plenty of water helps your kidneys flush away toxins and relieves the strain on your digestive system.

✔ If you suffer from sleepless nights, try eating sleep-inducing foods such as milk, yogurt, fromage frais, bananas, and lettuce.

✘ Avoid alcohol, caffeine, and nicotine before bedtime, as they can cause sleeplessness. A good rule is to avoid caffeine after 3pm in order to give your body time to neutralize it and dispose of it.

♥ If you have dark circles under your eyes, try this trick. When you're in the shower, take time to massage the area under the collarbone. Run your fingers under the bone, extending to your shoulders. This is believed to stimulate the lymph glands, which, when sluggish, can contribute to dark circles under the eyes.

RECIPES black-eyed peas and walnut spread (page 98), tasty tuna snack (page 99), Italian salad (page 104), summer pudding (page 113), strawberry starter smoothie (page 114)

DRY EYES

Dry-eye syndrome is a common condition. Symptoms may include dry, red, irritated eyes and a gritty, sandy sensation. This is usually due to reduced tear production and poor-quality tears. A lack of vitamin A may cause eye secretions to dry up, so eating foods rich in this vitamin helps maintain healthy eye moisture. Good sources include eggs, butter, herrings, anchovies, milk, and mackerel.

✔ Beta carotene is converted into vitamin A in the body and so can contribute to eye health. It's easy to tell which foods contain beta carotene—just look for brightly colored fruit and vegetables, such as bell peppers, spinach, tomatoes, broccoli, oranges, peaches, and papaya.

✘ Any foods that rob your body of moisture, such as sugary or salty foods, are best avoided, so stay away from potato chips, fast foods, or processed foods. Nicotine also reduces levels of oxygen and nutrients that reach the eye, so avoid smoky places.

RECIPES fresh fruit salad (page 92), weekend omelet (page 93), mediterranean oven-roasted vegetable soup (page 94), sundried tomato soup (page 96), warm chickpea and tuna salad (page 105)

STYES

A stye is a painful pimple that develops when a gland at the edge of the eyelid becomes infected. It can form on the inside or outside of the lid, and can occur at any age. It is not usually harmful to vision and generally heals within a few days. Normally, only the immediate area is swollen, causing tenderness and inflammation. Sometimes the entire eyelid may swell. The affected eye may water constantly and there may be increased sensitivity to light. To help prevent a stye occurring, and to combat the infection that caused it once it appears, you should load up on fresh fruit and vegetables to ensure that your immune system is strong.

✔ Foods such as spinach, guava, papayas, oranges, kiwi fruit, bell peppers, and strawberries contain vitamin C and beta carotene, both important for boosting the body's defenses.

♥ If you feel the beginning of a stye, an old folk remedy is to rub a friend's gold wedding ring underneath the eye. It's not known why this works, but it does seem to prevent the stye forming.

RECIPES mediterranean oven-roasted vegetable soup (page 94), baby spinach and radicchio salad (page 97), sesame beef rice and paper rolls (page 99), baby spinach, potato, and egg salad (page 103), perfect start (page 114), an apple a day (page 115)

EYE HEALTH FOR COMPUTER USERS

Computer users are particularly vulnerable to dry eyes, along with eye strain and fatigue, for two main reasons. One, they tend to blink less often than non-computer users (about seven times a minute, compared with the normal 22 times a minute). Two, the tiny muscles in the eye that control focusing are relaxed only when we look into the distance. Close-up focusing keeps the muscles constantly tense. Ideally, computer users should take a short break every 20 minutes to look out of a window. Adjusting the monitor so that it is below eye level means the upper lid is lower and so covers more of the eye surface, reducing evaporation. Trying to be more conscious of blink rate, air circulation, and glare, and making a more ergonomic work area, all help reduce symptoms of eye strain and dryness while using the computer.

recipes, treatments, and therapies

The first step to achieving natural beauty is to take the time to consider the many properties and uses of wholesome, nutritious food. Once you begin to appreciate all the benefits that vegetables, fruits, grains, and herbs can provide, the next step is to make the most of your newfound knowledge. In this chapter I've provided you with more than 90 delicious recipes to try, all of which are highly beneficial for the skin, hair, and nails. They're easy to prepare, and tasty to eat, so there's nothing stopping you from making the most of the healthy, fresh ingredients that nature provides.

Natural beauty doesn't have to stop at the dining table. Take a look at the 40 or more beauty treatments and recipes in this chapter. Each one explains how natural ingredients can help tackle skin, hair, and nail problems and there's useful information on applying and storing the mixtures.

If you've ever had a pampering beauty treatment, you'll know there's nothing better for your well-being. In this chapter you can take the opportunity to relax, learn about massage and meditation, and even create a spa in your own home! It may feel like an indulgence, but once you develop the habit of pampering yourself in some small way, you'll look and feel healthier, and be better equipped for dealing with life's stresses and strains. Each day, set aside a little time to use the knowledge that you've gained from this book—and enjoy living every day being naturally beautiful.

breakfasts

fresh fruit salad

Making a fresh fruit salad may be time-consuming, but it's a delicious way to start the day.

2 kiwi fruit
2 bananas
3 oranges
2 apples
2 pears
6 strawberries
handful blueberries and raspberries
1 mango
flaxseeds, pumpkin seeds, and sunflower seeds (optional)
honey (optional)
natural yogurt (optional)

Peel and chop all the fruit into small pieces or segments. Place in a large bowl and mix until the juices and fruits run into each other. Add the seeds, honey, and natural yogurt if desired. Serves 2.

healthy fry-up

Eating healthily is not just about fruit and vegetables. You'll get a lot of nutrients from eggs and tomatoes—such as protein, iron, B vitamins, and lycopene. Serve with wholewheat toast for some fiber.

4 eggs (organic free-range if possible)
4 tomatoes
2 slices wholewheat toast (optional)

Fill a large skillet with water and bring to a simmer. Using water instead of butter saves on calories and unnecessary fat. Roll the eggs, still in their shells, in the water for 30 seconds, so that the whites will remain together when you poach them. Remove and set aside for 30 seconds. Add the tomatoes to the pan, then break the eggs and simmer until the yolks are firm. Remove the tomatoes when the skins begin to split. Serve on wholewheat toast if desired. Serves 2.

oatmeal with prunes and apricots

Research has shown that people who eat oatmeal during the winter months are less likely to suffer from the "winter blues," depression, and lethargy of seasonal affective disorder (SAD). Oatmeal contains B vitamins and protein and is a great way to start the day, especially if you're prone to energy slumps.

5 oz organic oats
16 fl oz milk
16 fl oz water
handful pitted prunes
handful apricots
2 tsp organic sugar (if required)

Pour the oats into a saucepan and add the milk and water. Bring to a simmer, stirring occasionally. Cook as directed on the packet, adding milk as necessary to stop the mixture from becoming too thick. Add the prunes and apricots—chop them in half if they're too big. Cover the saucepan and let the mixture cook for another 60 seconds. Pour the mixture into a bowl, and add sugar (if desired) and extra milk to taste. Serves 1.

oatmeal with mixed fruit

A daily serving of oats helps stabilize blood sugar levels. If you're trying to quit smoking, oatmeal can help you kick the habit and fight cravings.

3½ oz ready-to-eat apricots, halved
3½ oz raspberries
3½ oz pitted prunes, halved
3½ oz blueberries
7 oz oats
bottled spring water
soft brown sugar for sprinkling (optional)

Place the fruits in a bowl, toss together, and leave. Place the oats in a saucepan, cover with plenty of water, bring to the boil, and allow to simmer for 5–10 minutes, stirring constantly, until thickened. Place in serving bowls, scatter over the fruits, and sprinkle with sugar if desired. Serve immediately. Serves 4.

smooth and sweet honey and berries

The World Health Organization recommends honey as a good remedy for stomach upsets and it is also an ideal skin-healer. With added berries, which are high in antioxidants, this morning starter is a tasty way to begin the day.

4 slices organic bread
6–8 tbsp thick honeycomb, plus honey to drizzle
4 tbsp natural yogurt
rind of ½ lemon, finely grated
2½ oz blueberries and raspberries
½ tsp grated nutmeg

Toast the bread until golden brown. Mix the honeycomb, yogurt, and lemon rind together. Spread a small amount of honey onto the toast, followed by a layer of the yogurt mixture. Scatter the berries over the topping, followed by another drizzle of honey. Grate the nutmeg on top. Serves 2.

alpine muesli with red and green grapes

Grapes are believed to purify the blood and cleanse internal organs and glands. They may also help treat long-term urinary problems.

2½ oz/1 cup rolled oats
ground cinnamon to taste
3 tbsp raisins
4 fl oz/½ cup skimmed milk
3 tbsp chopped walnuts
3 oz/½ cup seedless green grapes
3 oz/½ cup seedless red grapes

Place the oats, cinnamon, and raisins in a bowl. Add the milk. Cover and refrigerate overnight. Stir in the nuts and grapes when ready to serve. Serves 4.

strawberry spread

This is an ideal recipe for the weekend, when you'll have more time to prepare it. And it makes a great alternative to cereal or a breakfast fry-up.

4 strawberries, stalks removed
handful blueberries
1 kiwi fruit, peeled and quartered
1 apple, cored and quartered
1 orange, peeled and sectioned
¼ melon, cut into small segments
sunflower seeds or pumpkin seeds (optional)

Toss the fruit in a bowl and add sunflower seeds or pumpkin seeds if desired. You may also like to pour some organic yogurt over the top. Serves 1.

smoked haddock kedgeree with grilled tomatoes

Haddock contains protein, iodine, and B vitamins for strong, healthy hair. Teamed with tomatoes, this is a great breakfast for those who want a heartier meal.

5 oz smoked haddock fillet
1 egg (organic free-range if possible)
3½ oz brown basmati rice
2 large continental tomatoes
2 tsp fresh parsley, chopped
paprika pepper to taste

Place 2 fl oz water in a small pan. Add the fish, cover and steam for 7–8 minutes. Hard-boil the egg, then peel and chop. Place 8 fl oz water in a pan and bring to the boil. Add the rice, stir, and cover with a lid. Reduce the heat and leave to cook for 20–25 minutes, until the rice is cooked and the water absorbed. Halve the tomatoes and grill for 5–6 minutes. Stir the haddock, egg, and parsley into the rice. Serve with the tomatoes. Add the paprika. Serves 2.

weekend omelet

Weekends are an ideal time to enjoy a leisurely breakfast or brunch. An omelet provides plenty of calcium, which is important for healthy bones and teeth and resists osteoporosis. Calcium is also vital for nerve transmission and muscle function, and helps to maintain a proper pH (acid-alkaline) balance.

4 eggs (organic free-range if possible)
1 tbsp water
knob of butter
choice of filling (try finely chopped tomatoes, cheese, or red bell pepper)

Beat the eggs and water in a bowl. Heat the butter in a small non-stick skillet and pour in the egg mixture. Carefully stir the egg to fold the mixture and allow it to cook evenly. When it is nearly set, sprinkle on your chosen filling and fold over. Cut in half to serve. Serves 2.

soups, appetizers, snacks, and sauces

SOUPS

pea and fava bean soup

This is a rich and warming dish that features a fiery Moroccan paste called harissa, made with chili, garlic, and spices. Peas and beans are good sources of protein, vitamins, minerals, and fiber—all needed for healthy skin, hair, and nails.

7 oz frozen peas
7 oz frozen fava beans
32 fl oz vegetable stock
salt and freshly ground black pepper
8 small slices ciabatta bread
1 clove garlic, sliced lengthwise
4 tbsp olive oil
sour cream
harissa
Parmesan cheese shavings

Place the peas, beans, and stock in a large saucepan and bring to the boil. Cover and simmer for 30 minutes, or until the vegetables are tender. Pour into a food processor or liquidizer and blend until smooth. Pour back into the pan and heat through. Season. Place the bread slices on a grill rack and rub the cut side of the clove of garlic over them. Drizzle olive oil over the top and toast under the grill, turning once during cooking. To serve, place spoonfuls of sour cream on top of the soup, arrange two slices of bread on top, then spoon a little harissa over each soup. Scatter each soup with the Parmesan shavings. Serves 4.

mediterranean oven-roasted vegetable soup

This soup contains all the vitamins and minerals you need for healthy and glowing skin.

4 tbsp olive oil
2 zucchini, sliced
2 eggplants, diced
1 red and 1 yellow bell pepper, cored, deseeded, and chopped
2 cloves garlic, sliced
1 sprig rosemary
salt and ground black pepper
1 packet vine-ripened tomatoes

20 fl oz vegetable stock
4 tbsp green or red pesto
4 tbsp créme fraîche or soy cream
basil leaves to garnish

Preheat the oven to 400°F. Place the olive oil in a large roasting tin and heat in the oven for 3 minutes, until almost smoking. Add the zucchini, eggplants, bell peppers, garlic, rosemary, and seasoning. Turn to coat and bake for 20 minutes, stirring occasionally. Add the tomatoes to the pan, stir to coat, and bake for a further 25 minutes. Bring the stock to the boil in a large pan. Remove the vegetables from the oven and liquidize. Add the stock and whiz until roughly blended. Pour back into the pan and bring to the boil, stirring constantly. Season to taste. Spoon into warm bowls and spoon 1 tablespoon each of pesto and créme fraîche or soy cream into the center and scatter over the basil leaves. Serves 4.

carrot soup

Carrots are full of beta carotene, an important vitamin for healthy skin. They also contain phytochemicals that help to heal damaged or inflamed skin.

3 tbsp extra virgin olive oil
1 large leek, finely sliced
2 pints vegetable stock
4 large carrots, sliced (organic if possible)
3½ oz ground almonds
2 egg yolks (organic free-range if possible)

In a large saucepan, heat the oil and cook the leek for about 5 minutes, stirring constantly to stop it burning. Add the vegetable stock, carrots, and ground almonds. Turn the stove to simmer and leave the vegetables to soften. This should take about 10–15 minutes. Beat the egg yolks in a bowl. Blend the carrot and almond mixture in a blender or liquidizer. Pour into the bowl of egg yolks and beat. Pour the ingredients into the saucepan, heating the mixture gently. Serve with organic bread or croutons. Serves 4.

pumpkin soup

This is one of the tastiest and most comforting soups to make. As well as beta carotene, pumpkin contains lots of folic acid, and so is ideal for any woman planning to start a family.

2 tbsp extra virgin olive oil
1 oz unsalted butter
2 large white onions, finely chopped

2 cloves garlic, peeled and finely chopped
3 tsp curry powder
1¾ pints vegetable stock
2¼ lb pumpkin, deseeded, peeled, and cubed
4 tbsp créme fraîche

In a large heated saucepan, heat the oil and butter. When the butter has melted, add the onion and garlic, ensuring they don't burn. Add the curry powder and cook for 2 minutes, stirring continuously. Pour in the vegetable stock and bring to the boil. Add the pumpkin to the stock and simmer until the vegetables are soft and tender. Add the mixture to a food mixer and blend. Stir in the créme fraîche, mixing thoroughly. Add pepper to taste, if desired. Serves 4.

Thai sweet and sour soup *(below)*

Shrimps are an ideal addition to any meal. They're filled with anti-aging properties, helping you to achieve and maintain healthy, smooth skin.

1¾ pints fish stock
1 stalk lemon grass
2 limes
2 tbsp honey (organic if possible)
handful coriander leaves, chopped
1 lb shrimps, shelled

In a large saucepan, gently heat the fish stock. Crush the lemon grass thoroughly. Mix the juice of the limes with the honey and lemon grass and heat gently with half the stock for 5 minutes. Remove the lemon grass and pour the honey mixture into the rest of the stock. Add the chopped coriander. Simmer for 2 minutes, stirring continuously. Add the shrimps and gently poach for 5 minutes. Add more coriander leaves when serving, if you prefer. Serves 4.

sweet potato soup

Sweet potatoes are the unsung heroes of the root vegetable family. They're packed full of beta carotene and also contain vitamin E, which is essential for nourishing dry skin.

1½ lb sweet potatoes, peeled and cubed
2½ pints vegetable stock
sour cream and pepper, or chives (optional)

In a large saucepan, simmer the sweet potatoes in the vegetable stock until soft. Pour into a blender or food mixer and whiz until smooth. Pour the mixture back into the saucepan and simmer for 5–10 minutes. Add sour cream, pepper, or chives to taste, if desired. Serves 4.

mushroom and bean soup

This soup is ideal if your skin is looking tired and run-down. Kidney beans are a great restorative ingredient, helping to kick-start your system.

1 oz dried porcini mushrooms
2 celery sticks, chopped
2 large leeks, washed and chopped
1 large sprig sage
3 bay leaves
13 oz kidney beans
6½ oz live bio yogurt for consistency

Soak the mushrooms in 3 pints of boiled water for 15 minutes. Strain, reserve the liquid, and chop the mushrooms. Pour the liquid into a large saucepan and bring back to a simmer. Add the celery, leeks, sage, and bay leaves. Simmer for another 15 minutes. Strain again. Add the kidney beans and mushrooms and heat for 10 minutes. Stir in the yogurt and serve. Serves 4.

leek and lentil soup

This is a healing soup to restore a healthy color and vitality. Make up a batch and eat as much as you can if you've been feeling under the weather.

3 pints vegetable stock
7 oz lentils
1 tbsp extra virgin olive oil
7 oz organic back bacon, cut into thin shreds
3 large leeks, trimmed and finely chopped
2 cloves garlic, peeled and finely chopped

In a large saucepan, heat the stock, then pour in the lentils. Leave to cook for 20 minutes. In a separate pan, heat the oil and add the bacon. Leave to sweat for about 5 minutes. Add the leeks and garlic. Cook until soft. Add the bacon and vegetables to the stock. Simmer for 15 minutes and serve. Serves 4.

vegetable and bean soup

If you hate the thought of eating five servings of vegetables a day, this soup will help to give you some much-needed nutrients.

4 tbsp extra virgin olive oil
1 large onion, finely chopped
2 cloves garlic, peeled and finely chopped
3 pints vegetable stock
2 x 8 oz cans flageolet beans
2 large zucchini, trimmed and grated
4 new potatoes (scrub and grate just before use)
1 large carrot, grated (organic if possible)

Heat the oil in a large saucepan. Add the onion and garlic and stir for 5 minutes to avoid burning. Pour in the vegetable stock and stir until warmed through. Add the beans and grated vegetables and continue heating for 5 more minutes, stirring continuously. Add more oil if desired. Serves 4.

large shrimp and noodle soup

Low in calories, but high in health benefits, this soup is a light and tasty way to increase your calcium intake.

2½ oz thick noodles
3 tbsp olive oil
1 small butternut squash, peeled, deseeded, and cut into chunks
1 bunch scallions, sliced
1 clove garlic, chopped
1-in piece fresh root ginger, chopped
1 tsp turmeric
1 x 8 fl oz can coconut cream
1 tbsp coconut cream/1 tbsp tomato purée
32 fl oz chicken stock
6 oz large shrimp, cooked and peeled
2 tbsp fresh coriander, chopped

Place the noodles in a large bowl. Cover with boiling water and leave to stand for 20 minutes, stirring occasionally, until tender. Drain thoroughly. Heat the oil in a large saucepan. Cook the butternut squash for 5 minutes, stirring occasionally, until browned. Add the scallions, garlic, ginger, and turmeric and cook for 30 seconds. Stir in the coconut cream or tomato purée and chicken stock and bring to the boil. Simmer for 4 minutes until the squash is just tender. Add the noodles and shrimps and simmer for 3 minutes until heated through. Stir in the coriander, and serve. Serves 4.

sundried tomato soup

Tomatoes, dried, fresh, or canned are one of the healthiest fruits. Recent research has shown that they may help to reduce the risk of breast cancer.

4 tbsp olive oil
2 lb ripe plum tomatoes, halved lengthwise
2 cloves garlic, chopped
salt and freshly ground black pepper
32 fl oz bacon stock
3 tbsp balsamic vinegar
1 tsp brown sugar
2 oz sundried tomatoes, shredded
4 diagonal slices ciabatta bread
4 tbsp black olive tapenade
mixed chopped herbs

Preheat the oven to 300°F. Place the oil in a large roasting tin and heat in the oven for 3 minutes until almost smoking. Add the tomatoes to the roasting tin, skin-side down. Scatter over the garlic and seasoning. Bake for 40 minutes, until the tomatoes are dried and browned. Remove the tomatoes from the oven and add to a food mixer or blender, along with any pan juices. Add the stock, balsamic vinegar, sugar, and sundried tomatoes and blend until smooth. Return to the pan. Reheat. Meanwhile, preheat the grill. Place the bread slices on a grill rack and toast both sides of the bread. Spread the tapenade over each slice. Spoon the soup into individual bowls. Scatter over the mixed chopped herbs and serve with the toasted cibatta. Serves 4.

APPETIZERS/SNACKS

cashew stuffed potato boats

The potato boats can be made in advance and cooked off before serving if they are to be served hot. They can be frozen after filling to be used at a later date.

4 egg-sized potatoes (about 12 oz)
1 tsp of olive oil
1 small onion, finely chopped
1 clove garlic, finely chopped
3½ oz cashew nuts, chopped
1 oz wholewheat breadcrumbs
pinch mixed herbs
1 tsp tomato paste
salt and pepper

1 egg, beaten (organic free-range if possible)
extra oil for potato skins

Preheat the oven to 400°F. Boil the potatoes in their skins for 20–25 minutes until cooked. Cut in half, scoop out the potato, and mash with a fork. Gently fry the onion and garlic in a little oil until cooked. Mix the onion mixture with the nuts, breadcrumbs, herbs, paste, and seasoning, then stir in the mashed potato, add the beaten egg and mix together well. Brush the potato skins with the oil and heap the mixture equally between the halves. Bake for 10–15 minutes. Can be served hot or cold. Makes 8 well-filled boats.

creamy potato and artichoke salad

Artichoke is a superb liver cleanser, so this is an excellent side salad to serve at a wine-heavy meal to help the body's elimination processes.

2¼ lb baby new potatoes
3 fl oz walnut oil
2 tbsp white wine vinegar
2 tbsp Dijon mustard
4½ fl oz cream
salt and freshly ground black pepper
3½ oz red onion, thinly sliced
2 x 9 oz marinated artichoke pieces, drained

Cook the potatoes in boiling salted water for 15 minutes or until tender. Drain well. Cool, then cut the potatoes in half. Beat the oil, vinegar, and mustard in a bowl. Stir in the cream and season to taste with the salt and pepper. Combine the potatoes, onion, artichokes, and dressing in a bowl. Toss gently. Serves 6–8.

bruschetta with olives and tomatoes *(right)*

Olives are packed with essential fatty acids (EFAs), necessary for smooth, healthy skin. Basil is also good for women suffering from menstrual cramps.

1 large ciabatta loaf
5½ oz black olives, coarsely chopped
5 oz stuffed green olives, coarsely chopped
2¼ fl oz olive oil
5 oz sundried tomatoes, chopped
1 tbsp drained baby capers
2 anchovy fillets, drained and chopped
½ oz basil leaves, finely shredded
1 clove garlic, crushed
2 tbsp red wine vinegar
2¼ fl oz extra virgin olive oil to garnish
baby basil leaves to garnish

Cut the bread into ½-in thick slices, and brush with oil. Grill until lightly browned. Combine the olives with the remaining ingredients (except for the garnish) in a bowl. Place the mixture on top of the bread on a serving plate and garnish. Serves 10.

baby spinach and radicchio salad

This can be a side salad or a main course. It is especially beneficial for women, as the spinach can help to replace the iron they lose each month.

1 large radicchio lettuce, 1 baby spinach
1½ oz pine nuts, toasted sea salt flakes

For the dressing:
1½ oz raisins
3 fl oz extra virgin olive oil
2 tbsp red wine vinegar

Combine the raisins, oil, and vinegar in a small jar; shake well. Allow to stand for one hour. Wash and dry the lettuce and spinach leaves. Just before serving, toss in the pine nuts and add the dressing and sea salt flakes to taste. Serves 10.

rosemary potatoes

Like all herbs, rosemary has healing properties. Rosemary is recommended by herbalists, who believe that it can help treat colds, flu, and rheumatic pains. It also has uplifting properties, so this is a good winter side dish.

6½ lb desirée potatoes
2 tbsp olive oil
salt and freshly ground black pepper
1 tbsp fresh rosemary leaves

Preheat the oven to 350°F. Make ½-in cuts in each potato, slicing about three-quarters of the way through. Combine the potatoes with the oil in a large baking dish and sprinkle with the salt and pepper. Bake for about one hour. Increase the oven temperature to 400°F for about 15 minutes or until the potatoes are browned and tender. Sprinkle with rosemary. Serves 10.

mixed garlic mushrooms

Garlic is packed full of antioxidants, so adding garlic to a dish is an excellent way to increase your immunity. Try this dish if you feel a cold coming on.

1 lb flat mushrooms
3 fl oz extra virgin olive oil
1 lb brown mushrooms
1 lb button mushrooms
2 cloves garlic, thinly sliced
1 oz loosely packed flat-leaf parsley leaves
sea salt flakes
freshly ground black pepper

Preheat the oven to a moderately hot setting—around 400°F. Place the flat mushrooms in a large baking dish, drizzle with half the oil and roast for 10 minutes. Add the remaining mushrooms, oil, and garlic. Roast for a further 15 minutes or until the mushrooms are tender and lightly browned. Stir in the parsley and add salt and pepper to taste. Serves 10.

fresh fruit with maple-vanilla yogurt dip

Increase your daily intake of fresh fruit with this tasty and nutritious yogurt dip. You can use any type of yogurt, as long as it's low-fat.

18 fl oz vanilla low-fat yogurt
4 oz maple syrup
1 apple
1 pear
juice of 1 lemon
1 tbsp pistachio nuts, crushed
1 lb grapes

Combine the yogurt and maple syrup and place in the refrigerator to chill. Core and slice the apple and pear. Sprinkle with lemon juice to prevent discoloration. Place the yogurt in a bowl in the center of a large platter, drizzle with a few extra drops of maple syrup, and sprinkle with the nuts. Arrange the apple, pear, and grapes on the platter and serve. Serves 8.

black-eyed peas and walnut spread

Peas are an excellent source of vitamin C, iron, and B vitamins—all necessary for a healthy nervous system. The addition of walnuts helps to improve skin smoothness and softness. Walnut oils contain linoleic acid, which helps to maintain the skin's structure and keep it well hydrated.

1 lb frozen black-eyed peas
10 fl oz water
1 onion, chopped
1 red bell pepper, seeded and chopped

6 oz pumpkin, cut into ½–1-in dice (about 1 cup)
4½ oz walnuts, chopped
2½ fl oz sherry vinegar or wine vinegar
2 oz parsley, chopped
salt and pepper, to taste
16 leaves iceberg lettuce

In a medium saucepan, combine the black-eyed peas and water. Bring to the boil over a high heat, then reduce the heat to low and simmer, covered, for about 30 minutes, until the peas are tender but not mushy. Discard any liquid remaining in the pan and transfer the peas to a large bowl. Coat a large non-stick skillet with non-stick cooking spray and place over a medium–high heat. Add the onion, bell pepper, and pumpkin and cook, stirring occasionally, for 5 minutes. Turn the heat to low, cover the pan, and continue cooking for 5–7 minutes more until the pumpkin is just tender. Stir in the walnuts. Add the walnut mixture to the peas along with the vinegar and parsley. Stir and toss to combine, then season with the salt and pepper to taste. Allow to cool slightly. Spoon some of the pea and walnut mixture into each lettuce leaf. Fold the leaves in half for easy eating. Makes around 16 individual servings.

steamed lemon grass chicken and rice rolls

This easy-to-make recipe is filled with mood-boosting ingredients.

4 stalks lemon grass, halved lengthwise
3 chicken breast fillets, halved lengthwise
1 tsp sesame oil
2 red chilies, seeded and chopped
1 bunch gai larn (chinese broccoli), halved
10 oz plain rice noodle rolls

Place the lemon grass in the base of a bamboo steamer. Top with the chicken and then brush the chicken with the sesame oil and sprinkle with the chili. Put the lid on the steamer and place over a saucepan of boiling water. Steam for 3 minutes. While the chicken is steaming, place the gai larn and rice noodle rolls in another steamer of the same size. Place the rice noodle steamer on top of the chicken steamer and cover. Steam for a further 5 minutes or until the chicken and gai larn are tender. Serve with small bowls of soy sauce and wedges of lime. Serves 4.

spicy chicken salad in witlof

Witlof is a very popular salad accompaniment in Germany, where this curly-leaved member of the endive family hails from. It has a tangy taste and is packed with skin-saving nutrients. You can use endive as an alternative.

1 tbsp sesame oil
10 oz chicken, minced
1 tbsp fish sauce
2 tbsp lime juice
1 tbsp palm sugar

1 tbsp vietnamese mint, finely chopped
1 tbsp fresh coriander, finely chopped
4 baby witlof, separated

For the paste:
2 coriander roots, coarsely chopped
pinch salt
3 cloves garlic, peeled
2 tsp finely grated ginger
10 white peppercorns

To make the paste: in a small blender, spice grinder, or mortar and pestle, blend or pound all the ingredients together until fine. Heat the oil in a wok or large skillet and add the paste, stirring until fragrant. Add the chicken, stirring until lightly browned. Add the fish sauce, lime juice, and sugar to the pan and simmer gently, uncovered, for a few minutes or until the mixture has slightly thickened. Stir in the mint and coriander. Divide the mixture evenly among the witlof leaves. Makes about 24 individual servings.

stuffed bell peppers

Peppers help increase your metabolism, so include them in your diet if you're watching your weight.

2 tbsp olive oil
1 red onion, chopped
1 clove garlic, chopped
3½ oz split red lentils
10 fl oz vegetable stock
3½ oz organic cheddar cheese, diced
freshly ground salt and black pepper
2 oz roasted and salted pistachio nuts, shelled and chopped
2 tomatoes, chopped
bunch fresh chives, snipped
4 red bell peppers, halved and deseeded

Preheat the oven to 425°F. Heat half the oil in a large skillet and cook the onion for 5 minutes. Add the garlic and lentils and cook for one minute. Add the stock and bring to the boil, cover, and simmer for 25 minutes, stirring occasionally until the lentils are tender and the liquid is absorbed. Remove the skillet from the heat and stir in the cheddar, seasoning, nuts, tomatoes, and chives until well blended. Spoon into the pepper halves. Place the peppers on a baking sheet and drizzle over the remaining oil. Bake for 30 minutes, until the peppers are tender. Serve with mixed salad. Serves 2–4.

tasty tuna snack

Tuna is a great afternoon snack, as it contains lots of essential fatty acids (EFAs) necessary for good skin. This easy-to-make snack will fill you up, so you'll be less likely to reach for the cookie jar!

½ tin tuna (in water or sunflower oil)
½ lemon
2 small tomatoes, chopped
1 celery stick, finely chopped
½ carrot, chopped
lettuce

Place the tuna in a small bowl and squeeze lemon juice all over. (You can add low-fat mayonnaise if you prefer, but lemon juice is tastier and healthier.) Combine the tuna, tomatoes, celery, and carrot and mix. Place on top of the lettuce leaves. Add more lemon juice, and pepper to taste, if desired. Serve with 1 slice of rye bread. Serves 1.

vegetarian flan

Packed full of vitamins and nutrients, this is a fantastic winter meal, particularly if you've been suffering from colds or other infections.

2 tbsp olive oil
2 zucchini, thickly sliced
1 red bell pepper, cored and sliced
1 red onion, peeled
3½ oz wholewheat flour
pinch salt
2½ oz margarine
2½ oz sundried tomatoes
1 tbsp Dijon mustard
2½ oz Gruyère cheese, grated
2 eggs, beaten (organic free-range if possible)
3 fl oz soy milk
2 tbsp fresh chives

Preheat the oven to 400°F. Pour the oil into a roasting tin and place in the oven until smoking. Add the zucchini, bell peppers, and onion. Roast for 30 minutes. Sift the flour and salt into a bowl. Rub in the margarine until you have a breadcrumb consistency. Stir in 3–4 tablespoons of water until the dough is smooth. Chill for 20 minutes. Remove the vegetables from the oven. Add the tomatoes. Stir and let cool. Lower the oven temperature to 375°F. Roll out the pastry and line an 8-in fluted flan tin with greaseproof paper and baking beans. Bake for 10 minutes. Remove the beans and paper and bake for 5 minutes. Spread the mustard over the pastry case and sprinkle on the cheese. Arrange the cooked vegetables on top. Beat together the remaining ingredients and pour the mixture over vegetables. Bake for 30–40 minutes. Serves 4.

sesame beef rice and paper rolls

Snow peas are high in protein. By adding them to this recipe, you'll be aiding your digestive system and helping your body deal with any stress.

1 tsp olive oil
14 oz rump steak
1 tsp sesame oil
1 tsp soy sauce
2 bunches spinach, leaves only
2 tbsp sesame seeds
12 round rice paper wrappers
3½ oz snow peas
soy sauce for dipping

Heat the olive oil in a skillet over a high heat. Add the steak and cook for 2–3 minutes on each side or according to preference. Set aside for 2 minutes, and

then thinly slice the steak and place in a bowl with the sesame oil and soy sauce. Place the spinach leaves in a saucepan of boiling water and cook for 5 seconds, then drain and squeeze any excess liquid from the spinach. Roughly chop the spinach and combine with the sesame seeds. Dip the rice paper wrappers in hot water for 5–10 seconds or until soft. Remove and pat dry. Place the beef, spinach, and snow peas along the centre of the rice paper. Fold one end over the filling to form a base, then roll the rice paper from the side to enclose. Repeat with the remaining mixture and serve with the soy sauce. Serves 4.

vegetable rice paper rolls with chili dipping sauce *(left)*

Eastern food is low in fat and calories but extremely high in taste. This recipe is packed with nutrients, all of which help to lower cholesterol, calm nerves, and encourage digestion. The perfect party food!

2 oz vermicelli noodles
2 medium avocados
1 medium carrot
1 bunch chives
24 round rice paper wrappers
3 red radishes, grated
2½ oz bean sprouts, trimmed
24 large mint leaves
2 cloves garlic, crushed

chili dipping sauce:
4½ fl oz white vinegar
7 oz superfine sugar
1 tsp salt
2½ fl oz water
1 clove garlic, crushed
1½ oz red onion, finely chopped
2 oz cucumber, seeded
    and finely chopped
1 tbsp fresh coriander leaves, chopped
1 small fresh red chili, chopped
1 tbsp cashew nuts, toasted and chopped

To make the sauce: bring the vinegar, sugar, salt, and water to the boil in a medium saucepan. Continue to boil, uncovered, for 2 minutes. Pour the vinegar mixture over the remaining ingredients in a medium bowl. Allow to cool.

Place the vermicelli noodles in a bowl of hot water for 10 minutes or until softened. Drain well. Thinly slice the avocados. Cut the carrot into long, thin strips. Cut the chives to the same length as the carrot. Cover a board with a damp tea towel. Place a sheet of rice paper in a bowl of warm water until softened. Place the rice paper on the tea towel, put a slice of avocado, some of the carrot, radish, bean sprouts, a mint leaf, some garlic, chives, and noodles in the center of the sheet. Fold the bottom half of the rice paper up. Fold in one side, then roll over to enclose the filling. Repeat with the remaining rice paper wrappers and remaining ingredients. Place the rolls on a plastic-wrap-lined tray, cover with a damp paper towel, and refrigerate until needed. Serve with the chili dipping sauce. Serves 24.

SAUCES

classic tomato sauce

If you prefer your sauces homemade, this one is packed with goodness!

12 tomatoes or 4 x 14 oz cans peeled tomatoes, lightly crushed
1 tbsp olive oil
1 clove garlic, crushed
2 small onions, chopped
8 fl oz/1 cup red wine
2 tbsp oregano, basil, or marjoram leaves, chopped
cracked black pepper and sea salt

If using fresh tomatoes, place in a saucepan of boiling water and boil for 1 minute. Drain, peel, and chop, reserving any liquid. Heat the oil in a deep skillet over a medium–high heat. Add the garlic and onion and cook for 4 minutes or until soft. Add the tomatoes, wine, herbs, and seasoning, and bring to the boil. Simmer for 35 minutes if using fresh tomatoes (20 minutes for canned). Leave to cool and then refrigerate for up to 3 days. For longer-term storage, freeze in portion sizes ready to defrost and use. It can be kept frozen for 4–5 months.

lemon parsley-dill marinade

Lemons cleanse the blood and calm the nerves. They also help the body absorb iron, and so reduce the risk of anemia.

5 fl oz extra virgin olive oil
2 tbsp dry vermouth
1 tbsp garlic, minced
2 tbsp lemon pulp, all membrane and skin discarded
2 tbsp fresh chives or scallions, sliced
2 tbsp fresh Italian parsley, minced
2 tbsp fresh dill, minced
½ tsp freshly ground black pepper

Combine all the marinade ingredients in a food mixer and blend briefly until thoroughly combined and well minced. Alternatively, all ingredients may be minced very finely by hand and beaten together. Keep in the refrigerator to chill and store. Serve over chicken or fish dishes. Serves 4.

ginger marinade sauce

Ginger is ideal for mums-to-be, as it helps overcome morning sickness. It has a warming effect and can ease the aches and pains of an impending cold.

3 tbsp soy sauce
½ tbsp dark (roasted) sesame oil
1 large garlic clove, minced or pressed
1 tbsp ginger sea seasoning
¼ tsp hot sesame oil
½ tsp Chinese 5-spice powder

Add all the ingredients together in a blender or mixer and blend until smooth. Add to stir-fry vegetables or salads. Makes around 8 servings.

main courses, side dishes, and salads

tofu vegetable salad

Tofu is a good source of protein and is packed with calcium, which is important for strong, healthy bones. So this salad is brilliant if you can't eat dairy foods.

13 oz packet firm tofu, drained
5 fl oz bottled Italian salad dressing
2 medium zucchini
1 medium red bell pepper
1 lb spinach, trimmed
8 oz cherry tomatoes
2 tbsp fresh chives, chopped
1½ oz Parmesan cheese, flaked

Cut the tofu into 1-in cubes and combine with the dressing in a large bowl. Cover and refrigerate for 10 minutes while you cut the zucchini and bell peppers into long thin strips. Combine the tofu mixture with the vegetables and the remaining ingredients in the bowl. Toss gently to mix. Serves 4.

chicken salad with soy dressing

An average serving of chicken provides more than half your daily requirement of protein. The vegetables in this salad are filled with energy-giving vitamins.

1 tbsp peanut oil
4 chicken breast fillets
14 oz Chinese cabbage, shredded
4 shallots, sliced
12 oz snow pea sprouts

For the dressing:
2½ fl oz peanut oil
2 tbsp soy sauce
1 tsp sesame oil
1 tsp fresh ginger, grated
1 clove garlic, crushed
½ tsp sugar
2 tbsp lime juice

Heat the oil in a skillet. Fry the chicken until browned on both sides and cooked right through. Slice thinly. Combine the chicken, cabbage, and onion in a bowl. Top with the peas. Combine the dressing ingredients and drizzle over. Serves 4.

beef and noodle salad with chili lemon grass dressing

This tasty soup is low in fat but high in protein and energy-boosting nutrients such as iron, zinc, and B vitamins.

1 lb beef fillet steaks
10 oz hokkien noodles
2 tsp vegetable oil
1 lb baby bok choy, chopped
1 lb choy sum, chopped
1 bunch Chinese broccoli, chopped
1 small Chinese cabbage, shredded
7 oz bean sprouts

For the dressing:
2 tbsp lemon grass, chopped
2 small fresh red chilies, seeded and sliced
2 tbsp soy sauce
2 tbsp lime juice
1 tbsp fresh ginger, grated
1 tsp sugar

Add the beef to one-third of the combined dressing ingredients in a bowl. Cover and refrigerate for 10 minutes. Drain the beef and fry until browned, as desired. Pour boiling water over the noodles, stand for 5 minutes, then drain. Heat the oil in a wok or large skillet, quickly stir-fry the bok choy, choy sum, and broccoli until just wilted. Combine the beef with the noodles, vegetables, cabbage, sprouts, and remaining dressing in a bowl. Toss ingredients together. Serves 4.

lime, tomato, and scallop salad

Limes are high in vitamin C, and so, served with scallops, this salad provides all the nutrients needed for healthy and strong hair and nails.

8 oz dried rice noodles
1 lb white scallops

1 tbsp sweet chili sauce
1 tbsp lime juice
8 oz asparagus, trimmed and chopped
11 oz yellow teardrop tomatoes, halved
1 oz flaked almonds, toasted

For the lime dressing:
4½ fl oz peanut oil
1 tsp brown sugar
2 tbsp fresh coriander leaves, chopped
1 tbsp fresh mint leaves, chopped
2 small fresh red chilies, seeded and quartered
2½ fl oz lime juice

Place the noodles in a large heatproof bowl, cover with boiling water, and leave standing until just tender, then drain. Rinse under cold water and drain. Grill the scallops in batches, until they change color, occasionally brushing with the combined chili sauce and 1 tablespoon of lime juice. Steam the asparagus until just tender, rinse under cold water, then drain. Combine the lime dressing ingredients. Gently toss the noodles, scallops, and asparagus in a large bowl with the tomatoes and the lime dressing. Sprinkle with almonds. Serves 4.

baby spinach, potato, and egg salad *(right)*

This makes a super lunchtime salad as it's filled with lots of iron—important for the transport of oxygen for healthy skin, nails, and hair. It's also high in protein to maintain a healthy immune system.

1½ lb tiny new potatoes, halved
4½ fl oz olive oil
6 eggs (organic free-range if possible)
4 bacon slices, chopped
7 oz baby spinach leaves
2 tbsp white wine vinegar
4 anchovy fillets in oil, drained
2 tbsp Parmesan cheese, coarsely grated

Preheat the oven to 425°F. Combine the new potatoes and 2 tablespoons of the oil in a large baking dish. Bake uncovered for 25 minutes. Meanwhile, place the eggs in a medium saucepan, cover with water, and bring to the boil. Simmer, uncovered, for 10 minutes. Drain. Rinse the eggs under cold water, shell, and cut into quarters. Cook the bacon with the remaining oil in a large heated skillet until crisp, and then drain on absorbent paper or towels. Gently toss the bacon in a large bowl with the potatoes, eggs, and spinach leaves. Blend or mix the white wine vinegar, anchovy fillets, and Parmesan cheese, and drizzle over the salad. Serves 4.

baked feta and roasted tomato pasta salad

A light but filling salad, this is good for vegetarians who want to increase their intake of cancer-fighting nutrients. In addition, the pine nuts protect against heart disease and benefit the skin.

10 oz firm feta cheese, chopped
4½ fl oz olive oil
1 lb cherry tomatoes
13 oz penne pasta
1½ oz pine nuts, toasted
½ oz/¼ cup firmly packed small fresh basil leaves
2 oz black olives, seeded and sliced

Place the feta in a large piece of foil, bring the sides of the foil up around it and drizzle with 2 tablespoons of the oil. Enclose the feta in the foil. Place the parcel at one end of a shallow baking dish. Combine the tomatoes with 1 tablespoon of the remaining oil in the same baking dish. Bake uncovered in a very hot oven for about 15 minutes or until the tomatoes are soft. Meanwhile, cook the pasta in a large saucepan of boiling water, uncovered, until just tender, then drain. Combine the pasta with the tomatoes, feta, and any pan juices in a large bowl, and stir through the remaining oil, pine nuts, basil, and olives. Serves 4.

lima bean, tomato, and rocket salad

The lima beans in this salad will help to neutralize any acidity in your stomach—a common problem, especially if you've been eating a lot of meat.

1 lb 10 oz egg tomatoes
2 x 10 oz cans lima beans, rinsed and drained
4 oz rocket, trimmed and roughly chopped
2 tbsp silvered almonds, toasted

For the dressing:
2 cloves garlic, crushed
6 fl oz olive oil
4½ fl oz lemon juice
½ oz parsley, crushed
1½ tbsp sugar
3 tsp sweet paprika
1 tsp chili powder

Halve the tomatoes lengthwise, remove the seeds, and thinly slice. Combine the tomatoes, beans, rocket, and dressing ingredients in a large bowl. Mix well. Serve topped with the almonds. Serves 4.

Italian salad (*below*)

This tasty salad includes apricots, which are not only rich in beta carotene and other nutrients, but will release energy slowly into your system to help avoid the mid-afternoon slump.

3½ oz dried apricots, sliced
7 oz asparagus tips
15 oz new potatoes, sliced
4 slices Parma ham
2½ oz Italian salami
3½ oz sunblush tomatoes, chopped
2 little gem lettuces

For the dressing:
3 tbsp olive oil
4 tbsp balsamic vinegar
2 tbsp honey (organic if possible)
salt and freshly ground black pepper

Beat the dressing ingredients in a bowl. Add the apricots and marinate for 30 minutes. Meanwhile, cook the asparagus tips in a pan of boiling salted water for 5 minutes until tender. Drain and rinse under cold water. Boil the new potatoes in salted water for 10–15 minutes, or until tender. Drain and allow to cool. Cut the ham into pieces and halve the salami. Wash the lettuces. Arrange the lettuce leaves on a platter and top with sliced potatoes, asparagus tips, ham, tomatoes, and salami. Drizzle the apricots and dressing over just before serving. Serves 4.

oven-baked vegetable salad

This nutritious dish is perfect if you've been burning the candle at both ends!

2 medium eggplants
1 tbsp salt
5 tsp olive oil
2 medium zucchini
1 red bell pepper
1 yellow bell pepper
3½ oz pine kernels
2 cloves garlic, chopped
4 ripe plum tomatoes
1 rosemary and rock salt foccacia loaf, diced
1½ oz flaked Parmesan cheese

For the dressing:
salt and pepper
4 tbsp olive oil
3 tbsp red wine vinegar
2 tbsp egg-free mayonnaise
3 tbsp shredded basil

Slice the eggplants in half. Place in a colander set over a plate. Sprinkle over the salt, and cover. Stand for 1 hour. Preheat the oven to 400°F. Squeeze the excess juices from the eggplant, then rinse under cold water. Pour the oil into a roasting tin and place in the oven for 2 minutes. Add the eggplant, zucchini, and bell peppers and cook for 40 minutes. Stir in the pine kernels and bake for 10 minutes. Remove and allow to cool in the tin. Stir the garlic, tomatoes, and bread into the vegetables and transfer to a serving dish. Beat the dressing ingredients in a bowl. Drizzle the dressing over the salad and toss to coat. Scatter over the Parmesan. Serves 4–6.

shredded beet and feta salad

Beet has long been used to help purify the blood. It is also ideal for women going through the menopause, as it helps to regulate hormone levels.

3½ oz sultanas
2 medium zucchini
13 oz uncooked beet
2 medium carrots
1 endive lettuce
2 avocados
6 oz feta cheese, crumbled

For the dressing:
4 fl oz olive oil
3 tsp Dijon mustard
juice and grated rind of 2 oranges
salt and freshly ground black peppercorns

Place the sultanas in a bowl. Beat together the dressing ingredients and pour over the sultanas. Allow to soak for 30 minutes. Cut the zucchini into strips. Grate the beet and carrots. Wash the endive lettuce and break into leaves. Halve the avocados, pit, peel, and cut into slices. Mix together the salad ingredients in a large bowl. Drizzle over the dressing and serve immediately. Serves 4–6.

warm chickpea and tuna salad

Chickpeas contain the phytonutrient isoflavone, which may help to prevent cancer. Tuna is an excellent hair-growth food; include it in your diet at least three times a week to enjoy its full benefits.

6 oz dried chickpeas
2 tbsp olive oil
4 fresh tuna steaks
3½ oz green beans, trimmed
1 romaine lettuce, sliced
15 anchovy fillets in oil, drained
16 pitted black olives, halved

For the dressing:
4 fl oz cranberry juice
6 tbsp olive oil
2 tbsp clear honey
1 tbsp Dijon mustard
sea salt and ground black pepper
2 tbsp flat-leaf parsley, chopped

Place the chickpeas in a large bowl and cover with plenty of cold water. Leave to stand for 6 hours or overnight. Drain and place in a large saucepan, cover with water, and bring to the boil. Boil rapidly for 10 minutes. Reduce the heat, then cover and simmer for 1½ hours until tender. Drain and allow to cool. Heat the oil in a skillet and cook the tuna steaks for 4 minutes on each side, until just tender. Meanwhile, blanch the beans in boiling salted water for 5 minutes, until tender. Drain and refresh under cold running water. Mix together the beans, lettuce, anchovies, and olives in a large bowl. Divide between serving plates. Arrange a tuna steak on top of each. Quickly beat together the dressing ingredients and drizzle over the salad. Serves 4.

multicolored rice salad

This salad provides more than three times the recommended adult daily intake (RDA) of vitamin C, necessary for sturdy blood vessels and a strong immune system. It is also a great stress-reliever, as the honey in the dressing will help calm nerves and induce sleep.

1 red bell pepper
1 green bell pepper
1 yellow bell pepper
7 oz long-grain brown rice
8 oz brown rice bread
olive oil
4 ripe tomatoes on the vine, diced
2 medium zucchini, grated
2 bunches basil leaves, torn

For the dressing:
9 tbsp olive oil
1 clove garlic
5 tbsp honey
2 tsp pure maple syrup
sea salt and ground black pepper

Core, deseed, and quarter the bell peppers. Place the them on a grill rack, skin-side uppermost, and cook for 10 minutes until the skin is charred. Place the bell peppers in a plastic bag, seal, cover with a tea towel, and leave to stand for 5 minutes. Unwrap the bell peppers, remove the skins, and slice thinly. Cook the rice in a large pan of boiling salted water for 25–30 minutes, until tender. Drain, refresh under cold water, and drain again. Cut the bread into chunks. Heat the oil and fry the bread in batches for 2 minutes, turning, until golden. Drain on kitchen paper. Mix the rice, bell peppers, bread, tomatoes, zucchini, and basil leaves in a large bowl. Divide between serving plates. Place the dressing ingredients in a screw-top jar and shake well. Drizzle over the salad and serve. Serves 4.

couscous medley

Avocados are thought to be a "complete" food, as they are particularly rich in vitamin E, an important nutrient for healthy skin, hair, and nails.

7 oz couscous
7 oz smoked streaky bacon
1 red onion, diced
2 avocados, peeled, pitted, and diced
4 tbsp pumpkin seeds

For the dressing:
6 tbsp olive oil
2 tbsp cider vinegar
4 tbsp fresh mixed herbs, chopped
1 tbsp tahini paste
juice of 1 lemon
sea salt and ground black pepper

Place the couscous in a large bowl and pour over just enough boiling water to cover. Leave to stand for 45 minutes until the liquid is absorbed and the couscous is cool. Using a fork, break the couscous into fine grains. Grill the bacon for 10 minutes, turning occasionally, until golden. Remove from the heat and snip into strips. Stir the onion and avocado into the couscous. Beat together the dressing ingredients and toss through the salad. Divide the couscous between serving plates. Scatter over the bacon and pumpkin seeds. Serve immediately. Serves 4.

warm winter salad

Potatoes are an important inclusion in your diet if you are a smoker, or are exposed to secondhand smoke on a regular basis.

12 oz new potatoes
8 tbsp olive oil
3½ oz pancetta
7 oz flat mushrooms
7 oz cherry tomatoes
4 oz mixed salad
4 oz Lamb's lettuce

6 tbsp balsamic vinegar
salt and black pepper
2½ oz fresh Parmesan shavings

Cook the new potatoes in a pan of boiling salted water for 15 minutes until tender, then drain. Meanwhile, heat half the oil in a skillet and cook the pancetta for 5 minutes, turning once, until crisp. Remove from the heat. Add the mushrooms and cherry tomatoes and heat gently. Place the salad leaves in a large salad bowl and snip in the hot pancetta. Lift the mushrooms, tomatoes, and potatoes from the skillet and add to the salad. Add the remaining ingredients to the pan and heat through. Pour over the salad and toss. Serves 4.

pork fillets with date and hazelnut stuffing

This meal has a lot of mood-supporting B vitamins; the lean meat will raise the level of dopamine in the body, which helps to lift moods and increase motivation, and the dates are good for mind and emotions. The hazelnuts contain high levels of vitamin E, a good anti-aging ingredient. Serve cold with salad for the perfect al fresco meal.

2 pork fillets
3½ oz pitted dates, chopped
1 oz hazelnuts, chopped
12 streaky bacon slices

Preheat the oven to 375°F. Slit the pork fillets lengthwise. Mix the chopped dates and hazelnuts together and spoon the mixture into the center of each fillet. Lay 6 of the bacon slices horizontally on a clean board. Put a pork fillet lengthwise along the bacon slices and then wrap the slices around the fillet. Repeat the same process with the second fillet. Put the fillet in a lightly oiled roasting tin and roast for 40–45 minutes, or until the juices run clear when the meat is pierced with a skewer. Transfer to a serving plate and allow to cool slightly before carving. Serves 2.

marinated chicken with prune salsa

Eating prunes is ideal for your digestive system, and a great way to fulfil your recommended daily intake (RDA) of iron. The lime in the salsa will enhance the absorption of iron, and also improve the health of all body tissues.

4 skinless chicken breasts

For the marinade:
1 tbsp olive oil
1 tbsp soy sauce
1 tbsp tomato paste
1 tbsp honey

For the salsa:
5 oz prunes
1 raw chili, finely chopped
1 medium tomato, deseeded and chopped

1 tbsp olive oil
juice of ¼ lime
1 tbsp each coriander and mint

To make the salsa: place the prunes in a pan of water and bring to the boil. Allow to soak for about 1 hour. Combine the chili, tomato, olive oil, and lime juice. When the prunes are ready, chop roughly, removing and discarding the stones, then add to the salsa and chill. Mix the marinade ingredients together and spread over the chicken breasts. Leave for about 1 hour, turning the breasts over halfway through so that the marinade covers the chicken completely. The chicken can be baked at 425°F for about 20–25 minutes, or grilled, or "dry-fried" in a heavy grill pan, or barbecued. Before serving, add the coriander and mint to the salsa. Serves 4.

exotic kedgeree

Regular consumption of fish lowers your cholesterol levels—it is estimated that it can reduce the risk of heart disease by approximately one-third. Aim to eat fish at least three times a week. Fish is also good for hair, skin, and nails.

7 oz Basmati rice
15 oz smoked haddock fillets
1 tbsp olive oil
½ onion, chopped
1 clove of garlic, chopped
1 tsp curry paste
2 oz sultanas
1 oz almonds, chopped
salt and pepper to taste
2 tbsp of coriander, chopped

Wash and drain the rice. Cook in a saucepan of boiling water for 10–12 minutes, then drain. Cook the fish in its own juices, by baking or microwaving; skin the fillets and flake the fish. Gently fry the onion and garlic in the oil until soft. Stir in the curry paste and cook for about 1 minute, then add 4–6 tablespoons of water, the sultanas, and almonds, and gently simmer for a few minutes until the sultanas are plump. Gently stir together the rice, the flaked fish and juices, and the onion mix, and season. Mix in the coriander before serving. Serves 4.

baked fillet of sole

Research suggests that omega-3 fatty acids found in oily fish may counteract certain types of allergies. Eating oily fish can help relieve symptoms of eczema and psoriasis. Aim to eat some type of oily fish at least three times a week for smooth, healthy skin.

7 oz fillet of sole
lemon juice, as desired
½ oz dried onion flakes
sprinkle chopped parsley
1 clove garlic, finely chopped
salt and pepper to taste
paprika to taste
½ fl oz light soy sauce

Pre-heat the oven to 375°F. Place the fish in a baking dish and brush with lemon juice. Sprinkle over the dried onion flakes, parsley, garlic, seasoning, and paprika. Drizzle liberally with the soy sauce. Bake for about 25 minutes. Serves 4.

seafood pasta pesto

All seafood contains magnesium, which keeps muscles toned and strong.

1 lb fresh spaghetti
2 oz butter
12 oz large shrimps, shelled
7 oz small tomatoes, halved
1 jar fresh pesto sauce
8 oz tub mascarpone cheese
salt and freshly ground pepper
basil leaves

Bring a large pan of salted water to the boil. Add the spaghetti, stir until separated, and bring to the boil again. Boil rapidly for 3–5 minutes, until al dente. Meanwhile, melt the butter in a large pan and warm the large shrimps and tomatoes for 3 minutes, stirring occasionally, until golden. Stir in the pesto, mascarpone cheese, and seasoning, and bring slowly to the boil, stirring until heated through and smooth. Drain the spaghetti and toss in the sauce. Spoon onto warmed serving plates and scatter with the basil leaves. Serves 4.

mussels in ginger and lemon grass broth

Mussels contain ingredients that help strengthen the liver, so this meal is a good choice if you've been overindulging in processed foods or alcohol.

24 fl oz fish stock
2 tbsp shredded ginger
2 stalks lemon grass, finely chopped
2 tsp lemon rind, shredded
2 lb mussels, cleaned

Place the stock, ginger, lemon grass, and lemon rind in a saucepan over a high heat. Bring to the boil, then add the mussels and cook for 2–3 minutes or until the mussels have opened. Discard any mussels that don't open. Serve the mussels in deep bowls with the broth and some bread. Serves 4.

spinach salad with warm garlic dressing

Spinach strengthens the blood and cleanses it of toxins to keep your skin in good condition.

8 oz baby spinach leaves
3½ oz semi-dried tomatoes
12 slices sourdough baguette
olive oil

For the dressing
3 tbsp olive oil
3 cloves garlic, sliced
2 tbsp salted capers, rinsed

1½ oz linguarian olives
2 tbsp lemon juice
2 tbsp thyme leaves
cracked black pepper

Place the spinach leaves and tomatoes on serving plates. Place the baguette slices on a tray and drizzle with a little olive oil. Grill or toast for 1 minute or until lightly browned. Add the garlic, capers, olives, lemon juice, thyme, and pepper to the olive oil in a pan and cook for 1 minute or until heated through. Pour the warm dressing over the salad and top with the grilled baguette. Serves 4.

lemon and parsley fried fish

Lemons help to cleanse the blood, strengthen the circulation, and calm the nerves. Teamed with the fish, which contains key B vitamins, this makes a great immune-boosting meal, too.

2 tbsp lemon rind, finely grated
¼ tbsp flat-leaf parsley, chopped
cracked black pepper and sea salt
4 fillets white fish
olive oil

Combine the lemon rind, parsley, and seasoning in a bowl. Press the lemon and parsley mixture onto both sides of the fish. Heat a little olive oil in a large skillet over a high heat. Cook the fish for 1–2 minutes on each side, or until cooked to your liking. Serve with lemon wedges and steamed greens of your choice. Serves 4.

barbecue pork san choy bau

Eating meat is recommended if you're feeling run-down, or are anemic, as it contains high levels of iron.

2 tbsp sesame oil
2 tbsp shredded ginger
4 shallots, sliced
1 lb Chinese barbecue pork (cooked), sliced
2 tbsp hoisin sauce
2 tbsp soy sauce
bean sprouts
iceberg lettuce cups
extra hoisin sauce to serve

Heat the oil in a skillet or wok over a medium–high heat. Add the ginger and shallots and cook for 1 minute. Add the pork, hoisin, and soy sauce and cook for 3 minutes or until heated through. Place a small pile of bean sprouts on each lettuce leaf. Top with the barbecue pork mixture and serve with extra hoisin sauce. Serves 4.

chicken breast baked in olives, lemon, and capers

This is an ideal low-fat meal to aid digestion, and it contains plenty of antioxidant vitamins and phytonutrients to improve skin tone.

7 oz cherry tomatoes, halved
2 oz small lingurian olives
2 tsp grated lemon rind
2 tbsp salted capers, rinsed
2 tbsp olive oil
cracked black pepper and salt
2 chicken breast fillets

Preheat the oven to 425°F. Combine the cherry tomatoes, olives, lemon rind, capers, oil, and seasoning, and place in the base of a baking dish. Top with the chicken and spoon a little of the olive mixture over it to coat. Place in the oven and bake for 20 minutes, or until the chicken is cooked, turning the chicken once. Serve with boiled potatoes, and greens. Serves 2.

apple, vegetable, and quorn curry

This recipe is full of soluble and insoluble fiber to help keep your digestive system healthy and reduce blood cholesterol levels.

24 fl oz vegetable stock
2½ oz sultanas
2½ oz dried bananas, sliced
2½ oz pitted dates, halved
2½ fl oz olive oil
2 x 10 oz quorn pieces
2½ oz cashew nuts
1 red onion, cut into thick slices
2 carrots, cut into sticks
2 green apples, cored and thickly sliced
2 tbsp medium curry paste
7 fl oz coconut cream
salt and ground black pepper

Place the stock in a bowl and add the sultanas, bananas, and dates. Allow to soak for 30 minutes. Meanwhile, heat half the oil in a large skillet and cook the quorn pieces for 5 minutes, turning occasionally, until golden. Keep warm. Add the nuts to the pan and cook for 2 minutes. Transfer to a plate. Add the remaining oil to the pan and cook the onion and carrots for 5 minutes or until golden. Add the apples and cook for 5 minutes. Stir in the curry paste and cook for 1 minute. Add the dried fruit mixture and quorn and bring to the boil. Simmer for 25 minutes. Stir in the coconut cream and seasoning. Serve with boiled rice and scatter over extra cashew nuts. Serves 2.

rice jumble

This is a vegetarian dish that everyone can enjoy. It will provide you with a valuable amount of your daily nutritional needs.

2 tbsp extra virgin olive oil
2 red onions, thickly sliced
1 red and 1 green bell pepper, cored, deseeded, and sliced
6 oz long-grain brown rice
15 fl oz vegetable stock
2 medium zucchini, shredded
3½ oz cherry tomatoes, halved
salt and freshly ground black pepper
3½ oz vegetarian white cheddar cheese, diced
3 tbsp coriander, chopped

Heat the oil in a large pan and cook the onion and bell peppers for 5 minutes. Add the rice and cook for 2 minutes. Pour in the stock, bring to the boil, cover, and simmer for 20 minutes, stirring occasionally. Add the zucchini, tomatoes, and seasoning, cover and simmer for a further 10 minutes. Stir in the cheddar and coriander and serve immediately. Serves 4.

lentil and red onion quiche (right)

Lentils contain magnesium, iron, zinc, and calcium, and are particularly important for vegetarians. This recipe will help you control your blood sugar levels.

For the pastry:
7 oz spelt plain flour
pinch sea salt
13½ oz butter

For the filling:
2 oz red lentils
2 tbsp olive oil
2 red onions, sliced
2½ oz ready-to-eat apricots, sliced
3½ oz vegetarian cheddar cheese, grated
2 oz pecan nuts
5 fl oz soy milk
sea salt and ground black pepper

Preheat the oven to 375°F. Make the pastry and roll out to line an 8-in round fluted flan tin. Prick all over with a fork, line with greaseproof paper, fill with baking beans, and bake blind for 10 minutes. Remove from the oven, remove the beans and paper, and bake for 5 minutes. Place the lentils in a large pan, cover with cold water, bring to the boil, and simmer for 5 minutes. Drain. Heat the oil in a large skillet and cook the onion until softened and caramelized. Remove from the heat and stir in the lentils and sliced apricots. Scatter half the cheese over the base of the pastry case. Spoon in the onion and lentil mixture and scatter over the remaining cheese. Arrange the nuts on top.

Beat together the remaining ingredients and pour into the pastry case. Bake for 30 minutes, or until golden and set. Can be served either hot or cold with a salad. Serves 4.

salmon steaks with sesame seed crusts

This is a tasty, skin-enhancing meal, with the added benefit of helping your hair and nails grow stronger. By adding sesame seeds to the recipe, you'll boost your calcium intake to help ensure strong, healthy bones.

4 salmon steaks
juice and grated rind of 1 lime
salt and freshly ground black pepper
3 tbsp sesame seeds
2 tbsp flat-leaf parsley, chopped
1 sliced white rice cake, made into crumbs
2 tbsp sunflower seeds
1 red chili, deseeded and finely chopped
3 tbsp olive oil

Place the salmon steaks in a shallow dish. Pour over the lime juice and rind and season. Turn to coat and leave to marinate for 10 minutes. Mix together the sesame seeds, parsley, rice-cake crumbs, sunflower seeds, and chili in a large bowl. Remove the steaks from the lime juice and dip in the sesame seed mixture, coating well. Heat the oil in a large skillet and cook the steaks for 3–4 minutes each side, until golden. Remove from the heat and serve on a bed of salad leaves. Serves 4.

tofu risotto

Tofu is an excellent source of protein and calcium, which makes this a meal highly recommended for vegetarians, who can be at risk of missing out on these nutrients in their daily intake.

2½ fl oz olive oil
8 oz organic tofu, drained and diced
1 red onion, chopped
1 clove garlic, crushed
7 oz long-grain brown rice
32 fl oz vegetable stock
3½ oz pitted apricots, sliced
2½ oz organic sultanas
2½ oz organic raisins
6 oz vegetarian double Gloucester cheese, grated
fine sea salt and black pepper
1 oz fresh basil, chopped

Heat half the oil in a large pan and fry the tofu, turning occasionally until browned. Using a slotted spoon, transfer to a plate and set aside. Add the remaining oil to the pan and cook the onion for 5 minutes. Add the onion, garlic, and rice and cook for 2 minutes. Add half the stock, bring to the boil, and simmer, stirring occasionally until absorbed. Add half the remaining stock, the apricots, sultanas, and raisins, and simmer until the stock is absorbed. Add the remaining stock and simmer until almost completely absorbed and creamy. Stir in the tofu, cheese, seasoning, and basil and heat through. Serves 4.

chicken and broccoli in mushroom sauce

If you're avoiding eating red meat, increase your protein intake by eating chicken at least two or three times a week. Broccoli is one of the richest plant sources of iron, and is also high in vitamins C and E, and calcium.

3 tbsp vegetable oil
10 oz fresh broccoli spears
4 tbsp butter
8 oz fresh mushrooms, sliced
1 lb chicken broth
2½ fl oz non-fat dry milk
2 oz flour
½ shallot, sliced
nutmeg
6 tbsp Parmesan cheese, grated
2 oz fresh breadcrumbs (½ slice wholewheat bread)
2 tbsp parsley, finely chopped
1 lb cooked chicken, cut into chunks

Preheat the oven to 375°F. Add the oil to a pan. Steam the broccoli spears until tender. Drain and blot dry on paper towels. Place the broccoli in a medium non-stick skillet and fry over a medium heat. Melt 1 tablespoon of butter. Add the mushrooms, cover, and cook for 7–9 minutes, or until the mushrooms have released all their juices. Uncover and increase the heat to high. Allow the liquid to evaporate. Set aside. In a small bowl, combine the chicken broth and non-fat dry milk. Set aside. In a medium saucepan, melt 3 tablespoons of butter over a medium-high heat. Stir in the flour and cook for 1 minute. Add the chicken broth mixture and stir with a wire whisk. Bring to the boil, and then add the shallot, nutmeg, and 3 tablespoons of Parmesan cheese. Add the cooked mushrooms and set aside. In a small bowl, combine the breadcrumbs, 3 tablespoons of Parmesan cheese, and parsley. Set aside. Lay the broccoli spears on the bottom of the prepared pan. Evenly distribute the chicken over the broccoli. Pour the mushroom sauce over. Sprinkle the breadcrumb mixture on top. Bake for 25 minutes. Serves 6.

fish in sleeping bags (left)

This is a quick and easy way to increase your levels of essential fatty acids (EFAs). By adding various herbs to the recipe, you'll also aid your digestion and cleanse your kidneys and liver.

4 sole fillets
butter, as desired
1 tbsp coriander
1 tbsp parsley
juice 1 lemon
4 tomatoes, thinly sliced
1 lemon, thinly sliced and rind removed
2 bell peppers, cored, seeded, and thinly sliced
sea salt and pepper to taste

Preheat the oven to 425°F. Lay a large sheet of foil on a baking tray. Rub the fillets with butter, then sprinkle with the coriander and parsley and pour lemon juice over them. Place the tomato and lemon slices on the fillets, adding

seasoning to taste. Place the bell peppers over the fillets. Fold the sides of the foil to meet in the middle and roll close, until the fish are completely covered. Bake for 20 minutes. Serve with new baby potatoes and beans. Serves 4.

pasta and yogurt dressing

Pasta is a good source of carbohydrates, B vitamins, and, if using wholewheat pasta, insoluble fiber. This is an ideal meal after you've been to the gym, as it will help your body relax and repair itself.

1 lb pasta shells, cooked
5 oz snow peas, blanched
8 oz cherry tomatoes, halved
1 x 14 oz can tuna in spring water, drained

For the dressing:
9 fl oz natural low-fat yogurt
1 tbsp lemon juice
¼ tsp dried rosemary leaves
1 tsp dried basil
1 tsp dried mustard powder
½ tsp poppy seeds
1 tbsp fresh parsley, chopped

Combine the pasta, snow peas, tomatoes, and tuna in a large serving bowl. Place the dressing ingredients in a screw-top jar and shake until well combined. Pour over the salad and toss until the ingredients are combined. Serves 6.

nutty oven-baked monkfish

Adding nuts to meals is a good way to increase levels of essential fatty acids (EFAs) and natural oils. Without these fats and oils, your skin becomes dry and flaky, and is more vulnerable to premature aging.

8 monkfish tails
3½ oz baby spinach leaves
4 tomatoes, skinned, deseeded, and chopped
pinch nutmeg
salt and freshly ground black pepper
42 fl oz olive oil
1 tbsp cider vinegar
10 fl oz dry white wine
2½ oz unshelled pistachio nuts, shelled and chopped
3 tbsp soy milk
3 tbsp pesto (ready-made, if you prefer)
2 tbsp pumpkin seeds

Preheat the oven to 400°F. Place 4 of the monkfish tails on a worksurface. Place the spinach leaves on top of each monkfish tail. Top with the tomatoes, nutmeg, and seasoning. Place the remaining monkfish tails on top. Secure with string. Pour the oil into a roasting tin and place in the oven for 2 minutes to heat.

Remove from the heat and add the monkfish tails. Return to the oven and bake for 20–30 minutes, until the fish is just flaking. Remove the monkfish from the pan with a fish slice and keep warm. Place the pan on a hob and stir in the vinegar and wine. Bring to the boil and simmer until reduced by half. Stir in the remaining ingredients and heat through. Arrange the monkfish tails on hot serving plates. Spoon over the sauce. Serve with new potatoes or green beans. Serves 4.

mixed vegetable skewers

This is a good meal for vegetarians, or meat-eaters can simply add chunks of chicken. This dish is packed full of health-giving antioxidants and other nutrients.

2 red or yellow bell peppers, cored, seeded, and cut into large chunks
4 red onions, sliced and cut into quarters
1 lb mushrooms, peeled and cut into quarters
1 lb pineapple chunks (can be canned variety)
8 oz zucchini, thickly sliced

Preheat the grill to maximum. Thread the different ingredients in turn onto skewers. Brush with honey or olive oil, if desired. Place on a baking tray and grill for 4–5 minutes, turning as they cook. Serve with salad. Serves 4.

fruit and nut risotto

Cashew nuts contain lots of protein, unsaturated fats, and vitamins, which is good news for your heart.

2 tbsp olive oil
3 oz cashew nuts
1 red onion, chopped
1 clove garlic, crushed
9 oz risotto rice
10 fl oz dry white wine
24 fl oz vegetable stock
1½ oz walnut halves, chopped
1½ oz dried figs, halved
2½ oz apricots, chopped
3 oz fresh baby spinach leaves
7 oz Gorgonzola cheese, crumbled
1 tbsp mint, chopped

Heat half the oil in a pan and cook the nuts for 5 minutes, stirring occasionally until browned. Using a slotted spoon, transfer the nuts to a plate and keep warm. Heat the remaining oil in the pan and cook the onion for 5 minutes until softened. Add the garlic and rice and cook for 2 minutes. Add the wine, bring to the boil, and simmer for 5 minutes until the liquid is absorbed. Add two-thirds of the stock to the pan, bring to the boil, and simmer until absorbed, stirring occasionally. Add the walnuts, figs, apricots, and remaining stock. Bring to the boil and simmer, stirring occasionally, until the liquid is absorbed, and the rice is creamy and tender. Stir in the spinach leaves, two-thirds of the cheese, and all of the mint. Season to taste. Simmer for 2 minutes, until the spinach softens. Spoon the risotto onto serving plates, and scatter over the remaining cheese and cashew nuts. Serves 4.

desserts

mixed fall fruits with pancakes (below)

Traditionally, this dish includes special pancakes called "blinis," originally from Russia, and now available from specialist stores and delicatessens, but you can use any kind of ready-made pancakes, or you can make your own. To decorate, pieces of a kind of chocolate "plate" called a caraque have been used. As an alternative, you could add shavings from any good-quality chocolate.

1 red apple, cored and thickly sliced
1 pear, cored and thickly sliced
3½ oz blackberries
1 fl oz honey
1 oz butter
3½ oz raspberries
2 oz honey-dipped banana chips, broken into small pieces
2 oz superfine sugar
8 ready-made pancakes, warmed
confectioner's sugar
caraque

Place the apple, pear, blackberries, honey, and butter in a large pan and heat gently for 5 minutes or until the fruit is softened. Remove from the heat and stir in the raspberries and banana chips. Place the sugar and 3 teaspoons of water in a saucepan and heat gently until the sugar is dissolved. Boil until golden. Lightly oil a baking sheet and pour on the golden liquid. Allow to cool. Place a pancake on each serving plate and spoon over the fruit mixture. Top with a second pancake, dust with confectioner's sugar, then break the caraque into pieces and scatter on top. Serves 4.

mango, apple, and passion-fruit sorbet

High in vitamins and sweetness, this is a nutritious after-dinner treat.

3½ oz superfine sugar
17 fl oz apple juice
4½ fl oz water
1 x 14½ oz can sliced mango in juice, drained
4½ fl oz passion-fruit pulp (taken from 6 passion-fruit)
4 egg whites (organic free-range if possible)

Combine the sugar, juice, and water in a medium pan, then stir over a medium heat, without boiling, until the sugar dissolves. Bring to the boil and simmer, uncovered, without stirring for about 12 minutes, or until the syrup thickens slightly. (Do not allow the syrup to change color.) Blend the mango until smooth. Stir the mango and passion-fruit into the sugar syrup. Pour into an 8 x 12 in pan. Cover with foil and freeze until just firm. Beat the sorbet mixture in a small bowl with an electric mixer until thick and fluffy. Return to the pan, cover, and freeze until just firm. Repeat the beating process in a large bowl, add the egg whites one at a time, and beat until fluffy. Return the mixture to the pan, cover, and freeze until firm. Serves 4.

summer pudding

This recipe is crammed full of antioxidants to promote skin renewal and repair.

13 oz frozen blueberries
13 oz cranberry juice
12 slices wholewheat bread
confectioner's sugar
4 tbsp vanilla yogurt

Bring the blueberries and the cranberry juice to the boil. Grease 4 round dishes (such as kumquat dishes), and place the blueberries and juice to cover the bottom of each dish. Cut slices of bread to the same diameter as the dishes and place on top. Layer the bread and juice (3 slices per dish), and top with juice and blueberries. Place in the refrigerator to set. Turn out onto a flat dish. Serve with sprinkled confectioner's sugar and yogurt. Serves 4.

apple and almond fruit fool

This pudding contains folate, so it's ideal for would-be-mums.

10 fl oz semi-skimmed milk
1 heaped tbsp custard powder
1 level tbsp sugar
2 medium cooking apples
1 level tbsp sugar, to sweeten the apples
1 tbsp ground almonds
Few drops almond essence

To make the custard: add a little of the milk to the custard powder and mix to a paste, then add the sugar. Meanwhile, bring the rest of the milk to the boil. Pour the hot milk into the paste mix, carefully stirring as it thickens. Peel, core, and finely slice the apples and gently stew in a little water until soft. When cooked, either purée the apples or press through a sieve; sweeten with 1 tablespoon of sugar. Blend the apples, custard, ground almonds, and almond essence together and divide between the bowls. Leave to cool. Chill before serving. Decorate with dried apple slices, glacé cherries, almond flakes, and fresh mint leaves. Serves 4.

boysenberry and apple muesli-style crumble

Boysenberries help prevent varicose veins, premature skin aging, and urinary tract infections.

7 oz boysenberries
1 large apple, chopped
3 tsp superfine sugar

For the topping:
1½ oz natural muesli
1 tbsp all-purpose flour
2 tsp brown sugar
1 oz butter

Combine the muesli, flour, and brown sugar in a medium bowl, and rub in the butter. Combine the berries, apple, and sugar in a medium pan. Simmer, uncovered, until the apple is just tender. Divide the berry and apple mixture among 4 small ovenproof dishes. Sprinkle with the topping. Bake, uncovered, in the moderate oven for about 15 minutes, or until browned. Serves 4.

passion-fruit pineapple sorbet with mint sauce

Packed full of vitamin C, this light pudding is an ideal summer treat. You will need about 12 passion-fruit for this recipe.

1 large pineapple, peeled, cored, and chopped
3½ oz superfine sugar
9 fl oz water
4½ fl oz passion-fruit pulp (taken from 6 passion-fruit)
3 egg whites (organic free-range if possible)

For the mint sauce:
4½ fl oz passion-fruit pulp (taken from 6 passion-fruit)
5½ fl oz water
2 tbsp superfine sugar
½ oz firmly packed fresh mint leaves
½ tsp arrowroot

Blend or process the pineapple until smooth. Push through a strainer and discard the pulp. You will need 21 fl oz of juice. Combine the sugar and water in a medium pan and stir over heat without boiling, until the sugar dissolves. Bring to the boil, then simmer uncovered without stirring for about 10 minutes, or until the syrup is thick. Set aside to cool. Stir the pineapple juice and passion-fruit pulp into the sugar syrup, pour into a 8 x 12 in pan, cover with foil, and freeze until just firm. Quickly process the sorbet mixture and egg whites until smooth, pour into a 5½ x 8½ in loaf pan, cover, and freeze overnight. Combine the sauce ingredients with 1 teaspoon of water before serving. Serves 4.

Bramley apple and blackberry layer

The antioxidants in this tasty pudding contain anti-aging properties. The dairy products are a good source of calcium, helping to keep osteoporosis at bay.

15 oz Bramley apples, peeled, cored, and sliced
4 oz blackberries
2½ oz soft brown sugar
juice ½ lemon
½ oz butter
2 oz breadcrumbs
2 oz honey-coated nut mix, chopped
3½ fl oz vanilla flavor soy cream, chilled

Place the apples, blackberries, sugar, and lemon juice in a saucepan. Cover and simmer, stirring occasionally until the apples and blackberries have turned to a thick pulp. Remove from the heat and allow to cool. Melt the butter in a skillet and cook the breadcrumbs, stirring occasionally until golden and crisp. Remove from the heat and stir in the chopped nuts. Allow to cool. Spoon half the apple purée into 4 glasses. Top with the vanilla cream and sprinkle over the nut mixture. Chill until ready to serve. Serves 4.

juices and herbal drinks

get up and glow *(far right)*

If you don't feel particularly hungry at breakfast, try this great energizing smoothie. It'll keep you satisfied until lunchtime and it's extremely yummy!

1 banana
1 tsp honey
shaved nutmeg, as desired
7 fl oz milk (cow's or goat's, skimmed or semi-skimmed)

Put all the ingredients into a blender and mix until the banana is completely absorbed. Pour into a glass and add some more nutmeg to taste. Serves 1.

strawberry starter smoothie

If you're trying to eat healthily but still can't manage to make yourself a fruit salad every morning, this smoothie will provide you with more than your daily nutrient intake of vitamins A, C, and E. By adding seeds to the smoothie, you'll also ensure that you're getting enough essential fatty acids (EFAs), which are necessary for smooth skin and strong nails.

5 strawberries, stalks removed
handful of blueberries
handful of raspberries
1 banana
1 tbsp yogurt
handful pumpkin and sunflower seeds
10 fl oz apple juice (freshly squeezed or 100 percent)

Add the ingredients to the apple juice. Blend until the seeds are completed absorbed. Pour into a tall glass, and add ice if desired. Cheers! Serves 1.

green machine

An ultra-green juice that helps to maintain energy levels.

3½ oz broccoli
3½ oz kale parsley
1 apple
2 celery sticks

Juice and serve in a tall glass. Serves 1.

hard as nails

This drink is rich in silicon and potassium—valuable if your nails constantly break and chip.

1 medium parsnip
1 green bell pepper
small bunch watercress
½ cucumber
1 tbsp mint, chopped

Juice all the ingredients and serve over ice with a sprinkling of mint. Serves 1.

skin healer *(right)*

A sharp drink full of vitamins A and C, and minerals selenium and zinc.

½ grapefruit
1 large slice pineapple
1 kiwi fruit
2 oz frozen cranberries
2 oz frozen raspberries
lime wedge

Juice the grapefruit and pineapple. Blend with the kiwi and frozen berries. Throw in a lime wedge and serve with a straw. Serves 1.

perfect start

This juice is ideal if you don't have time for breakfast, as it contains so many vitamins and minerals that your recommended daily intake (RDA) is taken care of!

1 apple
1 pear
1 carrot
1 celery
1 kiwi fruit
ginger to taste

Juice all the ingredients. Leave in the refrigerator for 15 minutes to chill if desired, or add ice. For added sweetness and taste, you can put the mixture in a blender and add a banana and a handful of blueberries. Serves 1.

perfect skin

If you've been suffering from pimply skin, a celery juice is an ideal way to help the healing process.

1 carrot
1 apple
1 celery

Juice all the ingredients. Add ice to the mixture, if desired. Serves 1.

happy and healthy

Increase your intake of vitamin C with this tasty apple, carrot, and kiwi fruit mix. The ginger adds a spicy tang and can help settle an upset stomach.

1 carrot
1 apple
1 kiwi fruit
ginger (to taste)

Juice the first 3 ingredients. Add a small amount of the ginger to the juicer, adding more if desired. Serves 1.

an apple a day

This is a great skin-boosting juice with lots of antioxidants to help prevent premature skin aging. The essential fatty oils in the seeds also nourish and protect the skin, and there is plenty of fiber for a healthy digestive system, too.

9 fl oz apple juice
handful blueberries
handful raspberries
1 banana
1 kiwi fruit
2 oz pumpkin seeds
2 oz sunflower seeds

Put all the ingredients in a blender. Blend at a high speed until the mixture is smooth. Add ice if desired. Serves 1.

great start

Get your digestive system off to a healthy start each day with this tasty hot drink. The lemon and ginger are superb for kick-starting your digestive system and supporting your kidneys.

9 fl oz boiling water (add some cool water if desired)
3 lemon wedges
ginger, grated
honey (optional)

Put all the ingredients in a teacup. Add honey to taste, if desired. Serves 1.

cleansers and toners

Many cosmetic houses are now discovering that when it comes to cleansers, toners, and other beauty-enhancing products, nature got there first! Vitamin A, vitamin E, essential fatty acids (EFAs), and flavonoids—all nutrients found in the most common foods, such as vegetables, milk, fruit, nuts, and seeds—are being added to the latest cosmetic ranges. Many natural ingredients have a gentle peeling and cleansing action that is as effective as anything manufactured in a laboratory—and yet much kinder to your skin. For example, lemon is a good astringent and also contains antioxidant vitamins and phytochemicals that can help repair damaged skin and combat the aging effects of traffic fumes, cigarette smoke, and ultraviolet rays from the sun. Carrot juice replenishes the face and neck and can also help to alleviate eczema and acne. Grapeseed extract helps to counteract flaking, and has calming properties for inflamed skin. The properties of cucumber help remove excess grease as well as calming skin irritation and reducing puffiness around the eyes. These recipes utilize the skin-enhancing properties of the best natural ingredients, and whatever your skin type or problem—young or mature, dry or oily—there are treatments here that will work for you to cleanse, tone, and restore color, freshness, and vitality to your complexion.

milk and tomato juice cleanser

Tomatoes are a source of vitamins A, B, and C; minerals such as potassium and magnesium; and unique phytochemicals, such as lycopene. The high acid content in this recipe—from the lactic acid in the milk and the fruit acid in the tomato—gives this cleansing lotion a gentle peeling action. Test on the inside of the arm or wrist for any possible allergic reactions before using on the face. This cleanser is recommended for normal and oily skin types.

1 medium very ripe tomato
150 ml/5 fl oz fresh whole milk
bottled or spring water

Juice or blend the tomato. Strain through a piece of muslin and discard the pulp. Add the tomato juice to an equal amount of fresh milk. Store in a covered container or bottle in the refrigerator. Apply to the face and neck, using cotton pads, once or twice a day. Leave on for 10 minutes, then rinse with bottled or spring water, and pat dry.

return to youth

This cleanser is perfect for restoring vitality to mature, dry skin.

1 tbsp heavy cream
2 drops rose essential oil

Combine the ingredients and use as you would a cleansing lotion. It is gentle enough to be safely applied to the area around the eyes. Massage into your skin and remove with a warm, damp cloth. Apply moisturizer.

family cleanser

This cleanser removes excess oils, make-up, and dirt without stripping the skin of its natural oils. It is suitable for all skin types.

1½ oz/½ cup oatmeal
1 oz/⅓ cup sunflower seeds, finely ground
³/₄ oz/¼ cup almond meal, finely ground
1 tsp powdered peppermint or rosemary leaves, rose petals, or lavender flowers
dash cinnamon powder (optional)
water/milk/heavy cream (depending on skin type—see method below)

In a medium bowl, mix the dry ingredients together thoroughly. Using approximately 2 teaspoons of scrub mixture for your face and throat, or more for your body, add enough water (for oily skin), milk (for normal skin), or heavy cream (for dry skin) to form a spreadable paste. Allow to thicken for 1 minute. Massage onto your face and throat or body area. Rinse. Store any remaining cleanser in a zipper-lock plastic bag or plastic food container in a cool, dry place for up to 6 months, or up to a year in the freezer.

strawberry steam cleanser

Steaming not only brings a healthy glow to your skin, it is ideal for unblocking pores, too. If you're suffering from repeated outbreaks or problematic skin, try this recipe at least once a week to help clear your complexion.

1 tbsp lavender
1 tbsp red clover leaves
2 oz/½ cup fresh strawberries

Sprinkle the lavender, strawberries, and red clover leaves in a bowl of steaming water. Place your face over the steamy concoction and cover your head with a towel. Stay for 5–15 minutes. Rinse your face with cool water and pat dry.

cooling toner

The combination of calming cucumber and vitamin A-packed carrot will soothe and rejuvenate irritated skin. This toner is for sensitive skin types.

1 cucumber
4 fl oz/½ cup carrot juice
4 fl oz/½ cup camomile tea
4 fl oz/½ cup lemon juice

Juice the cucumber and mix with the carrot juice. Add the camomile tea and the lemon juice. Combine all the ingredients in a screw-top glass jar and shake to blend. Use a cotton ball to apply to your face.

rosewater and grapeseed toner

This sweet toner is suitable for all skin types. The grapeseed extract will help to exfoliate any dry, flaky skin, and the gentle astringent properties in the rosewater will tone the skin and help prepare it for moisturizing.

4½ fl oz rosewater
1 tsp vegetable glycerine
1 tsp pressed organic almond oil
12 drops grapefruit seed extract

Combine all the ingredients in a screw-top glass jar and shake well to blend. Apply to the skin and gently massage, beginning at your jawline and working upward. Leave for 1 minute. Rinse with lukewarm water. Store refrigerated for up to a month.

go green toner

In recent years many cosmetic houses have discovered the healing powers of green tea. Rich in antioxidants, this toner can help fight premature skin aging. It is also a good anti-irritant, and will soothe aggravated skin.

7 fl oz mineral water
4 tsp green tea leaves
1 tsp mint leaves
1 tsp lemon juice

Make an infusion with the mineral water, green tea, and mint leaves, then add the lemon juice. Strain the mixture and allow the liquid to cool. Pour into a spritzer bottle for easy use.

cool as a cucumber

Cucumber contains ingredients to help alleviate oily skin. Lemons are a great astringent to help your skin heal and renew itself. Egg white improves skin tone and tightens tissues, it also softens skin and refines pores. Use daily to keep shine under control.

½ cucumber
1 egg white (organic free-range if possible)
1 tbsp lemon juice
1 tsp mint

Combine all the ingredients in a bowl and blend well. Apply using a cotton ball. Your skin may feel slightly tight, so make sure you apply your moisturizer immediately afterward.

moisturizers and exfoliants

Natural nutrient-packed foods contain all the health-giving ingredients needed for the growth and renewal of skin, hair, and nails. Those same foods can be applied externally, too, where their revitalizing and protective properties will act directly to cleanse, moisturize, nourish, and replenish. As with the food you eat, always choose natural organic products, as these are free of additives, chemicals, and pollutants—substances you most certainly do not want on your skin!

everyday moisturizer

Moisturizer protects your skin from the elements, as well as replacing the moisture lost throughout the day. You should use this cream twice a day after cleansing and toning.

15 fl oz almond oil
3 oz cocoa butter
1 oz beeswax
4½ fl oz distilled water
1 tsp royal jelly
30 drops grapefruit seed extract oil

Combine the oil, cocoa butter, and beeswax and melt over a low heat, stirring occasionally. Remove from the heat and add the water and jelly. Blend in an electric blender until the mixture is thick and creamy. Add the grapefruit seed extract. Store in screw-top glass jars. This mixture lasts around 4 months, but discard if you notice signs of discoloration or mold.

all-over body pamper

Using essential oils can help hydrate extremely dry skin and return it to its natural moisture level.

10 drops lavender oil
10 drops Roman camomile oil
10 drops neroli oil
10 drops rosemary oil
10 drops carrot seed oil
2 fl oz almond, olive, or sesame oil

Apply the oil once a day after bathing or showering, while your skin is still damp. This will help your body retain moisture.

cocoa butter cream

This is excellent for pregnant women, and anyone else who suffers from stretch marks. Use after showering to retain moisture.

4½ oz grated cocoa butter
1 tsp almond oil
1 tsp light sesame oil
1 tsp vitamin E oil

Place all the ingredients in an ovenproof glass container and gently heat in the microwave or in a double boiler until the cocoa butter is melted and the oils are well mixed. Pour into a clean container and allow the cream to cool completely. You may need to stir the cream one more time after it has cooled. Store in a cool, dry place.

thirsty skin moisturizer

Avocado is not just a tasty fruit, it's a perfect treatment for tired or dry skin, as it replaces many of the oils that everyday life takes away.

4 tsp wheat germ oil
4 tbsp avocado oil
1 oz cocoa butter
1 tsp beeswax
½ tsp borax powder
2 tbsp rosewater
10 drops geranium essential oil
5 drops frankincense essential oil
5 drops sandalwood essential oil

Combine the wheat germ and avocado oil in a heat-resistant bowl and place in a saucepan that has been half-filled with water. Heat, adding the cocoa butter and beeswax, until the mixture has blended. Dissolve the borax in the rosewater and add to the mixture by stirring all the ingredients together. Remove from the heat and add the essential oils. Allow to cool before storing.

sugar delight

I discovered the use of sugar as an exfoliant while traveling, when I realized I had forgotten my usual brand. This blend is suitable for most skin types; you'll be amazed at how soft and smooth your skin feels afterward.

8 oz white cane sugar
8 fl oz vegetable glycerine or avocado oil
2 tsp aloe vera gel

2 drops lavender oil
2 drops orange oil

Combine all the ingredients in a bowl. Scoop some of the scrub into your hand and massage gently onto your skin for a minute (the scrub will actually tighten on your skin like a mask). Leave on for 3–4 minutes before rinsing. It can be used all over your body. Warning: some people develop blotchiness after using this scrub, but this is only temporary!

nutty body scrub

Using natural ingredients such as nuts and oatmeal will not only exfoliate your body without irritating it, the oil in the nuts will also provide a moisturizing film to help protect your skin from dehydration. For all skin types, particularly dry.

3½ oz ground nuts (try almonds or flaxseeds)
2 oz oatmeal
2 oz wholewheat flour
water for paste

Combine the dry ingredients in a blender until they are reduced to a coarse mixture. Pour into a screw-top glass jar. To use, scoop out a handful and place in a bowl, adding water to make a paste. Rub over your body to loosen any dry or flaking skin. This mixture can be stored in a freezer.

mid-week scrub

This recipe is perfect for exfoliating normal to sensitive skin. Oats are quite soft on the skin, and so make an ideal exfoliant, as you are far less likely to experience a sensitive reaction. This scrub is ideal if you like to exfoliate more than once a week.

2 tbsp oatmeal
2 tbsp cornmeal
2 tbsp wheat germ
water for paste

Mix all the dry ingredients and store in an airtight container. Make a paste by adding a splash of warm water to 1 tablespoon of the mixture.

shampoos, conditioners, and hair colorings

Natural remedies and treatments offer relief both to everyday stresses on your hair and to more specific problems. It is worth discovering the right shampoo and conditioner for you, as healthier hair will reward you with a greater sense of well-being. Whatever your hair type and problem—dry and frizzy, or oily and lifeless—there are numerous treatments that can improve its quality. By combining various ingredients you can deal with several complaints simultaneously, or tackle particularly stubborn hair conditions—head on!

dandruff elixir

Tea tree is a must-have for everybody. It can be used to treat pimples, cold sores, and cuts, and is also ideal for treating nits. Best of all, it is kind for those with sensitive scalps, so this mixture won't irritate your scalp in the way that many commercial anti-dandruff brands can.

4–5 drops tea tree oil
1 tbsp jojoba oil

Combine the ingredients in a screw-top glass jar with a tight lid. Shake well. After sectioning wet hair, dab the mixture onto a clean cotton ball and stroke along the scalp. Wrap hair in a towel and leave for 2 hours. Work shampoo into the hair with a little water to remove the oil. Rinse.

natural olive oil shampoo base

This is a great base shampoo. The extra virgin olive oil restores moisture to the scalp and hair shaft to nourish dry, thirsty hair. You can use this shampoo base on its own for clean, shiny hair, or you can add your own chosen herbs or essential oils to suit your hair's needs.

2 fl oz water
2 fl oz castile soap
½ tsp extra virgin olive oil

Mix all the ingredients together and pour into a shampoo bottle.

lavender shampoo

Lavender soothes an irritated scalp and stimulates the hair follicles. It also aids relaxation and engenders feelings of well-being.

3½ fl oz water
3½ oz fresh lavender
5 drops lavender essential oil
3½ fl oz natural shampoo base
2 tbsp glycerine

Place the water and lavender in a heavy-bottomed pan and mix together. Bring to the boil and continue to boil gently for at least 20 minutes. Leave to cool slightly, then slowly add the natural shampoo base and glycerine to the herbal mixture. Mix well. Pour into a container and leave to stand for a few days to allow the mixture to thicken. Use as you would your regular shampoo.

dry hair conditioner

Vinegar offers an extremely easy way to add shine to your hair. And adding rosemary and herbs helps to nourish dry, brittle hair. This is a good recipe if you suffer from flyaway hair during the colder months.

handful fresh rosemary
handful fresh mint leaves
8 fl oz cider vinegar

Drop the rosemary and mint leaves into a screw-top glass jar, and cover with the cider vinegar. Seal the jar and leave for 2 weeks. Strain the potion. After shampooing, pour a tablespoon onto dry hair and leave in.

conditioner for oily hair

Lemon is just as effective on your hair as it is on your skin. Its astringent properties absorb excess oil without damaging the hair or hair follicles.

1 lemon
2 fl oz cider vinegar

Wash, slice, and deseed the lemon. Whizz the lemon in a blender to a smooth pulp. Filter through muslin. Mix with the cider vinegar. After shampooing, blot your hair with a towel and rub the lemon-vinegar mixture into the scalp. Leave on for 5–10 minutes, then rinse with cool water.

essential oil leave-in conditioner

Improve the condition and increase the shine of your hair with these essential oils. I recommend using this at night for extra conditioning time, as the oils have relaxing, nourishing properties.

3 drops neroli oil
3 drops camomile essential oil
3 drops lavender essential oil
3 drops rosemary essential oil

Mix the ingredients in a small bowl. Shampoo your hair as normal. Towel dry and apply the mixture. Comb through and allow to dry naturally.

blonde moment

If you use products to lighten your hair and your true color is starting to show through, this mix of agents is ideal. The camomile and lemon juice work to subtly lighten your hair, and will condition colored or treated hair as well. Use also if your naturally fair hair color just needs a little brightening.

10 camomile tea bags
juice of 1 lemon
26 fl oz boiling water

Pour the water over the tea bags and allow to steep. Remove the tea bags and add the lemon juice. Allow to cool. Shampoo your hair as normal and towel dry. Pour the liquid over your hair. Some people leave the mixture in and blow-dry the hair immediately for better results.

dark-side hair colorant

Enhance the dark and mysterious side of your personality with this elderberry rinse. Elderberries also have cleansing and moisturizing properties. Use on dark hair to boost your natural color tones and give your hair a brilliant shine.

14 oz elderberries
26 fl oz water
1 tbsp cider vinegar

Add the elderberries and vinegar to the water and bring to the boil. After shampooing, pour the rinse over your hair and leave in. Dry as normal.

face and hair masks

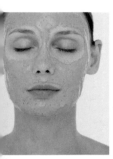

A mask made from natural ingredients is perfect for naturally beautiful hair and skin, so allow plenty of time for the nutrients to soak in and have their restorative effects. Papain, in pineapple, is a good exfoliant for flaking skin. Bananas are rich in anti-aging vitamins and other nutrients, and the rich natural oils in avocado are perfect for dry and normal hair. By mixing the right blend of ingredients, it is possible to tailor a mask for every individual skin and hair type.

face mask for normal skin

Egg and lemon together make an excellent purifying and skin-tightening mask. The lemon in particular will help abolish any occasional pimples or dry areas.

1 tbsp whisky
1 whole egg (organic free-range if possible)
1 oz non-fat dry milk powder
juice of 1 lemon

Combine all the ingredients and store in the refrigerator. When applying, spread the compound over the entire face, avoiding the eye area. Allow to dry. Remove with a damp face cloth. Use once a week.

face mask for dry skin

Use the egg yolk only—the high vitamin A content will nourish dry skin.

1 tbsp whisky
1 egg yolk (organic free-range if possible)
1 oz non-fat dry milk powder
juice of 1 lemon

Use the same method as for normal skin (above).

face mask for oily skin

Use the egg white only to help counteract pimples and treat oily skin.

1 tbsp whisky
1 egg white (organic free-range if possible)
1 oz non-fat dry milk powder
juice of 1 lemon

Use the same method as for normal skin (above).

face the day mask

Pineapple contains enzymes that not only exfoliate dry, flaky skin, but also promote healing. You can use papaya instead of pineapple, if you prefer—its enzymes perform a similar function, and can help prevent skin disorders.

1 slice ripe pineapple (or papaya)

Massage the fruit or juice onto your face. Allow to dry for about 10 minutes. Rinse with lukewarm water and pat dry. Apply your usual moisturizer for soft and smooth skin.

berry bright

Almond is a rich emollient. This face mask will help restore tone and vitality to your skin.

handful almonds
3 strawberries
½ cucumber
1 tsp honey
1 tbsp natural yogurt

Blend all the ingredients until smooth. Pull hair away from your face and apply the mixture to cleansed, damp skin. Leave for 15 minutes or until dry. Gently wipe off with a damp face cloth.

banana and cream anti-aging mask

Bananas are one of the most nourishing fruits available because they contain large quantities of magnesium, potassium, iron, zinc, iodine, and vitamins A, B (including folic acid), E, and F. Added to cream or yogurt and organic honey, this moisturizing mask makes an ideal anti-aging treatment for skin of all ages.

1 small banana
2 tbsp fresh heavy cream or natural yogurt
1 tbsp organic honey
1 tbsp oat flour
splash bottled or spring water

Mash the banana, using the back of a fork, and then add the cream or yogurt, honey, and flour. Stir the mixture. Gradually add the water, while continuing to stir. You may need to add a little more cream or yogurt or flour to obtain the consistency of heavy cream or yogurt. Apply the mask to a clean face, including the area around the eyes and the neck, and leave on for 30 minutes. Rinse off with lukewarm water and pat dry. This solution should be kept refrigerated and will last around 6 weeks.

strawberry strengthening mask *(left, below)*

Strawberries help to restore elasticity and vitality to your skin, so this recipe is just what tired-looking skin needs.

4 oz strawberries, very ripe
2½ oz cornstarch

Combine the ingredients to make a paste. Apply to the face, avoiding the delicate area around your eyes. Leave for 30 minutes and rinse off with cool water.

banana hair mask *(left, centre)*

Bananas contain minerals and other nutrients that help to restore vitality to your hair. The olive oil will replace lost oils and bring back the hair's natural shine.

1 ripe banana
1 tbsp olive oil

Mash the banana with a fork and add the oil. Apply the mixture to wet hair, from the roots to the ends. Massage all the way through your hair—give yourself a head massage! Wrap your hair in plastic wrap, or a hot towel (you can heat the towel in the microwave) and leave for 30 minutes. Rinse with warm water before shampooing and conditioning as normal.

hot hair mask

Jojoba oil is an antioxidant and contains properties to rehydrate and condition your hair and scalp. Use this hair mask treatment to restore softness to exceptionally dry hair. If your hair is dry with split ends, visit a hairdresser for a trim, then apply this mask. You'll notice the difference immediately.

3 tbsp pure jojoba oil

Warm the jojoba oil and apply it to your hair, starting at the ends and working up to the roots. Wrap your hair in a towel and relax for an hour, or leave the oil on overnight. Rinse and shampoo your hair as usual. You can do this once a week, or more often if your hair is extremely dry.

avocado hair mask *(left, top)*

Avocados are one of the miracle workers in Mother Nature's cupboard, and are packed with nutrients to maintain hair in good condition. With its natural oils, this hair mask is ideal for dry or normal hair.

1 avocado
1 tbsp olive oil (optional)

Mash the avocado, adding the oil to the mixture if desired. Apply to your hair, beginning at the roots and working toward the ends. Cover with a shower cap, and a hot towel if desired, and relax for 30 minutes. Rinse with warm water. Shampoo and condition as normal.

massage oils

Essential oils, when added to a carrier oil and used in a massage, have many therapeutic properties, including relaxation, detoxification, skin-repair, and revitalization. Essential oils can be used for face and body massage, added to a warm bath, or heated in an oil dish to release their aroma. Most oils are highly concentrated and must be diluted. Carrier (or base) oils are used to dilute the essential oils and to assist their absorption into the skin. For maximum benefit, use extra virgin or cold-pressed vegetable oils, such as mineral, grapeseed, safflower, sunflower, sesame, wheat germ, olive, and peanut oils.

STORING ESSENTIAL OILS

Store essential oils in brown or dark blue glass bottles (not plastic) with a close-fitting plastic screw-top, and place in a dark, cool place to prolong their shelf life. Keep essential oils out of the reach of children.

SAFETY PRECAUTIONS

! Essential oils are highly concentrated extracts so avoid contact with your eyes. (If any oil gets into your eyes, rinse it out with a few drops of pure sweet almond oil, not water, which does not mix with oil.) Always test first, on the inside of the arm or wrist, for possible allergic reaction. For safety, use only carrier oil when massaging around the eyes.

! Never take essential oils internally, and never apply to the skin without first diluting them in a carrier oil (see above).

! Never increase the recommended dose of essential oil.

! Do not go out in the sun for at least 6 hours after applying any of the following oils: ginger, lemon, orange, or bergamot. They can cause skin irritations if exposed to the sun.

! You should not use essential oils if you are (or might be) pregnant or are breastfeeding. Do not use on children under the age of two.

DIRECTIONS FOR USE

Blend all the ingredients well. Before using, place a few drops of the oil in the palm of one hand and warm it by gently rubbing your hands together. Ensure that the oil goes right to your fingertips. Then enjoy the self-massages and partner massages on page 126.

basic massage oil

These are the basic quantities of essential oil and carrier oil for a safe, soothing massage. Once you get accustomed to the scents of the different essential oils you can experiment until you find your perfect massage oil. A good combination is often one flower, one fruit, and one herb oil, diluted in a carrier oil.

8 tsp carrier oil of your choice
8 drops essential oil(s) of your choice

ultimate restorative

The mixture of lavender, rose, and jasmine is the perfect beauty refresher. The lavender helps to heal dry, bruised, or tired skin, as well as being a great antidote to anxiety, muscle tension, stress, and insomnia. Rose is gently uplifting and helps relieve nervous tension. The jasmine is revitalizing and produces a sense of optimism.

6 drops lavender oil
2 drops rose oil
2 drops jasmine oil
6–8 tsp grapeseed oil

sleepy head

We all know that camomile tea has soothing and soporific qualities. So what better than a bedtime massage with camomile oil to help put you in the mood for sleep? The other ingredients in this gentle blend will help to relax you and ensure that you wake up looking and feeling refreshed.

6 drops camomile oil
4 drops jasmine oil
2 drops rose oil
1 drop lavender oil
10 tsp grapeseed oil

meditative mood

The frankincense and violet oils in this blend help to induce a deep state of relaxation, and work well with the soothing properties of camomile. Violet can be used to treat various skin problems and is particularly known for its amazing ability to heal dry skin and treat bruises.

5 drops lavender oil
2 drops violet oil
2 drops camomile oil
2 drops frankincense oil
10 tsp safflower oil

something spicy

If you feel in an exotic mood, try this blend. Sandalwood has a moisturizing, tonic effect on the skin. It makes a great aftershave for men.

6 drops sandalwood oil
2 drops myrrh oil
2 drops jasmine oil
6–8 tsp grapeseed oil

stress relief

The combination of lavender, petitgrain, and frankincense in this blend makes it the perfect stress-reliever. Petitgrain is especially known for its convalescent effects on mind and body.

3 drops lavender oil
2 drops petitgrain oil
1–2 drops frankincense oil
8 tsp grapeseed oil

healing toner

This massage oil can be effective for stretch marks.

4 drops mandarin oil
1 drop fennel oil
1 drop frankincense oil
8 tsp grapeseed oil

joint relief

This blend can be added to cream or oil and applied to the skin to soothe sore and inflamed joints.

3 drops white birch oil
3 drops ginger oil
2 drops juniper oil
3 drops rosemary oil
8 tsp carrier oil of your choice, or 1 heaped tbsp scent-free moisturizing cream

cold relief

This massage oil is great if you have a cold—the scent of the eucalyptus will help clear congestion and the lavender will help you to relax. Make sure that the person receiving the massage is kept warm throughout.

2 drops eucalyptus oil
2 drops lavender oil
2 drops marjoram oil
2 drops ravensara oil
8 tsp carrier oil of your choice

happy days

Bergamot, geranium, and ylang ylang oils are particularly well known for their revitalizing and uplifting effects. All these oils are great for toning the skin.

2 drops bergamot oil
2 drops geranium oil
3 drops jasmine oil
2 drops petitgrain oil
2 drops rose oil
2 drops sandalwood oil
3 drops ylang ylang oil
10 tsp carrier oil of your choice

skin repair

Melissa oil is sometimes known as lemon balm. The oil was traditionally used in low concentration (as here) to heal eczema and other skin conditions.

2 drops geranium oil
3 drops lavender oil
2 drops marjoram oil
3 drops melissa oil
2 drops neroli oil
2 drops tangerine oil
3 drops ylang ylang oil
10 tsp carrier oil of your choice

scalp soothing

The combination of clary sage (known to help relieve cradle cap) and marjoram (which is good for relieving headaches and migraines) makes this blend perfect for a head and neck massage.

3 drops clary sage oil
3 drops lavender oil
2 drops marjoram oil
2 drops petitgrain oil
3 drops ylang ylang oil
10 tsp carrier oil of your choice

deep breath

Do not use this blend before bed, as the eucalyptus and peppermint make it mildly stimulating. However, it is also fantastic for clearing blocked sinuses and helping you to breathe deeply and calmly. If you leave out the carrier oil, you could use the blend as an inhalation (put 2–3 drops in steaming water, cover your head with a towel, and inhale the steam; stay like this for 5–10 minutes). Or, you could use it in a warm bath.

2 drops eucalyptus oil
2 drops lavender oil
2 drops peppermint oil
8 tsp carrier oil of your choice

self-massage

Receiving a massage, whether from a qualified therapist or your partner, is one of life's great delights. So, how often should you give yourself this treat? A massage is not an indulgence, but a necessity for health and well-being. When your neck is sore, your first thought is to rub it. You know, by instinct, that massage has the power to ease tension and aid healing. In fact, regular massage provides many therapeutic effects: it lowers blood pressure, boosts the circulation, eliminates toxins, prevents muscle spasms, and induces a state of mental relaxation and calm.

head massage

After a hard day's work, this form of self-massage promises to remove any lingering stresses from your body and mind. Take your time performing the massage—there's no need to rush. You can adapt the strokes to suit your needs or even make up your own.

TIP: You don't necessarily need to use oils for this massage, although you can certainly do so if you desire—you could always add them to your cleanser and perform this massage last thing at night when cleansing your skin.

step 1: Rub your hands together quickly, to create a ball of warm energy between them.

step 2: Cup your face in your hands, then slide your hands back through your hair.

step 3: Move your hands in large, rotating circles, pressing firmly against the scalp. Move your hands against your scalp—don't pull at your hair.

step 4: Press the heels of your hands against your temples, continuing the same circular movement. Leave your fingers in your hair and continue to press firmly against your scalp, rotating your fingers slowly. Continue this movement for as long as you wish.

step 5: Complete the massage by pressing firmly against the outside of your ears, ending at the earlobes. Gently tug your lobes —this restores vitality and energy.

face massage

If you've woken up looking as though you've boxed eight rounds with the world champion, this face massage is for you. It can help reduce puffiness and restore vitality to your skin.

TIP: Be careful not to tug or pull at your skin, and always work upward—against the pull of gravity!

step 1: Rest your hands on either side of your cheeks, with your fingertips resting lightly underneath your eyes. Imagine you are playing the piano and gently tap out musical scales underneath your eyes. This helps to eliminate any dark, puffy eye bags.

step 2: Lift your fingers and repeat the exercise on the area just below the previous one. Now work your way around your face: cheeks, chin, forehead, and temples.

step 3: Finish the face massage by cupping your hands over your closed eyes and breathing deeply.

step 4: Exhale. When ready, remove your hands and slowly open your eyes.

hand massage

The hands and arms take the brunt of everyday life. Yet we don't always give them the care and attention they deserve. Take time to appreciate them: don't just concentrate on hands and nails; stretch and relax the joints and muscles as well. Some therapists believe the hands are like a body map. Areas of the hands relate to specific body regions. By massaging the corresponding area on your hands you can alleviate pain or fatigue in those body regions.

TIP: If you're feeling fatigued or don't have time for a full massage, or even a short meditation, lightly hold the middle joint of your left middle finger between thumb and index finger. Maintain this hold for a few minutes. Repeat with the other hand.

step 1: With your left palm facing down, place your right hand on top of your left hand and grip the side firmly, kneading the top of the hand and the knuckles.

step 2: Turning your left hand over, cup the hand, and slowly but firmly knead the palm and joints with your right thumb.

step 3: Hold and gently pull each finger, working your way toward the fingernail. When you reach the fingernail, press hard on the nail, then quickly release it. This encourages energy to flow through the hand and should make you feel more alert.

step 4: Repeat the massage on the right hand.

step 5: To finish, link your fingers, turn your hands away from you and then straighten your arms. Try to stretch your fingers as far forward as you can.

foot massage

I find that most people are either "hands" or "feet" people—they prefer one or the other to be massaged. A foot massage can feel as beneficial and relaxing as a full-body massage, because your foot represents your entire body, including your internal organs, spine, and head.

TIP: *If you suffer from insomnia, give yourself a foot massage about 20 minutes before you go to bed. Add a few drops of lavender oil to a carrier massage oil, and knead your feet. This is an easy method of inducing relaxation and eliminating stress.*

step 1: Sit comfortably, to avoid getting cramp in your foot or hip. Choose a massage oil or body lotion, whichever you prefer, to add some much-needed moisture to your neglected soles and heels.

step 2: Rest your foot on the opposite knee and cup the toes and ball of your foot with your hands.

step 3: With your thumbs, press firmly in small circular motions, beginning at the base of the toes, slowly repeating the circles and working your way toward the heel.

step 4: Rub your heel firmly and slowly to release any stiffness or soreness caused by walking and standing.

step 5: Repeat the motion on the tops of your feet, working your way from your ankle toward your toes.

step 6: When you reach your toes, hold each toe individually, and gently massage it, pulling the toe outward.

step 7: At each toenail, press hard, before abruptly releasing the pressure. Repeat with the other foot.

simple stress-busters

Biologically, stress is a fact of life. In times past, stress hormones enabled us to hunt, and to survive in the face of danger. However, owing to our modern hectic lifestyles, and our continual need to be "alert," our bodies rarely have time to rest, and so we carry raised levels of adrenaline within our systems for long periods. Each time we are faced with a stressful situation, at work or at home, our adrenaline levels rise even higher. Scientists say that it's necessary —even healthy—to have some stress in our lives, but it's important to maintain some control over the level of stress we face each day. Excessive stress can cause heart disease, an impaired immune system, digestive problems, anxiety, depression, and feelings of helplessness or excessive anger.

importance of relaxation

Relaxation is the most important tool we possess in dealing with stress. Our problems are not likely to disappear overnight. But we can arm ourselves with the correct tools to reduce stress levels.

ARE YOU SUFFERING FROM STRESS?

Do you:
- have moist palms, feet, or underarms?
- have a fast pulse?
- have cold hands or feet?
- experience difficulty falling or staying asleep?
- experience shortness of breath?
- suffer from headaches?
- suffer from indigestion?
- suffer from asthma or hay fever flare-ups?
- suffer from constipation or diarrhea?

If you answer yes to three or more of these questions, you may need to take some time out to help your body recover from the effects of stress. Chronic stress, if allowed to go uncontrolled, poses a serious threat to health.

When did you last feel truly relaxed? The chances are your memory of relaxation is as distant as last year's vacation. Amid an already towering list of demands, we just don't seem to have time to relax.

Taking time to relax is as important as eating well. A relaxed body deflects illness and heals faster than one addled with stress. Relaxation prevents tension pain, as the muscles are no longer bunched like clenched fists. Best of all, a relaxed body and mind shows in the face, making you look healthier and more revitalized. You not only appear younger, but act younger too, as your body recovers energy normally channeled toward dealing with stress.

If you're reading this and thinking, "but I do relax," yet still are showing signs of excessive stress, it's likely that your version of relaxation is far removed from the type of relaxation your body really needs. If you consider relaxation to be a few hours in front of the TV after work, and drinking a couple of glasses of wine before collapsing into bed, you're actually doing more harm than good to your body. True relaxation time is quiet, calm time—just for you. It doesn't necessarily have to be hours of meditative silence: even a five-minute relaxation break can do you, your body, and your mind the world of good.

breathe for health and beauty

We breathe around 30,000 times a day, yet most of us do so incorrectly. Breathing well is the simplest way to relieve tension in body and mind. A deep breath pumps oxygen into the bloodstream for an instant injection of health that permeates throughout the body. One deep breath will clear your mind, reawaken your brain, and relax you completely.

Place one hand on your chest and the other on your navel and take a deep breath. If the lower hand doesn't move, you're not breathing deeply enough. Now take in a long, deep breath. As you breathe in, feel your abdomen rise and your fingertips part. Whenever you feel stressed, take time to check your breathing. If you've moved the focus of your breathing back to your chest area, spend time correcting your breathing technique. Eventually, you'll breathe correctly naturally; it just takes time and practice.

breathing exercise

Do this exercise whenever you feel that things are getting on top of you. Find a quiet spot to sit. You can sit cross-legged, or with your back to a wall, as long as your feet are resting comfortably on the floor and your back is straight.

● Let your breathing slow naturally.
● Place your hands side by side on your abdomen, fingertips meeting just below the navel.
● Take a deep breath through your nose and feel the oxygen reaching all parts of the lungs. Feel your abdomen rise under your fingers. Breathe out and feel your hands fall. Repeat this five times. Now let your breathing return to its natural rhythm.

You could include an affirmation, or positive thought, in this process to help you achieve a current goal. For instance, if you are about to go into a difficult meeting, say, "I am strong and talented and admired," with every in-breath. If you're feeling vulnerable, repeat "I am love," to create a feeling of love and warmth.

meditation for health and beauty

Daily meditation is another powerful tool to help you manage stress. It is important for well-being, helping to lower blood pressure, reduce stress, and eliminate fine lines and wrinkles. Meditating for as little as five minutes a day can be beneficial, but when possible aim for 20 minutes for a total mind massage.

Sit or lie comfortably. Close your eyes and begin the breathing exercise (above). Allow your thoughts to release with each exhalation. It may help to focus on a number or word so that your mind doesn't wander. Or try counting: with the first out-breath, count one, the next breath, two, and so on up to ten. Whenever your mind wanders, go back to one and start counting again. If you find it impossible to still your mind when your eyes are closed, try this method: light a candle and stare into the center of the flame. Blink when necessary and let your breathing be calm and steady.

home spa

If you've been lucky enough to spend a day or so at a health spa, you'll know that the relaxed and revitalized feeling you have at the end of your visit is unparalleled. The good news is that you don't have to spend a lot of money to enjoy bliss like this—with a little planning and the right supplies, you can achieve nirvana within your own four walls. Below are some guidelines to help you prepare for the perfect pampering spa day!

WHAT YOU'LL NEED TO DO

● Compile your shopping list (see the list opposite). Ensure that any items you need to buy are purchased in advance.

● Collect all the ingredients you need to prepare your chosen meals. Include lots of fresh fruits and vegetables—it may be your day of relaxation, but it's not intended to be for total indulgence!

● Prepare some drinks for the day. If you think you'll be bored drinking only water, add some strawberries or mint leaves to give taste and variety. If you plan to drink fresh juices and smoothies, buy your favorite fruits—ready to juice or blend just before drinking. Stock up on herbal teas as well. Try peppermint or green tea— these are good for the digestion and have calming properties.

● Prepare any beauty treatments, such as face and hair masks, cleanser, and moisturizer, that you plan to use, the night before.

● Prepare and bottle your favorite massage oil in advance.

● Stock up on tealights, candles, essential oils, or incense sticks to create a calming and relaxing ambience.

● If you have a problem or other issue that you'd like to work through, have a notebook and pen handy to jot down ideas and solutions as they come to you throughout the day.

● Create an oasis in just one room in your home: it can be your bedroom, living room, or your bathroom, if it is large enough.

● If you decide you want to have a solitary spa day, you need to ensure that you won't be interrupted. If possible, switch your telephone to answer machine. Don't turn on your TV or the computer. Switch the radio to a classical or easy-listening music station or stockpile some of your favorite, soothing CDs.

● Wear whatever you like, but just make sure it's comfortable. It doesn't matter how you look.

YOUR SPA DAY SHOPPING LIST

Plan to eat light meals and have plenty of water, herbal teas, and freshly made juices and smoothies throughout the day. You could use some of the recipes included in this book.

Your food for the day—compile a separate shopping list

Fresh flowers
A selection of herbal teas (including camomile)
An aromatherapy burner
Tealights, candles, and matches
A loofah or natural-bristle brush
An exercise video/CD (such as yoga or pilates)
Some relaxing music
A good book or a copy of your favorite magazine
Essential oils: grapefruit or lemon, lavender, camomile
A manicure and pedicure kit (nail clippers, emery boards, cuticle remover, orange sticks etc), plus a nail polish

Beauty products—you can prepare all/some of your treatments using recipes included in this book
    Facial cleanser
    Facial toner
    Facial moisturizer
    Face mask
    Body oil/cream plus a lighter lotion
    Hot oil treatment or conditioning mask for hair
    Relaxing bath oil

YOUR SPA DAY TIMETABLE

8.30 am: Try not to have too much of a lie-in, as you'll just feel drowsy and unmotivated. Start the day slowly with a cup of hot water and lemon—it'll kick-start your digestive system and is a good way to clear your skin if you suffer from repeated pimples.

9.30 am: Put some boiling water in an aromatherapy burner and add a few drops of grapefruit or lemon essential oils. These oils are relaxing and help to create clear, inspired thoughts. Sit calmly on a comfortable cushion and focus on the relaxation time ahead.

9.50 am: If you know yoga, perform a sun salutation. Repeat 10 times. Otherwise, try a little stretching. Reach both hands above your head, link hands, and stretch toward the ceiling. Then place your right foot behind your left. Reach your right hand above your head, toward the left. Swap legs and repeat on the opposite side.

10 am: Head to the bathroom for your morning ritual. Use a loofah or natural-bristle brush and body brush for at least 5 minutes. Always stroke toward the heart. Hop into the shower and wash your hair and cleanse your face and body. If you can bear it, turn the water to cold just before you emerge to sharpen your mind.

10.15 am: Apply body oil or body cream to your towel-dried body. Apply a hot oil or mask to your hair and wrap your hair in a heated towel. Get dressed in your day's clothing and head to the kitchen.

10.20 am: Make yourself a fruit salad, juice, or smoothie.

11 am: It's time to get moving! If you have an exercise video, or yoga or pilates tape or CD, play it and do at least 40 minutes of movement. Keep some herbal tea or water handy and sip slowly.

12 noon: Drink another cup of herbal tea or water. Spend some time focusing on how you're feeling. If your mind is busy with thoughts of tasks you must do, write them down in a list. If you have any particular worries, write those down too, along with any solutions that may ensue. Now fold the paper in half and put it aside to look at tomorrow. Today is a day of mental stillness and reflection, not action!

12.30 pm: Time for lunch. If you enjoy cooking, prepare one of the recipes in this book. But don't eat it off your lap in front of the TV. If you have a garden and it's a nice day, sit outside and savor every mouthful. Alternatively, set the table as though you were expecting guests. Set cutlery, condiments, even flowers if you like. Pour yourself a large glass of water, and enjoy your meal.

1.30 pm: Go for a walk around the block or in a nearby park. Or do some stretches, concentrating on clearing and focusing your mind.

2 pm: Sit in a comfortable position and slowly sip a herbal tea.

2.30 pm: Now it's time for some serious pampering. Cleanse your face using a suitable cleanser and pat dry. Apply a face mask, taking care to cover your neck and decolletage. Return to your spa room and lie down somewhere comfortable, making sure your back and neck are well supported. If you prefer, cover yourself with a light blanket. Try one of the breathing exercises on page 128.

3.30 pm: Bring yourself back to consciousness slowly, bringing awareness first to your arms and legs, then your body, neck, and face. Slowly shake your arms and legs and sit up. When you feel ready, stand up and pour yourself another drink of water.

4 pm: Rinse the mask off your face, and apply toner and moisturizer to your face, neck, and chest area.

4.30 pm: Pamper your hands and feet with a manicure and pedicure—using your favorite polish—to salon standard!

5 pm: Time for another stretch and a glass of water.

5.30 pm: You've got an hour before dinner, so make yourself comfortable on the sofa and read a favorite book or magazine.

6.30 pm: Prepare a light, tasty, and nutritious meal. Don't have anything too heavy—fish, chicken, or a salad is ideal.

7.30 pm: Run yourself a warm bath and add some relaxing oils, such as lavender. Turn up the music, light some candles or tealights, and immerse yourself fully in the bath. Enjoy the warmth and aroma for at least 20 minutes before getting out and drying yourself from head to toe. Apply body lotion and put on comfortable pajamas. If your hair is wet, dry it fully. If you like, give yourself a head, face, hand, or foot massage (see page 126). Scatter a few drops of camomile or lavender oil on your pillow and bedsheets and make yourself a cup of camomile tea.

9 pm: It's early, but it's time to hop into bed. Listen to some music or read for about 20 minutes before setting these aside and turning off the light. Enjoy a restful night's sleep and look forward to a new, revitalized you tomorrow morning!

7-day diet and treatment plan

I've found that if you enjoy living and eating healthily, it is not a chore—just a way of life. I hope you find this true for you. If you're truly dedicated to turning over a new leaf, I've devised a seven-day diet and treatment plan to help you get started. You know how great you feel after a vacation? Well, I hope that after seven days of feel-good treatments and healthy meals, you'll look and feel as if you've had that longed-for break.

day one

MORNING TREATMENT

As it's the first morning, greet the day with a smile. Even if you feel grumpy, this can trick your brain into releasing the "happy hormone," serotonin. Very soon you'll start to mean it!

breakfast: *fresh fruit salad (page 92)*
lunch: *chicken salad with soy dressing (page 102)*
dinner: *baked fillet of sole (page 107)*

EVENING TREATMENT

Facial exercises are designed to tone and strengthen the muscles. You can do these exercises while cleansing your face if you like. Add 2 drops of lavender oil to your cleanser to aid relaxation. Place the pads of three fingers of both hands on the area between your eyebrows, pressing lightly. Hold the pressure for a few seconds, then sweep your fingers toward your temples, pressing firmly all the time. Massage the temples with small circular movements.

day two

MORNING TREATMENT

Start the day by gently stretching from head to toe. Now sit at the side of your bed and slowly roll your head to your left shoulder,

then forward to your chest, then to your right shoulder. Repeat in reverse. Stand up and stretch your arms above your head, first the right hand, then the left. You should now feel awake and refreshed.

breakfast: *oatmeal with mixed fruit (page 93)*
lunch: *couscous medley (page 106)*
dinner: *marinated chicken with prune salsa (page 106)*

EVENING TREATMENT

The build-up of daily tensions places strains on our muscles, tendons, and joints. Relieve the day's stresses with a relaxing self-massage. Locate the site of tension (for example, shoulders, or lower back) and, using your favorite massage oil, gently rub the area. Feel your body relax.

day three

MORNING TREATMENT

Boost your circulation and improve the texture of your skin with skin brushing. Daily skin brushing, using a loofah or long-handled natural-bristle brush, will remove dead cells and unblock pores, as well as kick-starting the lymph system. Start from the soles of your feet and always brush toward your heart.

breakfast: *get up and glow (page 114)*
lunch: *vegetarian flan (page 99)*
dinner: *fruit and nut risotto (page 111)*

EVENING TREATMENT

This is my favorite end-of-day wind-down. Light a few candles, and play a soothing CD. To a warm bath, add 1 lb Epsom salts, with a few drops of relaxing essential oil. If you like, apply the Berry Bright face mask (page 122) and relax for 20 minutes. Bliss!

day four

MORNING TREATMENT

Add 1 drop of lemon essential oil, 1 drop of orange essential oil, and 1 drop of grapefruit essential oil to a vaporizer dish. Add warm water and light the candle. These oils are very invigorating and will get you going even on the coldest of mornings!

breakfast: *oatmeal with prunes and apricots (page 92)*
lunch: *mediterranean oven-roasted vegetable soup (page 94)*
dinner: *salmon steaks with sesame seed crusts (page 109)*

EVENING TREATMENT

Time for a steam! Cleanse with one of the toners suitable for your skin type, followed by the Strawberry Steam Cleanser (page 117) for a healthy glow.

day five

MORNING TREATMENT

Add 5 drops of rosemary essential oil to a bowl or basin of lukewarm water and, after your morning cleanse, splash your face several times. Rosemary is a great wake-up call for your skin.

breakfast: *alpine muesli with red and green grapes (page 93)*
lunch: *large shrimp and noodle soup (page 96)*
dinner: *exotic kedgeree (page 107)*

EVENING TREATMENT

Hold back the hands of time with a once-weekly anti-aging mask. After cleansing and toning, apply the Banana and Cream Anti-Aging Mask (page 122) and leave for 20 minutes. You can spend the time relaxing in a warm bath, or catching up on your correspondence, or even doing a bit of housework! Remove with cool water and apply your moisturizer immediately afterward.

day six

MORNING TREATMENT

If you've been skin brushing faithfully, your body should be feeling smooth and silky. But what about your face? Add some sugar to your cleanser and exfoliate for a baby-smooth face and neck.

breakfast: *strawberry spread (page 93)*
lunch: *tofu vegetable salad (page 102)*
dinner: *seafood pasta pesto (page 107)*

EVENING TREATMENT

Give your hair a treat and apply the Hot Hair Mask (page 123). Simply apply, wrap a warm towel around your hair, and leave for 20 minutes, or overnight if you prefer.

day seven

You've worked hard all week, so take your time with a long pampering session. Apply the Face the Day Mask (page 122) and leave it on while you read the papers. Rinse with warm water and pat dry. Apply your moisturizer for silky, smooth, radiant skin.

breakfast: *weekend omelet (page 93)*
lunch: *lima bean, tomato, and rocket salad (page 104)*
dinner: *pork fillets with date and hazelnut stuffing (page 106)*

EVENING TREATMENT

Switch off from the world and give yourself some special "me" time. Apply your favorite nourishing mask, exfoliate your entire body—including your feet, and you could even give yourself a manicure and pedicure.

detox

A few years ago, if you had mentioned detoxification—"detox"—most people would have thought you had an addiction to alcohol, cigarettes, or drugs. Today, detox has been hailed as the healthiest program you can put your body through, with impressive and long-lasting results. Whether you've been burning the candle at both ends, over indulging in alcohol and rich foods, or you just feel like giving your body a thorough "spring clean," a detox is an excellent way to kick-start a new health regime.

Toxicity, both internal and external, is a modern health concern. The incidence of many toxicity diseases—including obesity, skin allergies, and cancer—has increased in recent years. A toxin is basically any substance that creates irritating and/or harmful effects in the body, undermining your health or stressing the functioning of your internal organs and biochemical processes.

Through detoxification you clear and filter toxins and wastes and allow your body to enhance its basic functions, and so work more efficiently. Among its many benefits, a detox can increase your energy levels, alleviate fatigue, and promote weight loss.

At some time in our lives, almost everyone needs to detox, cleanse their body, and give their bodily functions a rest. Your body has a daily elimination cycle, mostly carried out at night and in the early morning up until you eat your first meal of the day. If you follow a regular, balanced diet, devoid of excesses, you'll need less intensive detoxification. However, when you eat a congesting diet high in fats, meat, dairy products, refined foods, and chemicals, detoxification becomes more necessary.

People with addictions to any substance may benefit from a detox program. Withdrawal symptoms that commonly occur with products including sugar, caffeine, and over-the-counter medications are precipitated by detoxification. Many of the toxins that we ingest or make are stored in the fatty tissues, which is why being overweight can indicate toxic overload.

However, although losing weight is a good method of detoxifying, during weight loss you tend to release more toxins, and thus need to give yourself extra protection by increasing your intake of water, fiber, and antioxidant nutrients, such as vitamins C and E, beta carotene, selenium, and zinc.

REASONS TO DETOX

You should detox if: you feel exhausted when you wake in the morning—despite having eight hours' sleep; you are constipated; your skin is pimply, particularly around the mouth and jawline; your eyes are constantly bloodshot; you drink more than 20 units of alcohol per week; you rarely, if ever, exercise; or you drink less than six glasses of water a day.

WHEN IS THE BEST TIME TO DETOXIFY?

We need to incorporate nature's cycles within our own cycles. We may notice that we have regular periods of congestion, and we may reduce or prevent these by following a more intensive detox program. Feeling tired or run-down, being constipated, bloated, or overweight are all signs that it is a good time to detoxify.

For women there is a particular need to detoxify for a few days a month in time with the menstrual cycle. But the seasonal cycle is the most important with regard to natural detoxification periods. Seasonal changes are the key stress times when we most need to reduce our consumption. If we can harmonize with these periods, we can do much to improve our health.

Warning: an intensive detox program is designed for a person who is healthy and eats well. Pregnant or lactating women should not take part in a strict detox program. Anyone with an on-going medical condition, such as diabetes or digestive or eating disorders, should seek specialist medical advice before considering a major dietary change.

THE LIVER

The liver is your most important detox organ because of its vital role in metabolism. It needs water and glycogen (the form in which glucose is stored) as glucuronic acid for many of its detoxification functions. A higher starch or carbohydrate diet with lower levels of protein and fats is helpful. This plan correlates with most detox diets. The B vitamins, especially B3 and B6; vitamins A, C, and E; the minerals calcium, selenium, and zinc; and L-cysteine are also needed to support liver detoxification. The herb milk thistle is believed to be particularly important for cleansing the liver.

MOVE YOUR BODY

Regular exercise is important to stimulate sweating and so improve waste elimination through the skin. Exercise also improves your metabolism generally and so aids overall detoxification. Regular aerobic exercise is the key to maintaining a "nontoxic" body, especially when you have over indulged with certain toxic substances. As with weight loss, exercise increases the release of toxins in the body, so it must be accompanied by an adequate intake of fluids, antioxidants, vitamins, and minerals.

BATHING AND BODY BRUSHING

Regular bathing is essential to open the pores and cleanse the skin of the toxins it has released. Saunas and sweatrooms are commonly used to help purify the body through enhanced skin elimination. Dry brushing the skin with a pure-bristle skin brush before bathing will cleanse the skin of old cells and invigorate the outer tissues. Exfoliation with a mild body scrub also removes dead skin cells and boosts circulation.

FOODS TO AVOID

Avoid or minimize your intake of foods such as red meat, cured meat, offal, refined and canned products, sugar, salt, saturated fats, and stimulants such as coffee, alcohol, and nicotine. All these substances place your digestive system under severe strain and may rob your body of vital nutrients.

YOUR DETOX DIET

Many nutritionists recommend a 28-day detox. Such a month-long program, whereby you are dedicated solely to rejuvenating your body, is ideal, but if you have a busy lifestyle, eat out frequently for business, or travel regularly, sticking to a strict detox diet may be difficult. Start with a week-long diet and follow the seven-day detox plan outlined on the following pages. Your diet should consist of high water content foods, such as cucumbers, bell peppers, onions, zucchini, celery, beans, tomatoes, lemons, and other fruits. Choosing organic foods during your detox (and indeed including as much as possible in everyday cooking) will reduce the amount of pesticides and artificial colorings your body ingests. If you find the detox plan relatively easy to keep to, continue it for another 14 days. From then on, it's permissible to reintroduce other foods, but take it slowly, so as not to overload your newly cleansed system.

Drink as much water as possible. If you already drink the recommended amount of 3 pints, or about eight glasses, of water each day, try adding another four glasses to this quota. You'll not only flush out the toxins in your body more quickly, but you'll also feel full, leaving you less likely to crave candy.

7-day detox plan

There's no denying that a detox program is highly beneficial, providing it is done sensibly. A bodily "spring clean" reduces the strain on your digestive system, enabling it to renew itself, and so prepare for optimum functioning.

The following seven-day detox plan includes a one-day fast (on day four). If you are well nourished and in generally good health, you can easily go without food for a day without ill-effects—provided you drink lots of fluids. But you may find you have less energy than usual, so aim to detox during a vacation or over a long weekend, when there are no demands on your time and you'll have a chance to take it easy.

You may notice you get a mild headache at some point during this detox. This is partly owing to your going without caffeinated drinks, such as tea, coffee, and colas, as headache is a frequent symptom of caffeine withdrawal. If you have been thinking about giving up cigarettes, why not do it now? To help you get started with your detox plan, I have listed a selection of recipes (see opposite page) that you can try for the different days of the diet. Each of the recipes is cross-referenced and can be found in this book. The recipes may include foods you've not tried before. Give them a go, and if you like them, you might want to include them in your diet on a regular basis.

Warning: this detox plan is not suitable for anyone with an eating disorder, or those such as diabetics, who must keep to a medical diet plan.

day one

The following are now on your "banned" list: ready-cooked meals, fast food, fried food, high-fat foods, added salt and sugar, chocolate, tea, coffee, alcohol, and cigarettes. Otherwise, choose any of the recipes in this book.

day two

Cut out eggs, meat, wheat products, potatoes, and dairy products (except bio or live yogurt). Include any of the following: rice, steamed fish, shellfish, lentils, millet, quinoa, soy products (including tofu, soy flour, and soy milk), olive oil, plain unsweetened bio or live yogurt, and as many fresh fruits and vegetables as you like. See the eating plan opposite for some suggested daily recipes that are suitable. Drink plenty of water, herbal teas, soy milk, and fresh fruit or vegetable juices. Or for a change, you might like to try dandelion tea, or Caro—a caffeine-free coffee substitute.

day three

Eat only fresh fruit (excluding citrus) and vegetables, and drink plenty of water, herbal teas, soy milk, and fruit or vegetable juices.

day four

This is the day of your fast, so avoid solid food but be sure to drink plenty of fluids (about 7 pints) including water, herbal teas, and fresh fruit (excluding citrus) and vegetable juices.

day five

As for day three.

day six

As for day two.

day seven

As for day one.

From now on, you can revert to your normal diet if you like, but to get the most out of this detox plan, try to include as many of the "good" foods listed for day two (especially fresh fruits and vegetables, and the juices made from them) and curb or end your consumption of items on the "banned" list.

SUGGESTED RECIPES FOR THE 7-DAY DETOX PLAN

Here are some suggested recipes for the detox diet. Some of the recipes will need modifying slightly to make them suitable for inclusion in your detox plan, and I have indicated any adjustments you will need to make alongside each recipe. Below are some general guidelines to help you tailor other recipes in this book, or indeed any other recipes that appeal to you, to your detox diet.

- Substitute semi-skimmed or skimmed milk with soy milk.
- Use unsweetened bio or live yogurt in recipes using yogurt.
- Use soy cream rather than créme fraîche or any other cream.
- Some recipes may include a small amount of sugar to sweeten, you can simply omit the sugar.
- Recipes often include salt for seasoning—omit this ingredient.
- Serving suggestions may include items on your "banned" list, such as cheese, mayonnaise, cream, sugar, or chocolate—you should always skip this option!

days one and seven

breakfasts: *fresh fruit salad (page 92), smooth and sweet honey and berries (page 93), smoked haddock kedgeree with grilled tomatoes (page 93), weekend omelet (page 93)*

soups: *carrot soup (page 94), leek and lentil soup (page 96), vegetable and bean soup (page 96), large shrimp and noodle soup (page 96)*

appetizers/salads: *bruschetta with olives and tomatoes (page 97), fresh fruit with maple-vanilla yogurt dip (page 98), steamed lemon grass chicken and rice rolls (page 98), stuffed bell peppers (page 99), vegetarian flan (page 99)*

main courses, side dishes, and salads: *tofu vegetable salad (page 102), shredded beet and feta salad (page 105), marinated chicken with prune salsa (pages 106–7), rice jumble (page 109), fish in sleeping bags (page 110)*

dessert: *summer pudding—serve with bio or live yogurt and resist the sprinkling of confectioner's sugar (page 113)*

juices and herbal drinks: *get up and glow (page 114), strawberry starter smoothie (page 114)*

days two and six

breakfasts: *oatmeal with prunes and apricots—use soy milk, and don't add any sugar (page 92), oatmeal with mixed fruit—don't add any sugar (page 93), alpine muesli with red and green grapes—substitute skimmed milk with soy milk (page 93), strawberry spread—use plain, unsweetened bio or live yogurt (page 93)*

soups: *mediterranean oven-roasted vegetable soup—be sure to use soy cream rather than créme fraîche (page 94), Thai sweet and sour soup (page 95), mushroom and bean soup (page 95)*

appetizers/salads: *baby spinach and radicchio salad (page 97), mixed garlic mushrooms (page 98), back-eyed peas and walnut spread (page 98), tasty tuna snack—don't add any mayonnaise (page 99)*

main courses, side dishes, and salads: *tofu vegetable salad—omit the Parmesan cheese (page 102), warm chickpea and tuna salad (page 105), multicolored rice salad (page 105), mussels in ginger and lemon grass broth (page 107), salmon steaks with sesame seed crusts (page 109)—serve with lemon parsley-dill marinade (page 101), tofu risotto—exclude the Gloucester cheese and don't add salt to season (page 110), mixed vegetable skewers (page 111)—serve with ginger marinade sauce (page 101)*

dessert: *fresh fruit salad—substitute natural yogurt with plain, unsweetened bio or live yogurt (page 92)*

juices and herbal drinks: *skin healer (page 114), an apple a day (page 115), great start (page 115)*

days three and five

juices and herbal drinks: *green machine (page 114), hard as nails (page 114), perfect start (page 114), perfect skin (page 115), happy and healthy (page 115)*

glossary

words in **bold** type also appear in this glossary

ALMOND MEAL, also referred to as almond flour, almond meal is used in many low carbohydrate recipes. It can be used as a whole or part substitute for many other higher carbohydrate flours in baking and cooking.

ALPHA-HYDROXY ACIDS (AHAs) these are naturally occurring acids, derived from the sugars in particular plants. For example: glycolic acid (sugar cane), lactic acid (milk), tartaric acid (grapes), citric acid (citrus fruits), malic acid (apples), and mandelic acid (bitter almonds). These acids aid skin maintenance by dissolving the cement that holds dead skin cells together, increasing cell turnover.

ANTHOCYANINS dark blue **antioxidants** that may reduce the "stickiness" of blood platelets and help prevent blood clots.

ANTI-MICROBIAL destroying or inhibiting **microbe** growth.

ANTIOXIDANT substance (nutrient or enzyme) that can "disarm" an oxidant—antioxidants neutralize the potentially damaging effects of oxidation. Key antioxidants are vitamins A, C, and E. Fresh fruit and vegetables, nuts, seeds, and wholegrains are all particularly rich sources of antioxidants.

ARYTENOIDS either of the two small laryngeal cartilages attached to the vocal cords.

AYURVEDA a traditional Indian **holistic** system of medicine and health care. The sanskrit term "Ayurveda" is composed of two words "ayus" (life) and "veda" (knowledge) and so the literal meaning of Ayurveda is science of life.

B-COMPLEX VITAMINS these consist of all the known water-soluble vitamins except vitamin C. Among the many functions of B-complex are energy production, metabolism, and cell division. A deficiency in one B vitamin often means that intake of all B vitamins is low.

BERGAMOT this is an **essential oil** that is traditionally used to treat acne, boils, cold sores, eczema, insect bites (or for use as insect repellent), oily complexion, psoriasis, scabies, varicose veins, ulcers, wounds, sore throats, thrush, infectious diseases, and depression. If using this oil to treat a specific problem area, do not expose the area of application to sunlight for 24 hours, owing to its phototoxicity.

BORAX POWDER also known as sodium borate, it can be used in emulsifying lotions containing beeswax, or mixed with water for household cleaning.

BROMELAIN a protein-digesting enzyme found in pineapple. It mimics the action of pancreatic enzymes and may reduce inflammation and swelling.

CAROTENOIDS pigments with strong **antioxidant** properties found in brightly-colored plant foods. They are converted into vitamin A in the body. Carotenoids include carotene (found in orange plant foods) and beta carotene (found in dark yellow and green plant foods).

CASTILE SOAP a gentle-cleansing hard soap, made almost entirely of water and olive oil.

ENDOCRINE SYSTEM regulates growth, digestion, and reproduction by controlling hormone levels in the body. It relies on endocrine glands that secrete substances directly into the bloodstream rather than through ducts.

ESSENTIAL FATTY ACIDS (EFAs) a group of fats (oils) essential for many vital functions, including healthy brain and nerve cells, balanced hormones, energy production, and well hydrated skin. EFAs cannot be created by the body, only obtained from the diet. Rich sources include nuts, seeds, and oily fish.

ESSENTIAL OILS also known as volatile oils, these are strong-smelling oils that give plants their characteristic odor and have many pharmacological actions.

FERMENTABLE CARBOHYDRATES comprise sucrose, glucose, fructose, lactose, galactose, maltose, and cooked starch. These are easily or relatively easily fermented by cardiogenic **microbes** in vivo and serve as substrates for bacterial acid production.

FLAVANOIDS a group of bio-active compounds, including quercetin, kempferol, rutin, and hesperidin with **antioxidant**, diuretic, and other wide-ranging properties. They reduce blood-cholesterol levels, and may protect against heart disease and some cancers.

FREE RADICALS by-products of metabolism that can cause

damage to cell membranes by oxidation of fatty acids. Free radicals are neutralized by **antioxidants**.

GAMMA-LINOLENIC ACID (GLA) is an **essential fatty acid (EFA)** in the omega-6 family that is primarily found in vegetable oils. EFAs are needed for normal brain function, growth, and development, bone health, stimulation of skin and hair growth, regulation of metabolism, and maintenance of reproductive processes.

GLUTATHIONE a **free-radical** scavenger dependent on selium for its **antioxidant** activity.

HOLISTIC the organic or functional relation between parts and the whole—for example, treating the mind and body as one.

HYDROLIPID SYSTEM maintains the pH value of the skin at the desired level of pH 5.5 and promotes cell regeneration.

IMMUNOSURVEILLANCE a term which is used to describe the immune system's role in cancer.

KERATIN a fibrous protein occurring in hair and nails.

KETONES compounds containing a carbonyl group attached to two hydrocarbon radicals. Ketones are very reactive substances. The simplest ketone is acetone (propanone).

LYMPHATIC SYSTEM the system of glands and vessels that drains fluid from the tissues of the body together with dead cells and bacteria.

MAY CHANG this **essential oil** is pale yellow in color with a lemony fresh and fruity scent. It is most valued for its anti-inflammatory and calming properties. It is also astringent, antiseptic, and hypotensive and can be used as an insecticide, stimulant, and tonic.

MICROBE a microorganism, or more commonly, germ.

MONOUNSATURATED OILS (OR MONOUNSATURATED FAT) a fatty acid that contains one double-bond in its carbon chain. Olive oil is a particularly rich source of monounsaturated fatty acids, which are also found in many animal, fish, and vegetable fats.

NEROLI an **essential oil** also known as orange blossom, as it comes from the white blossoms of a bitter orange tree. It has excellent anti-depressant qualities, and helps counteract anxiety, insomnia, and hysteria. It can also relieve dermatitis (dry skin) and premenstrual or menopausal symptoms.

OMEGA-6 AND OMEGA-3 These are **EFAs** made of unsaturated fatty acids. Omega-6 contains linolenic acid and is abundant in vegetable oils. Omega-3 contains alpha-linolenic acid, which is rarer in a modern diet and more beneficial than omega-6. These **EFAs** are best consumed in a ratio of 3:1.

PETITGRAIN is an **essential oil** extracted from twigs of a bitter orange tree. It is effective for treating low energy, insomnia, and fatigue; and also for relieving backache and muscular or nervous tension.

PHENOLIC ACIDS substances found in freshly picked vegetables and fruits, wines, and teas that encourage detoxification and inhibit the formation of cancer cells.

PHYTOCHEMICAL LYCOPENE this has been found to be the most powerful **antioxidant** of the dietary **carotenoids**. It is responsible for the red coloring in some fruit, such as tomatoes. It is believed to protect against several cancers, muscular degeneration, and heart disease.

PHYTONUTRIENTS nutritionally-important compounds found only in plants.

PROANTHOCYANIDINS belonging to the **flavonoid** family, they are one of the most effective **free-radical** scavengers known. Proanthocyanidins aid cell membranes, providing nutritional support to reduce capillary permeability and fragility. They also play a role in the stabilization of collagen and maintenance of elastin—two critical proteins in connective tissue that support organs, joints, blood vessels, and muscle.

PROSTAGLANDINS a group of complex fatty acids found in most human tissue. Prostaglandins act as local tissue hormones, regulating blood supply, acid secretion of the stomach, vascular permeability, platelet aggregation, and temperature regulation.

RAVENSARA this **essential oil** is referred to by Madagascans as "the oil that heals" owing to its antiseptic activity, as well as its help with respiratory problems. It is anti-infectious, antiviral, antibacterial, expectorant, and supporting to the nerves.

SEBACEOUS GLAND a skin gland associated with hair follicles. It produces sebum (an oily substance that protects against bacteria and lubricates the hair and skin).

SEROTONIN A mood-boosting neurotransmitter that is involved in numerous processes in the body, including sending out the signals that control appetite. Serotonin is derived from the amino acid **trytophan**.

TRYTOPHAN an amino acid that can be converted into vitamin B3 in the body. Can help to alleviate migraine and premenstrual tension.

index

Bold numbers indicate main
    entries

bibliography

Amanda Cochrane, *Perfect Skin: A Natural Approach* (Piatkuus, London, 2001)

Hazel Courtenay, *500 of the Most Important Health Tips You'll Ever Need* (Cico Books, London, 2001)

Pierre Jean Cousin, *Food is Medicine* (Duncan Baird, London, 2001)

Pierre Jean Cousin, *Natural Recipes for Perfect Skin* (Quadrille, London, 2001)

Stephanie Donaldson, *Home Spa: Top-to-Toe Beauty*

Treatments for Total Well-being (Lorenz Books, London, 2002)

Liz Earle, *New Vital Oils* (Vermilion, London, 2002)

Jospehine Fairley, *Organic Beauty* (Dorling Kindersley, London, 2001)

Kirsten Hartvig, *Eat for Immunity* (Duncan Baird, London, 2002)

Kathryn Marsden, *SuperSkin: Natural Ways to Super Healthy Skin* (Thorsons, London, 2002)

Natalie Savona, *Kitchen Shrink* (Duncan Baird, London, 2003)

Mo Siegel and Nancy Burke, *Herbs for Health and Happiness* (Time Life, Virginia USA, 1999)

Michael van Straten, *Super Boosters: Herb, Plant and Spice Extracts to Boost Health* (Mitchell Beazley, London, 2002)

Michael van Straten, *The Oracle Diet* (Kyle Cathie, London, 2002)

Amanda Ursell, *Beauty Superboosters: Foods and Massages to Boost Your Natural Beauty* (Mitchell Beazley, London, 2002)

Amanda Ursell, *The Complete*

Guide to Healing Foods (Dorling Kindersley, London, 2001)

Alfred Vogel, *The Nature Doctor* (Mainstream Publishing, Edinburgh, 1989)

Marcus and Maria Webb, *Healing Touch* (Godsfield Press, London, 1999)

Chrissy Wildwood, *Aroma Remedies* (Collins & Brown, London, 2000)

Janet Wright, *Stress Relief for Women* (Paragon, London, 1997)

acknowledgments

The author would like to thank everyone at Duncan Baird, especially Judy Barratt, Bob Saxton, and Lucy Latchmore, all of whom have been wonderful to work with on this project. Thanks also go to my agent Chelsey Fox for her advice and support. To Natalie Savona, my friend and "advisory" nutritionist who recommended that I write this book, thank you for your faith in me. Thanks also to my mother Colleen and my sister Cherie Bramley, who both volunteered to

type in many of the recipes in the book, with barely any bribery. And to Conn Prosser, who believes in me.

Picture credits
Duncan Baird Publishers would like to thank the following people, museums, and photographic libraries for permission to reproduce their material. Every care has been taken to trace copyright holders. However, if we have omitted anyone we apologize, and will, if informed,

make corrections in any future edition.

6 left Benelux/Zefa, London; **7 right** Emely/Zefa, London; **10** Marina Jefferson/Getty Images, London; **12** Miles/Zefa, London; **20** Michael Goldman/Getty Images, London; **67** Benelux/Zefa, London; **68** Picture Books/Robert Harding Picture Library, London; **70** Donata Pizzi/Getty Images, London; **78** Stockimage/Imagestate, London; **82** Emely/Zefa, London; **84** Tony

Anderson/Getty Images, London; **88** Michael Jordan/Imagestate, London; **90** Marina Jefferson/Getty Images, London; **118** Michael Goldman/Getty Images, London; **125** Michael Leis/Robert Harding Picture Library, London

The Publishers would also like to thank Nicolette Grobler (model) and Tinks Reding (make-up artist).